Clifford Owusu-Gyamfi

What is this Thing Called *Sunsum*?

Afrikanische Theologie
African Theology
Théologie Africaine

Band / Volume 10

LIT

Clifford Owusu-Gyamfi

What is this Thing Called *Sunsum*?

A Historiographical and Philosophical Investigation into the Nature of the Akan *Sunsum*, from its Pneumatological Conception to the Contemporary Argument of Quasi-physicalism

LIT

Cover image: Sunsum symbol

Publication supported by the Theological Faculty of the University of Geneva

This book is printed on acid-free paper.

Bibliographic information published by the Deutsche Nationalbibliothek
The Deutsche Nationalbibliothek lists this publication in the Deutsche Nationalbibliografie; detailed bibliographic data are available on the Internet at http://dnb.dnb.de.

ISBN 978-3-643-80334-4 (pb)
ISBN 978-3-643-85334-9 (PDF)

A catalogue record for this book is available from the British Library.

Flössergasse 10
CH-8001 Zürich
Tel. +41 (0) 76-632 84 35
E-Mail: zuerich@lit-verlag.ch https://www.lit-verlag.ch
Distribution:
In the UK: Global Book Marketing, e-mail: mo@centralbooks.com
In Germany: LIT Verlag Fresnostr. 2, D-48159 Münster
Tel. +49 (0) 2 51-620 32 22, Fax +49 (0) 2 51-922 60 99, e-mail: vertrieb@lit-verlag.de

Table of Contents

SUNSUM
(The Akan adinkra symbol signifying personality, energy, power, spirit, and purity)

DEDICATION

To my dear parents of blessed memory, John Kwadwo Owusu and Esther Ama Owusuaa, both from Wiamoase in the Asante region of Ghana. May they remain in our memory as long as life endures.

ACKNOWLEDGEMENT

As my research advisor, Prof. Christophe Chalamet, stated during my doctoral thesis defense: “Pride has a negative connotation in Christian cycles but today, you can be proud of your achievement.” His remarks reinforced the relevance of this study to the larger academic body as well as the Akan people of West Africa and beyond. For this, I am very grateful to Nana ‘Nyankopɔn Kwame and forever proud of this groundbreaking.

To have come this far has also been the contribution of many important persons of such I deem it a great courtesy to acknowledge their kindness and support in my studies. The first to mention are my late parents, Mr. John K. Owusu and Esther Ama Owusuaa, who both passed away in 2013 during my master's program at the University of Lausanne in Switzerland. Their passing came as a shock, sudden, and troubling. However, I had many reasons to celebrate their life of dedication to family unity, their selfless investment in my entire educational pursuit even when they did not have enough, the “I-can-do” spirit they instilled in me, and their exemplary life in the practice of the Christian faith. I do acknowledge them as heroes of my life. May their souls rest in perfect peace.

I also do acknowledge my brothers, sisters, nieces, and nephews who have always stood by my side in life. Their words of encouragement and support throughout the years have brought me this far. Words cannot express how wonderful they are to me especially my sisters Monica Owusu and Paulina Owusu-Sarpong. I take this opportunity to express my gratitude and to say a big “I love you” to them.

There are a few friends and organizations that I would like to acknowledge. I'd want to express my gratitude to Ndiouga Ndiaye, a Senegalese student I met in Lausanne. When I was still struggling to adjust in Switzerland, he hosted me at his hostel and helped me in a variety of ways. Let me thank François Tauxe and his family for hosting me in their home in Jougne, France, for six months when I first arrived in Switzerland for the first time. Others include Anne Kowlesseur, Patrick Moyowabo, Alexandre Vitorovic, Florence Brunner, Selam Salih, Samuel Sarpaning, Abigail Gyasi, Faustina Boansi, Joyce Serwaa Oppong, Pastor Gilbert Dewinter, Pastor Ulrich Frikhart, Pastor Dominique Frikhart, Albert Muller and family, Ricardo Ruiz and wife, Ribeiro Rui, Dr. Opoku Boateng, Dr. Robert

Osei-Bonsu, Dr. Brempong Owusu-Antwi, Dr. Dei Daniel, Pastor Abankwa Amoakohene, Pastor Seth Anokye, Wiamoase S. D. A Church, the Latinos Adventist Church of Lausanne, Adventist Church in Renens, JET Services and Centre Social Protestant (CSP), Fédération des Eglises adventistes du septième jour de la Suisse romande et du Tessin, Seventh-day Adventist International Church of Geneva (my current parish), and all others.

Preface

The present study forms part of the growing concern of using Africa's socio-religious context as a means for academic reflection. This growing concern has come as a socio-cultural and religious revival of what a majority of Africans consider as authentic self-definition. Already received in Ghana, notable scholars who have integrated religio-cultural ideas in interdisciplinary studies include Joseph Boakye Danquah, Kofi Abrefa Busia, John Pobee, Kofi Sarpong, Kwasi Wiredu, Kwame Gyekye, Kwame Bediako, Anthony Ephirim-Donkor, Robert Owusu Agyarko, and among others. All these scholars had one thing in common: to demonstrate the veracity of oral traditions for academic learning, and, more significantly, the importance of indigenous knowledge to the progress of Africa.

These significant contributers to Akan scholarship sparked my interest in contextual studies. I will particularly single out the works of Robert Owusu Agyarko, whose presentation at the International Conference on Pneumatology and Contextual Theology held at the University of Geneva in 2014 became the turning point of my whole theological and academic journey. Agyarko presented a paper titled: "'Sunsum' the Spirit of Life: Pneumatology in the (Akan) West Africa Context," with the aim of constructing a contextual Akan pneumatology based on the Akan concept of *sunsum* (spirit). This impressive contribution by Agyarko raised many interesting questions, leading to the present study.

In Africa, the notion of the spirit, whether in mythology or belief system, shows one thing: the universe is inspirited, and that we cannot ignore the spiritual. Therefore, it is very common to hear Africans talking about spirits and all sort of spells which in effect drive a religiosity based on power and protection. Even though the religious landscape in today's Africa has changed considerably and with some subtle focus on socio-economic and political concerns, the vast majority of the religions still emphasize the spiritual reality of the universe. For that we can be certain that the belief in spirits and the spiritual, whether they are real or not, is not a matter of contention among the majority of Africans, at least, not yet, because the vast majority of African societies affirm that whatever has a name must exist. As a matter of fact, the link between spiritual and physical existence embodies the factors through which most African communities orient themselves. So, we can consider the belief systems to be oral encyclopedias of knowledge and cultural identity.

This book is the first of two volumes of my findings on the meaning of the Akan concept of *sunsum* from a historical context. It has been the result of several years of reading, researching, and writing on the subject. I have divided the study into three main parts. The first part is the general introduction, which defines the statement of problem of the study. It also introduces the field of study, the scope of the research, and the research methodology. The general introduction further offers an introduction to Akan culture and worldviews by introducing and defining Akan anthropology and cosmology.

The second part explores the genesis of Akan scholarship and anthropology, beginning with the German missionary and philologist Johann Gottlieb Christaller and Robert Sutherland Rattray (1881–1938). Rattray was a Scottish anthropologist to Ghana (then Gold Coast) whose research focused primarily on the Asante tribe of the Akan. Christaller is credited as the architect of Akan Twi scholarship, while Rattray's name is associated with pioneering the study of Akan anthropology. This part further looks into the meaning and nature of *sunsum* in the works of Joseph Boakye Danquah, Eva L. Meyerowitz, Kofi Abrefa Busia, Helaine K. Minkus, and Anthony Ephirim-Donkor. These scholars contribute fresh conceptual insights to the study of *sunsum*.

The third part of the research focuses on contemporary criticisms and apologetics of the meaning of *sunsum*. Contemporary Akan thinkers use a critical approach towards understanding the nature and meaning of *sunsum*. The first problem is a linguistic problem. Should we translate *sunsum* into the English language as "spirit?" The study also discusses some commonly mistaken Akan terminology with *sunsum*.

Overall, it is my desire that this book will offer the reader with the fundamentals of Akan pneumatology. Some of the information in this book was written with the purpose of preserving some oral traditions that are rarely discussed. Again, a few of the chapters have been published in peer-reviewed journals with minor modifications. I hope that my contribution to the study of contextual pneumatology will inspire students and scholars to interact with African spirituality in a variety of academic domains and self-expressions.

FOREWORD

Theology wholly depends on language and is entirely practiced through language (or, better, through languages, since, as is well known, various artforms, beyond human words and human verbal discourses, also convey theological insights, and do so at times more powerfully than words). Since languages evolve, theologians cannot avoid assessing the adequacy of the terminology (as well as the syntax) they use. This is true of all discursive traditions, broadly conceived. Whether their historical roots are found in the distant past or not does not change anything, for language constantly evolves.

But traditions, including the Christian tradition, do not just evolve as language evolves: they also expand geographically, reaching lands and regions that previously knew little or even nothing of them. In this case new questions arise in relation to language: how should this or that term, that plays a role in a given tradition, be translated in the idiom of the region where this tradition has arrived? This is a question that is not at the forefront of many Western theologians today when they do theology. The terms they use have roots that reach very far back in time: the problem for them is, rather, how to say what these terms used to convey in new, fresh, and hopefully compelling ways. But when Westerners travel to different countries, especially to Africa, Asia, Oceania, or the Americas, or, even more powerfully, when people from these continents discover a new religious tradition (or a new philosophy), how should the key notions of this (foreign) religious tradition be translated within the language or dialect of that particular culture? Answering this question is everything, but easy or obvious?

It was a massive challenge especially for missionaries since the 16th and especially the 17th century. The problem becomes even more acute when one is attempting to translate notoriously difficult, polysemic concepts such as "spirit." Kirsteen Kim, of Fuller Theological Seminary, has brilliantly examined this particular question in relation to South Korea.[1] But the ques-

---

[1] "L'Esprit et les esprits. La question terminologique en Asie et ses implications pour une théologie du Saint Esprit," *Revue de théologie et de philosophie* 147 (2015): 67-87.

tion is of course not limited to this Asian country, or even to the Asian continent. "Spirit" is a basic and crucial dimension or reality in many human cultures. In the present work, Clifford Owusu-Gyamfi, a young Ghanaian scholar who completed his doctoral theological studies at the University of Geneva (Switzerland), surveys the complex ways in which the meanings of the term "spirit" have been interpreted among thinkers who belong to the Akan people, as well as among scholars from other ethnic backgrounds who have immersed themselves in Akan culture. A key term used in Akan culture to designate what English speakers call "spirit" is the term *sunsum*. Thus, the question was bound to come up: should this term, *sunsum*, be the term used by Christian missionaries as well as by Akan to refer to the Holy Spirit? Answering this question presupposed a close analysis of some of the rich, manifold connotations that this term carries. But what exactly are these connotations? What, in fact, does the word *sunsum* mean? And how should another Akan term that also denotes something of the "spirit," namely *honhom*, be understood? Might this other term (*honhom*) be an interesting candidate for pneumatological discourse in a Christian context? These are some of the main questions Clifford Owusu-Gyamfi pursues in the present work, in a manner that is both very detailed and searching. Perhaps unsurprisingly, the reader discovers that this term has been the object of much debate over the last century (roughly).

Why does such a study matter? Why is it important to analyze a term like *sunsum* (and, relatedly, *honhom*) in such a way? The answer is quite obvious: as Christianity continues to be a very important factor in Akan culture as well as, more broadly, in Ghana and neighboring countries, the process of searching for the most adequate (or the least inadequate) ways to convey the message of the Christian faith remains inescapable and urgent. This task is never finished. And at a time when religious experiences across the world often center on the life-giving Spirit, all of those who are committed to, or interested in, the work of expressing the gospel are urged to contribute to the task of reflecting upon the meaning of the key concepts that are commonly used to proclaim the Christian message, including, especially, a term such as "spirit" (or "Spirit"). Behind the historical survey provided in the present work lies a constructive theological task, which Clifford Owusu-Gyamfi clearly sees and to which his study helpfully contributes.

Whether the history of a key notion within Akan culture is of interest to you, whether you wonder about the many "harmonics" triggered by this notion and the interpretation of these harmonics by several leading Akan scholars from the last century up to the present, or whether you are interested in the task of thinking about "spirit" in an anthropological manner or in a theological manner (or both), this book will open new vistas before you and urge you to attend carefully to the meanings of the very rich, complex, and crucial Akan term *sunsum* and its cognates.

Christophe Chalamet
Professor of systematic theology, University of Geneva, Switzerland.

PART I

GENERAL INTRODUCTION

SANKOFA

"Go back to take"

Sɛ wo were fi na wo sankofa a yenkyi– "It is not a taboo to go back for that which is forgotten" (Akan maxim). The adinkra symbol means it is essential to learn from the past.

1. General Introduction

> *"May those Africans who are enjoying the benefit of a Christian education make the best of the privilege; but let them not despise the sparks of truth entrusted to and preserved by their own people and let them not forget that by entering into their way of thinking and by acknowledging what is good and expounding what is wrong they will gain the more access to the hearts and minds of their less favored countrymen"* — Johann Gottlieb Christaller, 1879.

This book is the result of a five-year research into African spiritual phenomena, involving a constructive anthropological, philosophical and theological investigation of the spiritual worldview of the Akan people of West Africa.[2] Akan is an ethnic group comprising several unique tribes whose current settlements are in the tropical areas of Ghana and the southeast of Cote d'Ivoire (Figure 1).[3] In both Ghana and Cote d'Ivoire, the Akan constitute the majority with an average population of more than twenty million citizens.[4] In this context, I use the term anthropology to refer to the numerous scholarly works, including approaches, that are employed in the study of the human being within the context of Akan societies, cultures, and be-

---

2 The term "Akan" is both singular and plural. The term expresses any person or group of persons or cultural group that belong to one larger ethnic group called Akan.

3 There are also few Akan found in Togo according to Louise Müller, "Ghanaian Films and Chiefs as Indicators of Religious Change among the Akan in Kumasi and Its Migrants in Southeast Amsterdam," in Robert W. Hefner, John Hutchinson, Sara Mels, Christiane Timmerman (eds), *Religions in Movement: The Local and the Global in Contemporary Faith Traditions*. New York: Routledge, 2013, p. 246.

4 Some prominent Akan figures in modern history include Kwame Nkrumah (1909-1972), the first prime minister of Ghana and father of African Nationalism, Kofi Annan (1938-2018), the seventh Secretary-General of the United Nations between January 1997 and December 2006, and Nana Addo Danquah Akuffo-Addo (b. 1944), the current president of the Republic of Ghana since 2016.

liefs, as well as their dynamic survival throughout human history. Philosophy is understood as the understanding of the rationality and concepts behind the beliefs, thought processes, and behavioral patterns of the Akan. Since religion shapes certain ideas, values and morals upon which people express their individuality and how they understand and relate to other members of their community, philosophy, as a branch of the discipline, gives these aspects a sense of situational meaning and expression. Theology, in this sense, involves a systematic understanding of the totality of the religious system as in belief in God, spirits, rituals and practices, and their implications on the moral and ethical life of the people in practice.

In this volume, I propose to investigate the Akan's religious notion in which the universe is animated and interpenetrated by an immaterial, dynamic, force, power, and "spirit" called *sunsum* (Rattray 1923; Danquah 1968; Gyekye 1987; among others). *Sunsum* is pronounced like the English "soon" and the Latin "sum" together.[5] The term is a multivalent and has various nuances in the studies of anthropology, philosophy, and theology. Several scholars accept the notion of *sunsum* as being responsible for basic essential functionalities in natural objects such as stones, trees, mountains, rivers, but also in human beings. It is generally held as the activating principle and the "spirit" of an object or person. For the purpose of convenience, let us call the Akan belief in spiritual phenomena as animism, even though the term is inadequate.

Scholars studying Akan religions and culture have tried to construct, deconstruct, and reconstruct the notion of the *sunsum*, particularly its ontological character, whether it is supposed to be called a "spirit" or an emanating force, or both. The results have brought several shades to the term. Despite the various nuances, contemporary scholarship focuses on two main ontological arguments. The first and most popular is the pneumatic character that designates the *sunsum* as a spirit, vital force, and the double of an individual that remains unseen in the astral realms (Rattray 1923; Minkus 1981; Gyekye 1987). The second, which is more recent, and a critique of the former is the quasi-physical or quasi-material character of *sunsum*. This is a new wave of philosophy that presents the Akan *sunsum* as not strictly a "spirit" but also a quasi-physical or quasi-material concept (Danquah 1944; Wiredu 1987).

---

5 In some books, it is spelled *sumsum*. I can only think of this as a linguistic inflection of the term *sunsum*.

Scholars from the pneumatic school of thought, which is underpinned by the term "spirit," designate the *sunsum* as a distinct immaterial substance or a spiritual entity. This conception stems from both Western and indigenous scholars studying Akan culture and religion (Rattray 1923; Minkus 1981; Gyekye 1987; and others). One of the most influential luminaries in this respect was the late Kwame Gyekye (10 November 1939 - 13 April 2019), an Akan indigenous scholar who favored and defended the pneumatic character of *sunsum*. Gyekye was a prominent scholar and modern philosopher who argued in favor of the pneumatic character of *sunsum* as both traditionally and philosophically accurate, even though he did recognize the multivalent nature of it. Gyekye was notable for his influence in shaping modern African philosophy. His approach to the interpretation of Akan religions and culture involved a critical analysis and comparative studies that provided an argument for a distinct African philosophy and identity. Gyekye, like several African philosophers, pursued a common interpretation that gives value to an African philosophical thought, rather than Western philosophy, as a yardstick for studying and practicing African philosophy. The dogma of an ontological inseparability between personhood and community was a hallmark of Gyekye's definition of an authentic African personality. To him, the community imposes identity upon the African child. For that reason, personhood is a communal spirituality. His compelling philosophical interpretation of the *sunsum* as a spirit, divine essence, and experience has heightened preference for the pneumatic character across the intellectual frontiers.

Quasi-physicalists, on the other hand, are intellectual questioners who, through analytic critique, question the nature of the *sunsum* and consider its translation into the English language as "spirit" to be inflected by the West. The scholar who championed this approach was the Akan scholar Kwasi Wiredu (3 October 1931 - 6 January 2022).[6] Wiredu remains one of the notable contemporary African philosophers in conceptual analysis. The centrality of his methodology was centered around a critique of some of the

---

6 Wiredu was a distinguished Ghanaian professor of philosophy at the Department of philosophy in the University of South Florida. He was trained in the studies of philosophy at the University of Ghana and Oxford University and gave lectures in several universities such as the University of Ibadan (Nigeria), UCLA, Richmond, Carleton College, and Duke, and held fellowships at the Wilson Center, Washington, D. C. and The National Humanities Center, North Carolina (Wiredu et al, 2006: xviii).

African concepts that he perceived as being ostensibly contaminated by Western "definite modes of conceptualization" (Wiredu 1998: 17).[7] Wiredu thought this came about as a result of the influence of foreign conceptual schemes, and the problem of indigenous susceptibility to Western education (Wiredu 1998: 1820; 1996: 136-144). Therefore, he saw the task of deconstructing African pedagogy as technically a "philosophical decolonization," which also is "necessarily a conceptual enterprise" and "fundamental conceptualization" (Wiredu 1998: 18). It was from this background that defined his rejectionist stance toward the pneumatic character of Akan spiritual realities to grapple with quasi-physicalism.[8]

Per Wiredu, the term "spirit" is polysemic in the English world and does not encapsulate the indigenous conception of the *sunsum*; for this reason, he cautioned Akan scholars to avoid translating *sunsum* into the English language as "spirit" (Wiredu 1987). His ability to analyze through the prism of Akan linguistics led him to propose that what many Akan speak of as "spirit" is not merely spirit per se, as understood in the English language, but rather something quasi-physical or quasi-material, meaning it lies between the spiritual and physical world and is often perceived and spoken of with physical properties. The nature of *sunsum* appears in Wiredu's conception as quasi-material, i.e., neither material nor immaterial. Thus, the Akan *sunsum* may appear to have physical qualities but does not (Müller 2008). Eventually, Wiredu rejects the pneumatic conception of *sunsum* by offering a constructive proposal of quasi-materialism as best describing the Akan worldview of what is supposed to be "spirit" and spiritual.

As a theologian, the aforementioned schools of thought are of a particular interest to recent contextual studies in African pneumatology. The current contextual Akan Christian pneumatology is the work of Robert Owusu-

---

7 While Wiredu maintains a sharp focus on the purity of Africa's traditional conceptual substances, it is however obvious that various political theories such as decolonialism and *sankofaism*, which are shaded by Kwame Nkrumah's neo-colonialism theory, have influenced him. The idea of a "go back to take" (Sankofa) to what is African opposes Westernization and its concomitant infiltration of colonialism in the educational system. Its target is to redirect Africa's educational pedagogy to its traditional values (Kwame Nkrumah 1970; Emmanuel Martey 1993; Kofi Poku and Nana Boaduo 2011; Wiredu 1996).

8 Wiredu is not the first scholar to view the *sunsum* as not being spirit. In this study, it has been argued that Joseph Boakye Danquah was the first Akan indigenous scholar who did not characterize the *sunsum* as pneumatic. The significance of Wiredu's work is how he shows from his analyses that *sunsum* is not spirit.

Agyarko, an Akan theologian, lecturer, and director of graduate programs at Central University in Ghana.[9] Agyarko has proposed that the Akan concept of *sunsum* may form the basis for contextual Akan Eco theology and pneumatology (Agyarko 2012, 2014). Agyarko's research interest has centered on contextual pneumatology, ecotheology, Christology, Trinity, and sociocultural reforms in West Africa. His spiritual theology from the Akan perspective has drawn attention to pneumatological discourses in African contextual theology, of which this present research is not an exception.[10] His work is an illustration of theological interest in the *sunsum* debate. It also points out the emergence of rigorous studies in contextual pneumatology among the Akan people.

Agyarko's contextual Akan Christian pneumatology tends to favor the pneumatic character of the *sunsum* at the expense of a critical and in-depth dialogue with the quasi-physical critique. Since the philosophy of quasi-physicalism remains the sole pervasive philosophical critique of the *sunsum* and continues to influence contemporary scholarship, it needs to attract the attention of scholars in Akan (African) pneumatology for proper investigation and dialogue.

The term *sunsum* has been enigmatic and ambiguous, and its meaning has puzzled many scholars studying Akan religions. Gyekye says it is the greatest difficulty in Akan metaphysics and a source of confusion (1987: 89). Ephirim-Donkor admits that *sunsum* is a paradox and even an enigma (Ephirim-Donkor 2016: 49). Few scholars have ventured, as far as possible, to investigate the meaning of the term. However, that is what my research has attempted to do. It begins by looking at the historical evolution of the term *sunsum* through the lens of scholars studying Akan religions in order

---

9 Agyarko is a Pentecostal pastor and an extraordinary researcher at the University of the Western Cape, South Africa. He currently serves as the coordinator of graduate studies at Central University, Kumasi branch in Ghana. Before assuming this position, he held the position of head of the department of theology at the Christian Service University College in Kumasi from 2013 to 2018. He also served as vice president and acting dean of the school of theology in 2004 at Pan African Christian University College (now Perez University College). Agyarko is currently serving as an ordained minister with the Church of God in Ghana. He is credited with planting seven Church of God communities in West Africa, namely, Burkina-Faso, Mali, Benin, Gambia, Guinea, and Senegal (Bill 2010: 375, 381, 386).

10 Some of his articles, "God of Life: Rethinking the Akan Christian Concept of God in the light of the Ecological Crisis" (2013), and "The Sunsum of Onyame: Akan Perspective on an Ecological Pneumatology" (Agyarko 2012).

to offer a new contextual pneumatology for the articulation of contextual Akan Christian pneumatology. The expectation is that acquiring an excellent grasp of the concept of the "spirit" will demonstrate how the theology of the Holy Spirit may be employed, contextually, in the Akan setting. The big question is focused on the nature of *sunsum*: What is this thing called *sunsum*? This question leads to an inquiry into the spiritual worldview of the Akan people.

2. INTRODUCTION TO THE MEANING OF RELIGION

> *"A people's interpretation of the universe is shown in conduct: in day-to-day activities, in human relations, and in rites; in avoidances as well as observances. The sociological field of religion and cosmology includes the emotions and beliefs prevalent in a social group regarding the super-natural, the overt behaviour, the material objects, and the symbols and rites associated with such belief"* – Kofi Abrefa Busia (1955: 22).

During my study, one of the most often questioned concerns was my use of the terms religion and culture. *Sunsum* is often expressed in religious and cultural orientations. As a result, my research begins with the task of addressing the meaning of religion and its relationship with culture within the context of Akan traditional settings as a crucial endeavor toward a correct understanding of Akan pneumatology. The second section of this chapter will look at the research methodology, which is largely historiographical in nature. This method was used to investigate ideas that have influenced and formed the thinking of researchers in order to gain the best possible viewpoint from the theories, interpretations, and approaches used by various scholars studying Akan religions and culture.

2.1. Meaning of Religion

Religion is a complex system of beliefs and practices that can have differing definitions from one cultural setting to another. Nevertheless, common to every religious system is the possession of certain transcendental experiences that impact meaningful beliefs and practices from one generation to the other. Religion may cover a set of illuminations that unite the people in practice in the community to achieve a common purpose. For these reasons, religion needs attention because it shapes certain ideas and behavioral patterns in an individual's worldview and provides a means of interpreting the behavioral patterns of a group of people.

Religion remains one of the oldest practices in human civilization. Bolaji Idowu (1913-1993), one of Africa's influential ethnographers and theologians in the indigenization of Christianity, is convinced that religion has always been with mankind, and it affects our innermost beings as well as events in life; minor or major (Idowu 1973). Religion has a universal interest that is "inevitable as a sphere of human life and activity." It is rooted deep in the nature of every person, thus, "an inherent urge in man which makes religion a matter of ultimate concern. It makes also for the common 'interest' in religion – whether the interest is in embracing it or in fighting a defensive battle against it" (Idowu 1973: 3).[11] Religion's transcendent power is undeniable, affecting all (consciously or unconsciously), and possessing in it a driving force of influence in a person's worldview. Such characterization of religion raises the question of whether religion is an ontological phenomenon. The answer lies in the next discussion on the definition of religion and its relationship with culture.

2.1.1. The Relationship Between Religion and Culture

Religion and culture often overlap each other, and many people often confuse one with the other. Generally, culture involves the behavior of a group of people who share some commonality and communality. The Center for Advanced Research on Language Acquisition defines culture as "the shared patterns of behaviors and interactions, cognitive constructs, and affective understanding that are learned through a process of socialization."[12] This ideology is given a broader interpretation by John Samuel Mbiti (1931-2019).[13] As a staunch Kenyan Anglican scholar and religious philosopher who served as an emeritus professor at the University of Bern and parish

---

11 For example, a person who adheres to atheistic conceptions is forced to talk about religion in one way or the other to establish a point in atheism.

12 The Center for Advanced Research on Language Acquisition, http://carla.umn.edu/culture/definitions.html Last visited 22. 03. 2020.

13 Professor Mbiti shown a great appreciation for African religious and cultural studies. He recounted how his intellectual quest for academic excellence was sparked by the story of Ghana's pioneer African educationist Dr. Kwegyir Aggrey (1875-1927). For more details check (Musopole 1994: 18).

priest in Burgdorf, Switzerland, and who had intimated knowledge of African sociology, Mbiti defines culture as follows:

> The word culture covers many things, such as the way people live, behave and act, and their physical as well as their intellectual achievements. Culture shows itself in art and literature, dance, music and drama, in the styles of building houses and of people's clothing, in social organizations and political systems, in religion, ethics, morals and philosophy, in the customs and institutions of the people, in their values and laws, and in their economic life (Mbiti 2015: 7).

Mbiti's definition infers culture as having expression within a social movement and covering an integral whole of something that is generally acceptable within a specific social group. Based on these explanations, one's cultural affiliation becomes a social heritage rather than a biological makeup.

It has also been discussed that religion has inherent dynamic force that influences a person's way of life; that means the relationship between culture and religion is conditioned by each other. Religion has a unifying effect on culture. Christopher Dawson (1889-1970), a historian of religion and culture, in his book *Religion and Culture* maintains the central unifying effect of religion on culture as the guardian of tradition, preserver of moral law, and educator and teacher of wisdom (Dawson 2013: 37). He further maintains that it is religion that holds society in its fixed cultural patterns (Dawson 2013: 37). It seeks to give meaning to culture and expresses the depths of cultural lifestyle. In some parts of the world, cultural elements such as naming ceremonies, marriage, kingship, puberty rites, funerals, and farming have religious significance and are maintained by formidable religious sanctions (Dawson 2013: 37).

Culture and religion have a mutual interaction but are not same. The relation between religion and culture is always a two-sided one, says Dawson: "The way of life influences the approach to religion, and the religious attitude influences the way of life" (Dawson 2013: 43). Even in secular societies where the reception of religion may suffer repugnancy, people continue to embrace certain vital rudiments of religion. Various wedding ceremonies, swearing in of state officials and certain customary laws are characteristics of religious illuminations. Religion is a vital force that brings together all that are of vital importance in the life of people into close relationship so that every economic and social way of life has its corresponding form of religion (Dawson 2013: 43).

Whereas one may assume that religion and culture have a model of mutual relationship, we cannot assume a general conception that every culture has a religion. With reference to the Akan, religion is central, all-pervasive and involves a lot of communal ties (Pobee 1979: 44). In fact, it is so closely tied up with the totality of their existence and worldviews that it becomes a matter of impossibility to separate religion from communal activities. Marriage, farming, puberty rites, music and arts, naming ceremonies, kingship, funerals, etc., are all absorptive of religion. So, the question about religion among the Akan, like in most world societies, is an ontological phenomenon that pertains to the question of being.

2.2. African Traditional Religions (ATR)

African traditional religions encompass several territorial traditional religions. The term African traditional religions, as used in this research, refers to the indigenous religious beliefs and practices of Africans that distinctively define the spiritual and moral complexities of African people that are handed down from generation to generation. The question as to whether there is truly an African traditional religion has been researched and scholars in this field of study have unanimously embraced the large measure of homogenous features in the various traditional religious practices on the continent. Such features include the general belief in the supernatural, ideas about man, society, and nature (Idowu 1973; Asare Opoku 1978; Mbiti 1991). The conviction that the universe is arrayed by varying degrees of spiritual entities and forces that impinge on the natural order of things, including the affairs of humanity, is a general fundamental belief in most African traditional religions (Green 1983). A human being, by definition, is made up of both body and spirit. Community also involves the spirits of the departed family members as ingrained in the invocation of ancestral spirits through the pouring of libation and other sacrifices made to the dead (Asare Opoku 1978: 9).

Another general characteristic of African traditional religions is the explanation of human misfortune and suffering as caused by retributive spirits of some moral offenses or malevolence of spiritual entities. Misfortunes like droughts and famine may be considered as punishment from the gods for an act of sacrilege. In such a situation, after inquiries are satisfied, pacification and sacrificial ceremonies are performed to appease the gods for help. Human predicaments such as poverty, illness, death, hardships, etc. could be attributed to malicious acts of wicked spiritual entities or by malevolent beings such as witches and sorcerers that use spiritual powers (Green 1983). Though this is not always the case, it is the most popular belief.

African traditional religion is a heritage, with its own historical patterns from the past. Its structure is generally founded on five main pillars according to Mbiti:

1. *The belief system*: This is the most essential part of the religion. Beliefs shape the worldview of adherents. It involves belief in God, spirits and forces, human life, life after death, reincarnation, etc.
2. *Ceremonies and festivals*: These essential group activities express the belief system in practical terms. They mark events in the past and sometimes involve recreational activities where people celebrate through singing and dancing. On other occasions, they are moments of mutual sorrow. Examples of ceremonies include funerals, naming ceremonies, marriage ceremonies, etc.
3. *Religious objects and places*: Religious objects include amulets, charms, talismans, etc. that are meant to serve as instruments of spiritual power. Religious places are sacred places reserved for religious meetings and appointments. They may include natural shrines like mountains, rivers, forests, or man-made shrines.
4. *Values and morals*: These are social ideals that safeguard the harmony of the society. They maintain interpersonal relationships with members in the community and also involve people's worldview of their environmental surroundings. African folklore, proverbs, and taboos are the most common depositories of values and morals.
5. *Religious functionaries or leaders*: These are experts who have excellent knowledge about religious systems. By their knowledge, they preserve religious traditions and pass it on to their successors. They also preside over ceremonies and rituals. Functionaries "hold offices as priests, rain-makers, ritual elders, diviners, medicine men, and even as kings and rulers" (Mbiti 1991: 12).

African traditional religions are practiced by millions today on the continent, making it a contemporary reality (Asare Opoku 1978: 9). Contrary to what early Western anthropologists considered as primitive and savage religion, African traditional religion has become resourceful for unearthing Africa's pre-Christian spiritual heritage (Idowu 1973: 109-112). African traditional religion is studied in upper primary and tertiary institutions alongside the study of many major world religions such as Christianity, Islam, and Judaism. The length of its appreciation, generated by keen interests in contextual theological studies, philosophy, and the social sciences, even in the world outside the African continent, attests to why it needs constant scholarly engagement.

If someone should ask whether African traditional religions are so significant at all to Africa's theological studies, the obvious answer is seen in the heightened interest of scholars in pre-Christian religious traditions that is taken seriously as worthy for shaping indigenous Christian lifestyle and learning. This heightened interest in African indigenous religious spirituality, once "deemed unworthy of serious theological consideration in missionary times, now [occupies] a central place on the African theological agenda" (Bediako 1999: 2). As a hermeneutical praxis in Africa's theological studies, African traditional religions seek to find a holistic interaction with Christian doctrines.

2.3. Akan Traditional Religions

Akan traditional religions are a sub-religion of African traditional religions. It possesses such complex spiritual heritage that defines behavioral patterns and spiritual values for the Akan. The Akan religious experience defines how Akan people express themselves in their belief systems and practices. The concept of *sunsum* is an aspect of the belief system among the Akan that has informed the scope of my research work.

One historical phenomenon that I want to address at this moment is the convergence of Christianity and the Akan traditional religions. Most Akan profess Christianity today, and many scholars have failed to see the essential distinction between the Akan traditional religions and Christianity; the former is typically cultural while the latter is adequately faith based – at least within the African context.[14]

[14] Christianity is also "typically cultural;" it is not simply "faith based." With Christianity, the colonizers brought their culture, and they often confused their faith with their culture.

Christianity arrived in Ghana in the 15th century when it was ushered in by the Catholic Church as part of the global movement of Christianity and colonialism. Missionary work and colonialism were inseparable in the sense that Christianization of Africa was part of the colonial agenda. The initial Papal bull, "Dum Diversas," issued by Pope Nicholas V on 18 June 1452 to King Alfonso V of Portugal, gave the king the authority to enslave and evangelize the third worlds. This inception gave way to the theology of *salus animarum*, or a theology of the conversion of those without faith (Gibellini 1987: 63-64). From 1820, rigorous missionary activity emerged among the Akan people by the advent of the Protestant missionaries. The Basel Mission Society was established in 1828 at Akropong-Akwapim from whence the Akan traditional religions began to gradually decline over time as the dominant religion.

The emergence of Christianity in Ghana, therefore, was a historical conquest. In Ghana today, about 5.2 percent of the general population adhere to African traditional religions.[15] This translates into more than one million adherents of the traditional religions among the Akan. Despite their limited numbers, traditional religions' moral principles and ethics continue to serve as the foundation for many Christian expressions in Ghana, and both are thought to complement each other.

When indigenous religions gave way to Christianity, which was also a tool of colonialism, Western scholarship emerged. The information obtained in the new settlement was used by Europeans to bolster Christianity as well as the colonial rule. From Bible translations to the works of early European anthropologists, colonists were able to establish ideological imperialism that favored Westernization while undermining Africa's religio-cultural traditions. As a result, contemporary African research is concerned with ensuring authentic African religio-cultural values through a critical examination of current ideological narratives from colonial Africa. And it is against this backdrop that my research of the Akan *sunsum* took a historiographical approach.

---

[15] http://countrystat.org/country/GHA/contents/docs/2010_Population_Report.pdf. Last visited Jan. 02, 2020.

2.4. Historiographical Approach

One of the earliest subjects of study for European scholars in Ghana was the concept of *sunsum*. Erstwhile Europeans used ethnographic research methods to enhance a better understanding of *sunsum*. Ethnographic field observation helps scholars to capture or gather observable information from a contextual point of view. In recent scholarship, the approach has shifted to subjective analysis. Instead of objective accounts of field study, many scholars today use analytical studies to serve as the basis for criticizing and reinterpreting traditional concepts. In recent studies, a broad spectrum of academic disciplines in anthropology, philosophy, history, and political science as well as students of religion have all closely engaged in approaching the *sunsum* concept using this analytical methodology. Nevertheless, the subjective analysis has given weight to a despairingly linguistic conundrum that is progressively occupying the central debate of the contemporary argument of the pneumatic character of *sunsum* and the philosophy of quasi-physicalism in recent scholarship. The results have led to alternative ways of perceiving the nature and meaning of *sunsum*.

By using a historiographical approach, I want to trace the various ideas that have shaped the nature and meaning of *sunsum* in Akan studies.[16] Collingwood noted that "the right way of investigating mind is by the methods of history" (Collingwood 1946: 209). To investigate the nature and definition of *sunsum* from a historiographical approach brings to view the importance of history to intellectual analysis. Conceptualization of the term historiography calls for an understanding of the concept of history.

The term history has a Greek root meaning exploration, research, or inquiry of information. Since ancient times, history has had various contextual and conceptual definitions by different historians. Greek historians like Herodotus, Polybius and Thucydides all gave accounts of past events as worthy of remembrance. The definition of history goes beyond events of the past. Gustaaf Renier defines history as 'the story of the experiences of men living in societies" (Renier 1950: 33). English historian Edward Carr defines history as "a continuous process of interaction between the historian

[16] The historiographical approach to the study of *sunsum* was first used by Louise F. Müller. She is a Lecturer at LUCAS Leiden University Centre for the Arts in Society, Department for African Languages and Cultures in African Culture, History and Philosophy. She is also a research fellow at the University of Kwazulu-Natal in South Africa.

and his facts, an unending dialogue between the present and the past" (Carr 1990: 55). The "process of interaction" between the historian and his environment is dynamic due to the continuous changing of society and its impact on the views of the historian. The impact of social dynamics on ideas is a reality that makes history so important to understanding the evolution of concepts.

From the above definitions, it suffices to note that there is no one clear definition of history. However, the underlying concept is about the actions of people in society in the context of time and place. The vastness in the nature of history has informed the development of the historiographical approach, which is the methodological study of history. Merriam-Webster dictionary defines historiography as "the writing of history based on the critical examination of sources, the selection of particulars from the authentic materials, and the synthesis of particulars into a narrative that will stand the test of critical methods" (Merriam-Webster Dictionary). This definition applies to the study of religions and religious ideas over time. Within the study of Akan pneumatology, the different times and specific contexts have all contributed to how scholars perceived the nature and meaning of *sunsum*. Hence, a historiographical approach will help to gauge the value of a systematic evolution of how scholars have understood *sunsum* and the various circumstances that formed their understanding.

There are historiographical tools that have aided in the advancement of the study of history including, but not limited to cultural history, history of ideas, and intellectual history.

2.4.1. Intellectual History and the History of Ideas

There is no single, globalized definition of intellectual history, cultural history, and the history of ideas (Bavaj 2010; Gordon 2013). This complexity is informed by the multidisciplinary nature of each approach. However, the clear concept of the above approaches is understood in the comparison and contrast of the approaches. Intellectual history constitutes the study of intellectual patterns, ideas, and intellectuals over a specific period (Gordon 2013). The above definition recognizes the nexus between intellectual history and the history of ideas. Even though the two terms are sometimes used interchangeably, they differ in the concept of definition. The history of ideas looks at how large-scale historical concepts develop and transform over time (Skinner 2013). As such, historians of ideas pursue one major idea by organizing the historical narrative in the contexts of the time. A classic example of the history of ideas is portrayed by Arthur Lovejoy's book, *The Great Chain of Being: A Study of the History of an Idea* (2009). One merit of the history of ideas is that it permits an individual to acknowledge the commonalities that exist in thoughts despite the contextual differences (Gordon 2013). On the other hand, the history of ideas fosters a Platonist attitude concerning thoughts. The insistence that ideas are similar regardless of the contextual variations portrays a Platonist attitude. The history of ideas is quite nuanced as it is marred with internal inconsistencies and tensions (Gordon 2013).

On its part, intellectual history contrasts the history of ideas in various ways: it repels the Platonist narrative. It principally recognizes the existence of the physical world in defining ideas (Bavaj 2010). Intellectual history regards the contextual conditioning of historical ideas. Intellectual historians assert that ideas are understood within some larger contexts, such as the context of intellectual biography, linguistic or cultural dispositions, institutional change, or social struggle (Skinner 2013). Nonetheless, some intellectual historians follow in the path of the history of ideas in the sense that they exclusively adopt the "internalist" approach, and thus advance thoughts in relation to other thoughts, consequently disregarding the external world (Bavaj 2010). The advancement of thoughts in relation to previous thoughts often helps in the appreciation of the connection that may exist between two or more different realms of intellectual study, which could have been previously ignored (Gordon 2013). This is illustrated by the relationship between political and metaphysical concepts of causality, or scientific and theological ways of elucidation. Any attempt by historians to align themselves to either pure historians of ideas or intellectual historians has become almost impossible. The dominant school of thoughts mirrors the exploration of Platonism. The major focus is on the conceptual contexts, while "contextualism" has been merely given lip-service (Gordon 2013). The take-home message in this discussion is that the study of intellectual history involves multidisciplinary approaches and that the history of ideas and intellectual history cannot be effectively studied in isolation of each other. The methodological approaches involved do not only overlap but are also beneficial for understanding the connection that exists between them.

2.4.2. Intellectual History and Cultural History

There has been a noticeable shift from the study of political and social history to the study of cultural history. It has been observed that there is a very thin line between cultural history and intellectual history (Burke 2008). Cultural history constitutes the study of the vast culture of human society. These include, but are not limited to fine arts, religious beliefs and values, human sexuality, national symbols, and commemorations or rituals (Gordon 2013). One of the explanations about the origin of cultural history is drawn from the French "Annales" school in the early twentieth century. Exponents of the school sought an understanding of the long-duration patterns of European life (Gordon 2013). They compared the experience of the larger populace alongside the conventional historiographical concern about the schemes of the political elites. Cultural history seemed to have gone into oblivion, but in the 1970s and 1980s it re-emerged (Burke 2008). The central focus of the inquiry was the socio-economic "structuralism" that plagued the society, especially in Europe and North America. The second wave of cultural history was championed by the likes of Carl Schorske, Robert Darnton, Natalie Zemon Davis, and Lynn Hunt (Gordon 2013).

The use of a historiographical approach – cultural history, history of ideas, and intellectual history – is suitable for this research to investigate, analyze, and offer critique of the historical definition of *sunsum* according to scholars of Akan religions. The approach draws from the early years of colonial ethnography and ethnology, through postcolonial theoretical, analytical, and theological interpretivism of the *sunsum* concept. In this light, my research has offered a critical examination of both the limitations and potentialities of the methods of the scholars and how relevant these methods are to both current and future scholarship in the study of *sunsum*.

Scholarly contributions to the study include authoritative sources such as books, articles, monographs, and other materials touching on the subject. Despite employing a historiographical approach, I was unable to access resources such as autobiographies, memoirs, diaries, etc. The reason for this is that if such materials existed, I was unaware of them at the time of my research. But with the available materials, a comparative textual analysis of the pneumatic and quasi-physical schools of thought has been studied to demonstrate that *sunsum* is not always a "spirit" even though it has over the years enjoyed such pneumatic character. Nevertheless, my conclusions do not dismiss *sunsum* from pneumatological discourses as my research has recognized *sunsum* as an emanating force or one that is associated with spiritual beings.

Further, the context of my research focused on the Akan ethnic group. However, as an Akan myself, and of the Asante cultural group, I am not altogether safe in talking about the Akan people without my own Asante biases. In as much as this study is not limited to the Asantes, I deem such presuppositions inevitable but fruitful since I am an Asante and possess a firsthand experience of the Akan culture. The Asante ethnic group constitutes the majority among the Akan and has impressive ethnographic literature. This came about as a result of the introduction of the study of anthropology in the Asante region in the early twentieth century. My biases in this sense should not be taken as cultural arrogance but a limitation of how much literature and information I have been exposed to.

Finally, since some Akan people are in la Côte d'Ivoire, Togo, and in the diaspora, it has not been the purpose of my study to explore all these Akan territories. This study focused only on the Akan people living in Ghana. Where necessary, references have been made to some Akan communities living outside Ghana, but these fields do not occupy the main context of this research. Ghana, which hosts the largest and most diverse Akan roots, is the field of study as stated in the study.

Summary

The research methodology has answered the question of the difference between religion and culture as a methodological problem in understanding the context of my research. The overall research methodology is a historiographical approach to investigate and analyze the meaning and nature of *sunsum* in Akan scholarship. This has involved a constructive anthropological, philosophical, and theological investigation of the concept of *sunsum* and its implications for theological reflections. All these methodologies are meant to point out the direction of my research and the conclusions that I will draw as a result.

3. Introduction to the Akan Worldviews

> *"These traditional African cultural worldviews represent the ideas, folk wisdoms, and beliefs of African people; they are what elders are claimed to have said, which were not documented but passed down through succesive generations via oral tradition. Although these ideas may have been arrived at on the basis of reasonable arguments, they were not documented and hence are lost. It is difficult to try to recapture all these ideas accurately and the arguments underlying them."*— Polycarp Ikuenobe (*in* Wiredu 1980: 27).

In this chapter, I will outline the worldviews and cultural anthropology of the Akan people. In common with many sub-Saharan African societies, the Akan culture is a framework of social, economic, political, and religious systems diversified in artistic expressions for everyday life. The definition given in my research as Akan culture involves cultural particularities exclusive to the Akan. Despite the strong influence of westernization in Ghana, Akan communities continue to glory in their cultural heritage. Akan culture sheds light on day-to-day activities in present-day Ghana – including national affairs.[17] It is therefore of great necessity to set the basic framework to understand Akan religious-cultural traditions and to bring forward some of the implicit rationalities behind all that unfolds in the relationship between the spiritual and physical world. To do this will require a systematic definition of the contextual premise of Akan worldview in understanding the formulation of any Akan pneumatology.

The basic idea of worldview may cover the "concept of the supernatural, of nature, of man, and society, and of the way in which these concepts form

[17] One of such areas is the Akan language called Twi. The Twi language remains the most widely spoken language in Ghana. About half of the Ghanaian population comprises native Twi speakers, and about seventy-five percent of the general population speaks the Twi language. The Akan Twi has become the medium for many activities in marketing, media, and cultural exchange in Ghana."

a system that gives meaning to men's lives and action" (Busia 1955: 19). The worldview shapes one's thought for day-to-day fulfillment of life. It involves reality and the interpretation of cause and effects in life and beyond. The Akan worldviews are not independent of the total experiences of people's existence. The demands of a community, driven by holistic expressions in the languages, customs, and arts, form the basis of the Akan worldviews, and the continuity of these expressions predisposes their collective destiny.

In the following sections, we will look closely into the Akan worldviews to determine its various dimensions, lay the basic answers to the fundamental questions of the meaning and nature of *sunsum* and its implications to develop a new perspective for a contextual Akan pneumatology. In the end, we should be able to raise the necessary questions that will determine the basis for the anthropological, philosophical, and theological investigation of *sunsum* in this present study of Akan pneumatology.

3.1. Akan Cultural Anthropology

Knowing more about Akan anthropology begins with its cluster of unique cultural groups. Every Akan belongs to a specific group, colloquially called tribe. Major groups comprise Adansi, Akyem, Akwapin, Anyi, Aowin, Asante, Assin, Baule, Bron, Fante, Gomoa, Kwahu, Nzima, Sefwi, Twifo, Wassa, and the East Atlantic communities in Côte d'Ivoire (Pescheux 2003: 29–30; Ephirim-Donkor 2008: 56–57).[18] The Ghana Statistical Service estimates the Akan population to about 47.5 percent of the general Ghanaian population. The Asantes of the Akan make up the highest percentage of the general Ghanaian population. In terms of regional population, it ranks the

---

18 The Akan people of Côte d'Ivoire originated from the Asantes of Ghana. The Asante Kingdom was founded in the seventeenth century under the leadership of its famous king Osei Tutu I. His administration saw a drastic expansion of Asante territory in modern Ghana until his death in 1731. When his nephew and successor died after a short reign, a divisive war over succession to the throne broke out in Kumasi, the capital of the Asante Kingdom, between two royal families; this led to the death of the brother of the contesting queen mother, Awura Poku. To avoid further deaths, she led her people westward to their current settlement in Côte d'Ivoire (Shoup 2011: 109).

second most populous region after Greater Accra region in Ghana.[19] The Akan people of Cote d'Ivoire have their settlements in the south-east and central parts of the country with three major divisions: Central Akan, occupied by the Baoulé who make up the largest community with about 23 percent of the general population in Côte d'Ivoire. The Akan at the border comprise the Agni or Anyi, Abron, etc., and the Akan in the Ebrié lagoons are Ebrié, Abouré, Adioukrou, Appolloniens, etc. (Allou 2012; Kouadi 2016). There is a sizeable Akan population in the diaspora, including the Americas.[20]

3.1.1. Social Aspect of Akan Cultural Anthropology

Characteristically, the Akan share common trace of progeny and linguistics. Akan ancestry descends from an ancestress called *abrewa*, or "old woman." Traditional folklore regards her as the first ancestress and ancestral mother in the ancestral spiritual world (Ephirim-Donkor 2008). Based on this ideology, every Akan child bears a physio-material of the *abrewa* called *mogya* (blood), which eventually becomes the ideology behind Akan matrilineage of the eight consanguineal groups called *abusua* (Ephirim-Donkor 2010: 12, 30-32).[21]

An *abusua* is a social unit in which members of a specific lineage trace their existence to a common ancestress and share strong ties of kinship. That means the *abusua* identifies an Akan citizen to belong to a particular maternal ancestor. The *abusua* also underscores the ancestral cult where the

---

19 It is estimated that the Asantes constitute about 19.4 percent of the general population of Ghana according to the 2010 Population & Housing Census, Summary Report of Final Results, Ghana Statistical Service, May 2012, http://www.webdeploy.statsghana.gov.gh/nada/index.php/catalog/51. More information can be found in the 2021 Population and Housing Census (PHC). Last visited May 23, 2022.

20 Historians give accounts of Akan migrants in the Americas due to the transatlantic slave trade in the sixteenth to the nineteenth centuries. About 10 percent of the slaves shipped from Ghana to the Americas were Akan (Konadu 2010).

21 *Mmusua kuo* (clans) is the plural form of *abusua* (clan). Members of the *abusua* are called *abusuafoɔ* in the Akan languages. Each *abusua* has unique characteristics and taboos. However, the word *abusua* is often used in ordinary conversations to express friendly relations.

living and dead connect. The eight most popular consanguineal *abusua* with their totemic symbols and qualities are:[22]

Table 1: The Eight Akan Clans

Abusua (Clan)	**Totemic symbol**	**Symbolic quality**
Aduana[23]	Dog (with flames in the mouth)	Honesty and industriousness
Agona	Parrot	Eloquence and management
Asakyiri	Vulture	Calmness and patience
Aseneɛ	Bat	Diplomacy and faithfulness
Asona	Crow	Statesmanship and patriotism
Biretuo	Leopard	Bravery and Aggressiveness
Ɛkoɔna	Buffalo	Honesty and uprightness
Ɔyokoɔ	Hawk	Statesmanship, bravery and patience

Akan citizenship is by birth or affiliation into one of these matriclans.[24] The group ideology has a consequent expression of unity in diversity. Other

22 Conservation International of Ghana 2003: 2; Yankah 1995: 49; Awuah-Nyamekye 2014: 109.

23 The present researcher belongs to the Aduana clan of Wiamoase in the Ashanti region.

24 The grouping is expressed by the Akan proverb, *Abusua te sɛ nhwiren, egugu akuokuo*, meaning "The clan is like flowers, they blossom in clusters." Translated by Rattray (1916: 125). A person cannot renounce citizenship of an *abusua* as the proverb says, *Abusua nte sɛ asafo na yɛakɔ agyae*: "Clan membership is unlike club membership where one can withdraw membership." In some rare cases, an immigrant can attain Akan citizenship. An immigrant is known in the Akan language as *ɔhɔhoɔ* in the narrow sense; the term denotes a stranger because of the mere fact that the person is without Akan citizenship. Any person without Akan citizenship residing in Akan land is *ɔhɔhoɔ*. In its broader usage, any person (irrespective of a cultural group) can be a stranger in Akan land especially if one is not a citizen of the town. At some point, if a migrant desire a permanent residence within Akan community of residency, then affiliation to an Akan clan would be necessary for

commonalities among the Akan may include language, bilineal and matrilineal inheritance, unique naming ceremonies, traditional religion, festivals, and a monarchical succession of kingship and queenship (Pobee 1979: 44; De Graft-Johnson 1986: 83-84).[25]

3.2. The Human Being in Akan Anthropology

The Akan conception of the human being, personhood, and community is a social ontology. The social structure begins with the concept of the human being, known in Akan terminology as *onipa* (*nipa* is singular, and *nnipa* is plural). *Onipa* is the generic Akan term for the human being. Gyekye and Wiredu have identified the word as ambiguous because it expresses both the concept of the human as a "being" and the idea of a person as a degree of quality (Wiredu & Gyekye 1992). We can express these in two categories, i.e., descriptive and normative judgments. By descriptive judgment, *onipa* refers to the distinct features of a personal being called "human being" as opposed to an animal or a thing (Gyekye 2011). Phrases in the Akan language like *ɔyɛ nipa*, meaning "she is a human being," and *ɔnnyɛ nipa,* meaning "she is not a human being," distinguish the human being from what is not human.

The second category presents the human being as a person, the criterion for moral judgment. Normative judgments like *ɔyɛ nipa* – "she is a person" – suggest the individual represents commendable social norms and standards such as kindness, generosity, sympathy, etc. (Gyekye 2011). The opposite, *ɔnnyɛ nipa* – "she is inhuman" – indicates that the individual falls short of socially commendable norms and standards. It may suggest the person is unkind, corrupt, unloving, unfaithful, etc. These expressions of the human being provide the basic framework to construe Akan socio-religious and political structures.

---

protection and integration purposes. Since the Akan tradition has no allowance for proselytism, such affiliations are duly recognized. If the migrant is a woman, her children become part of the clan she is affiliated to, and the children have the right of inheritance from the mother's bloodline. If a migrant man espouses an Akan woman, the children are automatically Akan and have matrilineal rights. The Akan people from antiquity have recognized this form of affiliation or adoption as legal for community growth.

25 John Pobee, an emeritus professor at the University of Ghana, explains that the Akwapim of Larteh and Mampong are exceptionally patrilineal (Pobee 1979: 44).

Broadly, the Akan do not define a human being using physical components such as flesh and blood. The Akan indigenes perceive a human being as possessing immaterial, material, and social elements.[26] These are *ɔkra* (aw-krah'), denoting "life-force," *mogya* (mo-ja) meaning "blood," *ntorɔ* (n-to-ro) representing "fatherhood," *nipadua* (ni-pa-du-a) for "body," and *sunsum*, often translated as "spirit." *Ɔkra* and *sunsum* are immaterial by nature. The *'kra* is a life component responsible for life in the body.[27] It is "the innermost self, the essence of the individual person," and "the embodiment and transmitter of the individual's destiny (fate: *nkrabea*)." *Ɔkra* is the "spark of the Supreme Being," "the divine essence" and the state of "having an antemundane existence" with God (Gyekye 1987: 85). This definition of the *'kra* gives it a spiritual nature, although arguments surround its pneumatic nature. In Akan religions, the *'kra* is deathless and its separation from the body is death. It is the reason why Akan people esteem the human being with a significant degree of sacredness, beginning from the time of conception until the post-mundane life of the individual as an ancestor or ancestress. The *'kra* is the reason why Akan people say, "*Nipa nyinaa yɛ Nyame mma, obi ara nnyɛ asaase ba,*" meaning "All human beings are the children of God, and none is a child of the earth." Thus, God is the origin or Ancestor of every human being.

Following the spiritual essence are the social biogenetics responsible for the social experience. These are *ntorɔ*, which means "semen" and symbolizes fatherhood or character resemblance, and *mogya*, meaning "blood" and intimates *abusua* from the mother. These are biogenetics that give social affiliation to the Akan child. *Ntorɔ* is a genetic component emitted during sexual intercourse between a man and woman. Only males transmit *ntorɔ* (Rattray 1927: 319; 1929: 8). Its role accounts for the physiological mysteries of conception (Rattray 1923: 46). Akan traditional belief attributed the *ntorɔ* to a tutelary spirit from river gods (Denteh 1967: 91, 92). There are twelve river gods who have been identified as being responsible for the donation of the *ntorɔ* and are behind the proto-psychological character inherited from the father or members of the patrilineage (Denteh 1967: 96).[28] *Ntorɔ* is not responsible for the physical resemblance of the child

---

26 The term immaterial is used in this sense to denote non-physical and non-perceivable objects.

27 It is often shortened as *'kra*.

28 The twelve river gods or *ntorɔ* groups are: Bosompra (Tough/Strong/Firm), Bosomtwe (Human/Kind/Empathetic), Bosompo/Bosomnkóteaa (Proud/Audacious),

(Gyekye 1987: 226). Its operation is a spiritual input responsible for the individual's degree of charisma and the degree of "personal presence that each develops at the appropriate stage" (Wiredu 1992: 196, 197). At death, the *ntorɔ* returns to the father's family (Rattray 1957: 319). The *mogya* "represents a physiological bond to one's mother and an independent membership into her clan (*abusua*), or maternal lineage" (Neville & Co. 2009: 51). The Akan matrilineal system, already mentioned, is based upon the *mogya* ideology to legitimate a person's citizenship in Akan society and acquisition of ancestral status in the family.

The *nipadua* is only a physical material and the subject of perceptible experience of the whole human being. We can say it is that part of the human being that can be felt by physical touch. The word *nipadua* is a compound from *nipa* (human being) and *dua* (tree). The Akan perceive the figure of a human being like the shape of a tree with branches like hands and fingers, the leaves like the human head, the trunk standing like the body to the feet, and roots like the toes (Gyekye & Wiredu 1992). The *nipadua* has many biological components such as cells, tissues, muscles, and organs. Its formation begins from the womb after the immaterial and the biogenetics combine to form a fetus. The *nipadua* is temporal, suffers death and corruption, and there is no existence of it after death.

The next important aspect of the human being in Akan anthropology is the distinctive *sunsum*, an immaterial substance that defines personality and interacts and operates on various aspects of a person's whole life, including the social, emotional, mental, and spiritual faculties. Scholars consider *sunsum* as the basis of the Akan concept of personhood since it expresses the qualities peculiar to one's individuality – in both moral and ethical attributes (Asare Opoku 1978: 96). *Sunsum* has a variety of contextual interpretations because it is not exclusive to only humans. In a broader sense, the term integrates ontological and epistemological principles to define Akan cosmology.

Now, it is proposed to offer a general panoramic look at the various meanings and interpretations given to *sunsum* in Akan worldviews. Further study will reveal more critical analyses and different dimensions relating to

---

Bosomafram (Liberal/Kind/Empathetic), Bosommuru (Respectable/ Distinguished), Bosomkonsi (The Virtuous), Bosomdweróbe (Eccentric/Jittery), Bosomayensu (Truculent), Bosomsika (Fastidious), Bosomkrete (Chivalrous), Bosomakim (Fanatic), Bosomafi (Chaste) (Rattray 1923: 47, 48; Denteh 1967: 96; Asare Opoku 1978: 98).

the historiography of *sunsum*. Right now, I will move towards a comprehensive understanding of *sunsum* in the Akan worldviews. I will introduce the many definitions of *sunsum*, with a special emphasis on a literature review of the meaning and nature of *sunsum*.

3.3. What Is This Thing Called *Sunsum*?

My first approach is an inquiry into the spiritual worldview of the Akan people. *Sunsum* is enigmatic and ambiguous, and its meaning has puzzled many scholars studying Akan religions. Gyekye says it is the greatest difficulty in Akan metaphysics and a source of confusion (1987: 89). Ephirim-Donkor is an Akan scholar in religious studies and traditional chief of Gomoa Mprumem in Ghana. He has written a lot on the subject and admitted that *sunsum* is a paradox and even an enigma (Ephirim-Donkor 2016: 49). Part of the puzzle stems from different attempts to unravel its nature or to appropriate its conception in English translations. Few scholars have ventured, as far as possible, to investigate the meaning of the term. There is a unanimous conception that *sunsum* is a "spirit," except for recent studies in quasi-physicalism that challenges the pneumatic character to be incorrect and a conceptual blunder.

Generally, the Akan believe *sunsum* is a spiritual and dynamic substance that is present in natural objects, including human beings. It serves as the principle of animation, personality, and power for protection against spiritual attacks (Rattray 1955: 153). The idea of protection suggests that the *sunsum* is an astral vitality although it is considered to be the essence of the object in which it resides. Several Akan people accept *sunsum* as an activating principle of life in human beings and natural objects (Gyekye 1987: 75, 88, 98). It is an essence emanating directly or indirectly from God (Jawanza 2012: 79-80; Gyekye 1987: 73).[29] According to some scholars, *sunsum* is the operational force for morality and that which is responsible for character, genius, temper, and quality (Molefi 1996: 453). It is the subject of experience, and it determines the spirituality of an individual or object. It is responsible for the formation and transformation of personality (ego) and the character in dreams (Ephirim-Donkor 2010: 90; Gyekye 1987: 89, 90, 102; Molefi 1996: 453; Wiredu 1987: 161).

---

[29] The concept of *sunsum* emanating from God has been debated, thus this study will provide a rigorous examination.

3.3.1. Etymology of *Sunsum*

There are different etymologies of the word *sunsum*. J. B. Danquah suggests that *sunsum* is an evolution of *esu*, meaning character or nature in Akan language.[30] In Akan epistemology, *esu* expresses distinct features of an individual's personality or the nature of a thing. Akan words like *suban* (character) and *suman* (amulet or charm) have their root in *esu*.[31] Danquah describes *esu* as a form of "prime genetic basis for the origin of the social subject, i.e., man" (1968: 111). *Esu* is synonymous with personality, leaving little doubt as to why Danquah thinks *sunsum* is personality.[32]

Danquah again observes the connection between the word *esu* and water (*nsu*), river (*a/nsu*), and rain (*osu*) (1968: 111). The relationship makes *sunsum* a compound of three words, namely, *esu* "nature," *nsu* "river," and *mu* "inside."[33] The literal transliteration would mean "the nature/character/quality coming from the river." Other conceptions of *sunsum* agree with this meaning. Rattray, Busia, Ephirim-Donkor, and others think *sunsum* is a tutelary vitality. Akan traditional beliefs do not consider rivers and water bodies as only natural objects. Water is associated with tutelary deities called Abosom (pl. deities). The Abosom are spirits that re-

---

30 *Su* is a shortened form of *esu*.

31 Danquah gives more details about *esu*: "In a secondary sense, *nsu* also means vow, oath, or solemn promise. Other developed forms of *-su* are *susu* (measure), *nsusui* (thought), *suma* (hide, conceal), *sunsuma* (shadow), *sunsum* (looks, personality, ego), *esum* (darkness, literally, in or at the place of "*su*"), and *suman* (talisman, fetish, amulet, or "any protecting power"). *Suman* means literally "the world of "'*su*.'" If the Akim from *sumane* is considered, it may mean "'*su*' gone wrong" or "'*su*' bypassed." In the context of species or race, the connection of "*esu*" with *abusua* (family) is apparent in *a-bu-su-wa*, i.e., a bit or portion of "*su*" broken off, with *abusua* treated as a portion of the race. "*Su*" features in many compounds, e.g., *nisu* (tears, from *ani-eye and -su*); *bosu* (dew, form *ebo*, mist or fog and *-su*); *suban* (conduct, from *-su* and ban, form, shape, fashion, frame)" (Danquah 1968: 111, 112).

32 There is more to say about this in my discussion on Danquah in the subsequent chapters.

33 There are so many compound words among the Akan that a non-Akan may have trouble understanding. For example, Koofori is a compound of Kofi-Ofori, *Tweduampon* which is a compound of *Twere-dua-ampon*. Other words include, *konua* (*kɔn-mu-dua*) means yoke; *sunsuma* (*sunsum-ba*) (shadow), *ewiase* (*owia-ase*) meaning world, *nkrabea* (*nkra-bea*) denoting destiny, and many others.

side in rivers and bodies of water (Ephirim-Donkor 2016: 54). Their essence is spiritual and known to Akan people as *sunsum* and are identified with water. The Abosom help in human reproduction through the use of a spiritual element already known as *ntorɔ*. Akan people believe only males transmit *ntorɔ* during the act of sexual intercourse between a man and a woman.[34] Scholars like Rattray, Minkus, Busia, Meyerowitz, Wiredu, Ephirim-Donkor, etc. have all associated *sunsum* and *ntorɔ* with the Abosom, and the two terms are often nuanced with each other (Rattray 1923: 46; Wiredu 1987: 161). The intervention of the Abosom in procreation makes every Akan, according to Ephirim-Donkor, "the *Ɔbosom* willed into the corporeal environment" (2016: 83). Thus, their spiritual presence in the individual defines the spiritual attributes of personality in life. In effect, *sunsum* is the nature or character of the tutelary deity (river god) responsible for life forms.[35] The Akan people had a firm understanding of humanity's origins as a product of the divinities.

There is another common school of thought which holds that *sunsum* is nothing but a shadow or image (Meyerowitz 1951; Ephirim-Donkor 2016). This school of thought parallels the inherent *sunsum* to the shadow of a person on a surface projected by rays of light. Ephirim-Donkor writes: "So a human being, for instance, though not a Sunsum because he or she is a physical being, has a Sunsum nonetheless, which becomes visible under a light" (2016: 46). Ephirim-Donkor shares two ideas here. First, there is the imperceptible *sunsum* (spirit) hidden from the reach of the physical eye, and the second is the perceptible *sunsum* (shadow) which is a reflection of the inherent *sunsum*. This striking scenario points to *sunsum* as an unseen non-human agency, active, and revealed under the exposure of light as the double of the person (shadow). *Sunsum*, like the shadow, is intangible, beyond the control of tangible objects, and is an "active agency making it a spirit" (Ephirim-Donkor 2016: 40, 48). Those who advance the shadow thesis do so because the majority of Akan people call "shadow" *sunsum* in the local languages, even though the "shadow" is not identical with the intrinsic *sunsum*. This notion seems to be a misnomer. The Akan name for shadow is *sunsum ba*, "child of *sunsum*," or often shortened as *sunsuma*; hence

[34] For further studies on the relationship between water and Abosom, see Ephirim-Donkor 2016: 50-55.

[35] This understanding falls within the methodological framework of this research, and it is my purpose to critically probe whether the primal conception of the *sunsum* whether is indeed from the tutelary deities or God or both.

asunsumabo, "to cast stones at a shadow."[36] *Sunsuma* is a term given to the dark reflection of a physical object illuminated by light rays. The name also suggests the physical presence of the invisible *sunsum*. This does not mean the two are identical or same. Akan thinkers do not have a dichotomy of a mystical *sunsum* (spirit) and physical *sunsum* (shadow). After all, Akan people do not consider the shadow to be mystical although superstitious myths exist around it, and no ritual is ever associated with a person's shadow.

In connection with the shadow thesis of *sunsum* is darkness. The suffix of *sunsum* is *sum*, from *esum* (darkness). *Sunsum*, although not the same as darkness, may carry connotations of an intrinsic darkness and elusiveness (Ephirim-Donkor 2016: 48). Darkness is the antithesis of light; it conceals visible objects from the naked eyes. The Akan spiritual worldview carries a similar idea of privacy, secrecy, and a world of entities that are invisible to the naked eyes. Ephirim-Donkor says, "all ethereal phenomena are subsumed under Sunsum, because, figuratively, anything that people do not understand or observe and yet think to be *real* or *there* is time tested" (2016: 48). The spiritual agencies are invisible, but they are capable of revealing themselves in the corporeal world. The suffix *sum* (dark) is a reminder of the mystical nature of *sunsum*, which Ephirim-Donkor thinks is always a mystery (2016: 48).

Let us do a recap of the various meanings and etymologies of the term *sunsum*. The different meanings of the word reveal the difficulty that students of Akan religions confront in their attempt to find a common meaning of *sunsum*. There are more dimensions of *sunsum* to look at in order to understand the overall usage of the term among Akan people. I'll now look at how *sunsum* underlines the conceptual framework of the meaning of reality and its implications for ideas, values, and people's attitudes toward life.

3.4. *Sunsum* in the Akan Worldview

The first attempt to understand the Akan spiritual worldview will be a reassessment of its material and metaphysical conceptions. The two most fun-

[36] *Sunsuma* (*sunsum ba*) is a shade or shadow (Christaller 1881: 464). Among the Ga people of Ghana, *sunsuma* means "spirit," an equivalent of the Akan *sunsum*.

damental terms to consider are *wiase*, translated into English as the "corporeal world," and *sunsum mu*, translated into English as "spiritual."[37] *Wiase* is a compound of *owia* (sun) and *ase* (under/below), i.e., "under the sun." In other words, *wiase* involves all that pertains to the world under the sun. It is the world of natural objects comprising all objects under the category of visible objects that are observable in the world of natural phenomena (Gyekye 1987: 69). These may include animate and inanimate objects such as human beings, animals, trees and plants, rivers, stones and mountains, moon and stars, air and the sky, and all other things that are perceptible to human senses.

The metaphysical world, known as *sunsum mu* or the non-perceivable, involves all objects conceived and perceived in abstract terms and are physically nonconceptual (Wiredu 1987: 165; Gyekye 1987: 69). *Sunsum mu* is a realm other than the physical universe of matter. This assumption does not mean that *sunsum mu* is a specific universe outside our physical world; that explanation creates a dualistic view of the Akan universe. As we will explain later, the Akan universe is an inspirited world. *Sunsum mu* is mystical, comprising abstract realities, and beings including God, pantheon deities, spirits, forces, and other psycho-dimensional experiences such as dreams and divinations. In modern Akan linguistics, a phrase like *wiase mu nsɛm*, meaning "matters of the world," has become the generic phrase to convey Akan's cosmological interpretation of both the physical and nonphysical world.

From this background, we understand the basis of the Akan cosmological conception of the universe as a composition of matter and a metaphysical world (Gyekye 1987: 69). Despite the seemingly dualistic cosmological ideology, contemporary Akan thinkers argue that there is an interpenetrating unity between these two-dimensional worlds, making it

[37] Even though a majority of scholars have translated *sunsum mu* as "spiritual," I think it should rather be translated into English as "mystical" or "world of mystical forces." The usual connotation given to *sunsum mu* expresses mystical forces. This argument is highlighted in my research, and further discussions will be provided in the subsequent chapters in an attempt to show that both *sunsum mu* and *honhom mu* may be identical and are in fact often used interchangeably. However, the separation here should not be seen as awkward, as further discussion will show that the two are not synonymous and that one has an ephemeral phenomenon while the other is eternal – not limited by time and space. For clarity, we will abide by the ordinary understanding of *sunsum mu* as "spiritual world" until further critical analysis has been rendered.

one and conveying the idea of the universe as one inspirited universe. Akan religions postulate the physical universe as being ruled by the immaterial dimension of the world of powerful spirits and hypnotic forces that impinge on the material world; this conception explains why Akan people attribute physical causalities to the spiritual (to be described shortly). Reality is defined in connection with the spiritual world, although the physical world is also real (Minkus 1980: 182; Gyekye 1987: 69; Wiredu 1998: 29; Ephirim-Donkor 2010: 123). This definition of reality forms the foundation of Akan epistemologies and ontologies.

The Akan worldviews focus on the spiritual and physical world. First, the spiritual comprises of mystical entities and forces: God, pantheon deities, ancestors, and other spirits. These form the basis for pneumatological studies and represent an essential cue to the expression of Christian thoughts and learning among the Akan. The second is the physical world of natural objects, comprising the concept of the human being, animals, plants, and all other objects perceptible to the human senses. Natural objects are animated by the spiritual and the relationship between the two is ontological. We will look at these two main categories in order to define the various terminologies and how they help us to form the basis for further investigation.

3.4.1. The Supreme Deity (Onyankopɔn)

Akan spirituality is rooted in the belief of a unique God named Nyankopɔn or Onyame Kwame, "Great God of Saturday."[38] In other words, "He whose day (of birth or worship) is Saturday" (Danquah 1968: 30). He is the creator (*Ɔbɔadeɛ*), sustainer of life, the highest spirit-being, and progenitor of all, and whose essence lives in all. According to the Akan proverb, *Obi nkyerɛ abɔfra Nyame*, meaning, "Nobody teaches the child to know God," the Akan God is an absolute reality, self-revealing, and self-evident (Gyekye 1987: 70). Nyankopɔn is a suprasensible deity transcending all in God's absolute reality. The various myths attach anthropomorphic characteristics to God as the great ancestor (Nana Nyankopɔn). Among the Akan, belief in

[38] Nyankopɔn or Onyankopɔn expresses the same idea of the unique God of the Akan. Akan people often use the name Nyankopɔn interchangeably with the distinctive Nyame, the generic name for the deity. The designation of Nyame to God perhaps evolved from "nyame" or "anyame" (gods) to disassociate the Supreme God from the pantheon deities.

God as the creator affects everyday life and activities because they believe God is immanent in the universe and present in us. God rules both the *wiase* (material) and *sunsum mu* (spiritual) world.

3.4.2. The Pantheon Deities (Abosom)

Akan traditional religions believe in pantheon deities or tutelary gods. These are localized and geographical protective deities that identify themselves with a group of people in a given place. One of such deities is the great god of the Tano River, often known as Ta Kora in the Asante region.[39] Ta Kora is one of the children of Nyankopɔn (so ascribed to other popular divinities) and progenitor of several other deities (Rattray 1915: 146; 1955: 54).

The Akan pantheon deities entail myriad gods acting as intermediaries between human beings and Nyankopɔn. Their roles as intermediaries make them superintendents of daily affairs. The Akan explanation for this mediation is in the belief of the absolute sovereignty of the supreme God whom they should approach according to what he prescribes. Others argue that God cannot be approached lightly or bothered with trivial affairs of human beings; therefore, He works in tandem with the divinities that act in God's stead as mediators, i.e., the Abosom "pantheon of gods" (Pobee 1979: 46; Gyekye 1987: 68, 69).

---

[39] The Tano River is a legendary river in Ghana. It rises from Techiman in the Brong Ahafo region and flows southeastward about 250 miles (400 km) through Ehy Lagoon, Tendo Lagoon and finally Aby Lagoon in Ivory Coast to join the Atlantic Ocean. The river occupies great significance in the making of a shrine among the Akan people. It is esteemed to be the greatest of all the gods. Ta Kora is the religious name given to the god of the river. *Ta* is the shortened form of Tano, being the name of the river. *Kora* is an Akan word that means "to keep" or "mend," and that suggests the importance of this god as the keeper and protector of the people. *Kora* is most of the time confused with *akora*, which means an old man. According to legend, when "the Supreme Being was premeditating as to where he should set down the abodes of his children on earth, the goat heard of it and being a great friend of Bea [a river in Ghana] ran and told him that when his father sent for Tanno and him, he should rise up and go very quickly so that he should arrive there before his brother. So, when the children were called before their father, Bea came first and his father, as a reward, set his abode down in the coolness and shade of the forest country, whereas Tanno was given a home in the more open grass lands. In consequence, to this day the followers of Tanno, 'turn their back on', or 'hate', i.e. taboo the flesh of the goat" (Rattray 1915: 46, 47; Ref. Rattray 1955: 145-6).

The essential description of the pantheon deities as children of God makes them inherently powerful like God. As spirits, they can penetrate the natural world through natural elements and means. Hence, they are able to take temporary residence in natural objects such as stones, trees, rivers, mountains, etc. to exercise their external manifestation to the natural world, especially to the person they desire to use as a point of contact. Several Akan people perceive these suprasensible beings in nature as *sunsum*. Consequently, it is held that everything has *sunsum*, meaning everything can exercise power. In Akan religions, God is not in matter, neither is He a distant God from His creation as may be understood in deistic theories. God transcends all things; it is the deities who are identified as taking residence in natural objects. Therefore, animism can be a loose term to describe the Akan religions in general. But it cannot be ruled out that the concepts of panentheism and panpsychism are not in themselves principles of animism. How good are the pantheon deities to the Akan?

The deities are protective agents, and their work is to protect their people and the environment from harm. Nevertheless, they possess the potency to inflict evil. Breach of social norms (taboos) may incur the wrath of the gods, and without hesitation, they can respond with uncontrollable plagues. The situation will call for ritual sacrifices and pacifications to appease the gods to restore normalcy; this makes the nature of the gods partly good and evil. The lesser deities exercise absolute independent authority of their will, even though God created them (Gyekye 1996: 12).6

The Akan religions have officials who have excellent knowledge about the religions. Among them are the traditional priests or priestesses through whom the gods manifest their presence. Akan people call these individuals *Akomfoɔ*, meaning "traditional priests." Erstwhile missionaries confused their profession with witchcraft or fetishism. Their call to the priestly cult is personal and they serve as mediums for one or more of the deities.

3.4.3. Ancestors and other Spirits in Akan Cosmology

Next to the Abosom are the ancestors known in Akan languages as Nananom Nsamanfoɔ, or Mpanyinfoɔ. These ancestors are deceased family members. In the Akan religions, it is the matrilineal clan that confers ancestral status on the individual. These apotheosized beings, who were once among the living but have departed to *Asamando*, the spirit world of the dead, are said to be powerful to help their affiliates in the world. Their presence is summoned in prayer invocations through the pouring of libation, an act of summoning the benevolent spirits in the atmosphere. Ephirim-Donkor's book, *African Religion Defined: A Systematic Study of Ancestor Worship among the Akan* thematizes on the subject of the relationship between the departed souls and the living, which forms an integral part of the Akan traditional religions.

The reverence given to the ancestors is periodic and ceremonial. Akan people do not worship their ancestors as they do to the deities; this is because the ancestors do not possess ultimate powers in themselves, and neither are they counted among the deities. There are no altars erected for the ancestors except the ancestral stools believed to contain the *sunsum* of the ancestors. An Akan will bow down before an altar erected for a deity instead of bowing down before an ancestral stool. The religious space for the ancestors is only for benevolence and is very much communal. Ancestors are benevolent spirits like angels are benevolent spirits in Christianity. The concept of ancestors further expresses solidarity and communality since the Akan community "consists of the living, the dead, and the yet-to-be-born" (Pobee 1979: 49).

The ancestral cult has strong significance in terms of showing that life does not end in death. The general conception is that life is a journey and death is only a state of departure from the physical world to the spiritual realm of the dead (*Asamando*).[40] After the *'kra* separates from the body, it does not make its final abode with God in heaven as is understood in the doctrines of Judaism and Christianity about the return of the soul to God.[41]

---

40 This is not a separation per se because the belief in ancestors solidifies the bond between the dead and the living.

41 Ephirim-Donkor seems to propose the idea that the departed *ɔkra* lives in heaven, thus creating the impression of the return of the *ɔkra* to God (Ephirim-Donkor 1997: 87). However, a careful reading of Ephirim-Donkor reveals his use of heaven as a metaphorical interchange of the ancestral world (Ephirim-Donkor 1997: 52). Though his explanation makes sense, it does not justify the use of heaven as an accurate term in this context in the sense that such a terminology has no significant meaning in Akan traditional religion. It again carries an implicit theology that can mislead readers to think otherwise. Further critique on this is issued in Kofi Opoku Asare's review of Ephirim-Donkor's book *African Religion Defined: A Systematic Study of Ancestor Worship Among the Akan* (Asare Opoku 1998).

The *'kra* travels to the ancestral world, making the process of life among the Akan linear rather than cyclical.[42]

There are other spirits in Akan cosmology involved in human affairs apart from the ancestors. The religious belief that the universe is populated with evil spirits and powers that work to alter individuals' destiny is interwoven with many aspects of life. Each *'kra* enters the mundane world with a specific destiny imposed by God. The Akan idea of destiny is positive in the sense that it determines the totality of the various temporal events and occurrences that bring luck to the person. It is by default an existential condition of a person's spiritual and social wellness in life. The ability of evil forces to alter destiny exposes their evil nature and antagonism against human well-being. Few of these evil spirits are mentioned in Akan mythology, namely Sasabonsam: a forest monster, the prince of evil powers, and the master of evil acts (Pobee 1978: 48). Sasabonsam works in tandem with other cohorts, such as witches and evil dwarfs (*mmoatia*) who come under his command. Many human sufferings, such as sicknesses, accidents, barrenness, and all other suspicious ailments and misfortunes are said to be the result of their evil schemes. The dwarfs possess magical powers with which they can induce a person or lead one astray in the forest. Legend says they possess the secrets of healing and can train a person to become a magician.

3.4.4. The World of Natural Objects

The world of natural objects is the physical world of experience. As previously indicated, these are objects under the sun that are subject to the animation of the spiritual world (*sunsum mu*) as well as the natural laws of physics. The most important to our present study is the human being who is the criterion of judgment within a given social experience or geographical context and the focus of anthropological discourses.

---

[42] The departed *'kra* does not wander to seek for a place of abode. The Akan believe in various rituals performed for the dead as a send-off to the ancestral world, which may include funerals and forty-day celebrations. The departed *'kra* knows where it is going; indeed, there are only few instances whereby the departed *'kra* will wander around. For example, Akan people believe the spirit of an individual who died through an accident or suicide wander. These kinds of death are known as *atɔfowuo* (premature death). It means the person's destiny is altered. The *akra* of these individuals do not travel to the ancestral world; instead, they wander around revealing themselves to people occasionally.

To sum up this section, the recent spread of Christian ideas has disrupted the Akan worldviews, leading to a conflict of faith whereby many Akan Christian adherents are regularly caught in the web of the traditional religions. There exists a constant fear of evil spirits and malediction from the spiritual world. Consequently, many Akan Christians tend to consult the deities they have previously denounced for protection. While they do not quit the Church, their faith is rather shaped, partly, by their traditional worldviews. In a deeper sense, many of them are struggling with the question of identity. For this reason, many people wonder whether conversion to Christianity has adequately served its purpose.

Again, today's global influences, such as technology and education, are shaping how most Akan people perceive the world and live their lives. Sociologists and anthropologists have called this the social revolution. In part, we can see positive consequences regarding Ghana's integration into the larger global sphere of communication, trade, and international relations for the common good. On the other hand, global integration raises the question of being, social organization, and habits that we must readjust into new situations because of social changes (Busia 1955: 16, 17). Most of the time, the latter fails and spawns a double standard of life or multifarious conflicts (Busia 1955).

3.5. *Sunsum* in Akan Anthropology

3.5.1. The Origin of *Sunsum*

The previous discussions have highlighted the multiple enigmas associated with the meaning of *sunsum*. In this section, I will explore in greater length some of these difficulties, particularly the question of the origin of *sunsum*.

There are currently two schools of thought regarding the origin of *sunsum* that demands our attention. The first school of thought relates *sunsum* to the pantheon gods or tutelary deities, who through a male agent transmit their *sunsum* to a child. This conception reiterates the interpenetrating relationship between the spiritual and physical world. With that conception, *sunsum* becomes an essential quality of the deities that only males are capable of transmitting or passing to their offspring. The implication of this idea seems to be the reason why Akan people say that *Ɔbaa nni sunsum*, meaning, "a woman does not have *sunsum*," or what some accounts explain to mean men are more inspirited than women.[43] The rationality stems from the masculine mediumship of the *sunsum*. The deities choose males to transmit the *sunsum* for reasons that I will show later. For now, the *sunsum* makes each person bear the essence of the Ɔbosom (god). Ephirim-Donkor writes, "an *Ɔbosom*, as Sunsum (spirit), is transmitted through a father's semen (*huaba/ntoro*) during a sexual act analogous to spirit alightment during divination rites" (2016: 83). He then asserts a similar idea that "[t]he Abosom created life-forms that were of the same essence as themselves, comprised of the blood (Mogya) or matter, and spirit (Sunsum) as an activating agency" (2016: 152). Some scholars in this school of thought include Rattray, Mayerowitz, Busia, and Minkus. More will be said about these scholars in subsequent chapters.

The second school of thought is theocentric, which argues in favor of panentheism where God's *sunsum* vivifies the natural world. Danquah and Gyekye agree on this notion of the *sunsum* as a divine essence, even though they disagree in their conceptual understanding about the nature of *sunsum*. Danquah postulates: "Nyankopon is the Sunsum of Odomankoma, the Experience of Ultimate Being… Nyankopon is already an expression of Odomankoma, his Sunsum" (1968: 113). Gyekye likewise asserts that "*sunsum* derives ultimately from Onyame who, as the Supreme Being, is the Highest Spirit or Highest Power" (1987: 73). The concept of panentheism relegates the tutelary deities to positions of little involvement in life-forms. If anything, they, too, like all other things, are animated by the *sunsum* of God. Does that prevent them from transmitting *sunsum*? I intend to explore this question later. A contribution to this school of thought is Agyarko's Onyame *Sunsum* (God's spirit) and *Sunsum Kronkron* (Holy Spirit) pneumatology.

43 The maxim is used metaphorically and comparatively to show that females possess a small portion of the father's *sunsum*, hence are not high-spirited or able to transmit *sunsum* like men do. I intend to offer more details in Chapter Six.

3.5.2. Various Categories of *Sunsum*

3.5.2.1. *Sunsum* in Sleep Peregrination

The idea of sleep peregrination of the *sunsum* in dreams is common in Akan worldview. An astral voyage occurs when the *sunsum* temporally vacates the body during nightly peregrinations in dreams, returning or not returning to its owner (Asare Opoku 1978: 96; Appiah 1992: 157). A person is likely to die without the *sunsum*. This phenomenon happens when another spiritual force, such as a witch, attacks the person's *sunsum*. The *sunsum* is dynamic, making it liable to the manipulation of evil forces, either for good or evil purposes. Witchcraft is nothing but a *sunsum* that has become evil. The intrinsic vitality of *sunsum* is what makes witchcraft a superhuman phenomenon capable of attacking people during their sleep. The Akan use this rationale to objectify spiritual illness and misfortunes. Hence, religion and healing practices are indispensable. Some individuals are resistant to spiritual attacks. A person's *sunsum* can act as protective paraphernalia against witches if that person has a strong *sunsum* (*ne sunsum mu yɛ duru*). A strong *sunsum* is the most effective protection against witchcraft (Asare Opoku 1978: 97). Individuals with light *sunsum* (*ne sunsum mu yɛ hare*) are most vulnerable to witchcraft attacks.

3.5.2.2. *Sunsum* in Akan Mediumistic Experience

Akan mediumistic experience may also help in understanding the mystical operations of the *sunsum* and how a supernatural encounter with a human being has a close connection with the *sunsum*. *Akɔm* is a religious performance in Akan religions that entails the composition of a traditional ensemble of percussion, characterized by ecstatic experience of the supernatural in which a spiritual agent descends or alights on the Ɔkɔmfoɔ (traditional priest) who serves the deities. Akɔmfoɔ (pl.) are cultic priests who have a special call from the deities and who are trained to serve the deities' interest for the good of the community. Their primary roles involve mediation between the natural and spiritual worlds. Traditional priests are religious leaders who offer sacrifices and intercede on behalf of people in various prayer rituals. They possess healing abilities, can exorcize witchcraft, and can communicate with other spirits such as the ancestors. They live in shrines dedicated to the deities, and in some cases have intimate ties to the kingship.

Akɔmfoɔ command great authority because they occupy the "highest socio-religious and spiritual estate, vested in the esoterica of ritual application and processes" (Ephirim-Donkor 2008: 56). The Akɔmfoɔ undergo ecstatic prophesying when one or more of the deities take control of the consciousness through alighting, characterized by a state of trance or prophesying (*akɔm*). The Ɔkɔmfoɔ becomes the medium of speech for the deity when the trance status is reached. The priest under ecstatic experience loses consciousness, his body tingles, he becomes uncontrollable, exhibits unusual strength, dances, jumps, falls, rolls on the ground, and may display diverse paranormal gestures. Two or three, or more priests can experience spontaneous frenzy. Akan people judge this experience as the activation of the *sunsum* of the Ɔkɔmfoɔ by a spiritual agent. The deities inform the Ɔkɔmfoɔ about what they want or what to reveal through the *sunsum* (Gyekye 1987: 102). Without the *sunsum*, a person may lack transcendental rationality, or it may be impossible for any extrasensory experience to take place. The *sunsum* acts as a unifying force between the physical and spiritual, and often transposes itself into various dynamic interactions outside one's body.

3.5.2.3. *Sunsum* as a Revengeful Force

There is a strong assertion of a telepathic interception between people's *sunsum*. A majority of Akan believe a person's *sunsum* can intercept another. For example, legend says a husband's *sunsum* can seize his adulterous wife. It follows that the husband's *ɔkra* will alert his *ntorɔ*, who will inform the husband's *sunsum* to punish the woman. Hence, the saying *Me kunu sunsum akye me*, "My husband's *sunsum* has seized me." If the woman refuses to confess, the *sunsum* of the husband may kill her (Rattray 1955: 154). Some use this phenomenon as a basis for attributing an entitative character to the nature of *ɔkra*, *ntorɔ*, and *sunsum*. Further analysis will challenge this interpretation, and even if one considers them as entities, for argument's sake, then how many entities form the human being? The concept of consubstantial entities (hypostases) as found, for instance, in the Trinitarian conception, is absent in Akan anthropology. The various immaterial substances work in ways that are so mysteriously woven together to make a complete human being.

3.5.2.4. *Sunsum* in Akan Psychology

There is the psychological dimension of experience, which gives *sunsum* a psychical function. An Akan figurative speech goes like this, *Wo reku me sunsum*, "You are hurting my [soul] emotions." Hatred, anger, evil thoughts, and other emotional burdens may ramp up against oneself or someone because the *sunsum* is sensitive to these psychological effects. Evil thoughts, whether self-inflicted or inflicted by another person, can overshadow, or suppress the *sunsum* of an individual, resulting in sickness. In spite of this, this conception recapitulates why moral and ethical behavior is dependent upon one's *sunsum*. It also expresses the relationship between the mind and body. Akan culture has a process of carefully dealing with the ill-effects of the mind through a formal ceremony of confession called *Apo* festival. During this celebration, individuals express uninhibitedly to another – including the king – what they think about them, without apprehension. In a practical sense, a person's *sunsum* is supposed to be relieved from pain and evil thoughts (Rattray 1923: 153; Asare Opoku 1978: 97).

3.5.2.5. The Collective *Sunsum*: Sika Dwa Kofi (The Golden Stool)

Besides the operation of the *sunsum* in the different dimensions of individuals' lives, families and groups may also have their *sunsum*, which holds their souls together. The sacred stool, or *Sika Dwa Kofi,* is said to contain the *sunsum* of the Asantes (Figure 4). The history behind the stool epitomizes political power and patriotism among the Asantes. Legend says Ɔkomfo Anɔkye, the then supreme priest and friend of Osei-Tutu I, king of Kumasi and founder of the Asante nation, called for the stool from the sky, all covered partly with pure gold and rested on the lap of Osei-Tutu I, signifying the right of leadership of the Asante Confederacy.[44] Anɔkye decreed that nothing would harm the Asante nation as long as they kept the Golden Stool.[45] He further cautioned the Asantes to keep the stool from destruction

---

[44] Ɔkomfo Anɔkye was a traditional priest and one of the legends of the Asante kingdom whose spiritual powers and wisdom helped the leadership of Osei-Tutu 1 in the 17th century to unify the Ashanti nation. Ɔkomfo Anɔkye drafted the stratification of the Ashanti kingdom, kingship, and its constitution. He holds great prominence in Asante history, and many traditional songs hail his heroism.

[45] In 1900, the British attempted to seize the Golden Stool from the Asantes. On 25 March 1900, Sir Frederick Mitchell Hodgson, then British governor to the Gold

or from being stolen, else "as a man sickens and dies whose *sunsum* during life has wandered away or has been injured by some other *sunsum*, so would the Ashanti nation sicken and lose its vitality and power" (Rattray 1923: 289, 290).[46] The *Sika Dwa Kofi* represents the communal spirituality and serves as a unifying force or "a sacred place where the spirits could cool down, and the spiritual energy could flow openly between the ancestors, the clans and individuals" (Müller 2013: 123). Great reverence is attached to the Golden Stool, which is tightly guarded as a man will guard his *sunsum*, for whatever happens to it – good or bad – affects the nation (Asare Opoku 1978: 97, 98). The collective *sunsum* gives us another perspective to understand the *sunsum* and its operations. Further analysis will bring out answers to questions like the source of the collective *sunsum* of the Golden Stool and how it helps to understand the nature of *sunsum* for the development of a contextual Christian pneumatology.

3.6. Summary

This chapter has, in part, discussed the essential basic framework for understanding *sunsum* in Akan worldviews and anthropology. We have noted the multivalent character of *sunsum* and how the various meanings imply an extensive polysemy of the term. Akan cosmology is an inspirited world of spiritual and natural objects. The mystical, often known as *sunsum mu*, comprises varying degrees of spiritual entities and forces that exercise

---

Coast (Ghana), met the Asante leadership in Kumasi and requested to sit on the Golden Stool. The Asantes saw the request as open defiance of the kingdom since a foreigner has no right to the stool. Hodgson also made it clear to the Asantes that their king Prempeh I would be permanently exiled from the kingdom. The Asantes, led by Yaa Asantewaa, the queen mother of Ejisu, mobilized their army against the British. The war ended in severe fatalities on both sides, but the Asantes were defeated and Yaa Asantewaa, including several traditional leaders, were exiled to the Seychelles Island where she also died in 1921. The British could not retrieve the Golden Stool and never saw it. Read more from (Müller 2013).

46 Rattray recounts an attempt to replicate the Golden Stool by Adinkra, the king of Gyaman. He "saw or heard of the Golden Stool of Coomassie and made one similar to it. This so enraged the king of the Ashanti that he led an army against Adinkra, completely vanquished that chief near Bontuku (now French Ivory Coast) and cut off Adinkra's head. This caused that chief's golden stool to be melted down and cast into two masks representing Adinkra's face; the masks were then hung on each side of the Golden Stool" (Rattray 1923: 291).

power over the world of natural phenomena. Entities include 'Nyankopɔn (God), *Abosom* (deities), *Nananom Nsamanfoɔ* (ancestors), *Sasabonsam* (wizard), *Abayifoɔ* (witches), *Mmoatia* (dwarfs), and all animating forces belong to the *sunsum mu*. Along these lines, we understand *sunsum* to refer to all spiritual beings and forces in Akan ontology. Although the natural world of phenomena is real to the Akan, the spiritual is the realest because causal realities in the natural world are often attributed to the spiritual. Everything in its natural state is animated by *sunsum* to exercise power for either good or bad. Here lies the spiritual rationality behind the Akan socio-religious practices and beliefs and the factors which shape the Akan worldviews.

As to the question of the nature of *sunsum*, several questions need to be raised for further investigation. Should we understand *sunsum* in relation to the pantheon deities or directly from God, or both? How does that understanding affect the way Akan people perceive the nature of *sunsum*? These questions require a historical inquiry, and this will be the focus of the next chapter.

PART II

THE GENESIS OF AKAN ANTHROPOLOGY AND THE *SUNSUM* HISTORIOGRAPHY

OWIA REPUE
"Rising sun"
Adinkra symbol of life-spark, progress, warmth, renewal, development, and vitality.

4. The Big Bang of Akan Ethnography

> *"These people, the true Ashantis of the forest country, present the anthropologist with a peculiarly interesting and hitherto perhaps neglected task. The general idea would seem to be that this is a field of research that is so well trodden by alien feet as to offer little chance or opportunity of retracing thereon the tracks left by the original husbandmen"* – Robert S. Rattray.[47]

The previous chapter outlined the basic framework for understanding Akan anthropology and the concept of *sunsum*. The study raised questions about the nature and source of *sunsum* for further studies. This chapter begins a thorough investigation into the meaning and nature of *sunsum* to find possible answers to the questions raised in the previous chapter. The study will involve a historical understanding of the evolution of the meaning of *sunsum* since the early years of Akan scholarship to assess the various ideological trajectories and the contribution of scholars of Akan studies. The necessity of this investigation is that the meaning of *sunsum* has been ambiguous, in the sense that opinions exist and differ. There is also the problem of linguistics resulting from the English translation of *sunsum* as "spirit." It seems the word "spirit" has become the closest translation of *sunsum* into English. This is not done for the sake of convenience, but some argue that *sunsum* is philosophically equivalent to the English term "spirit." The result has propagated the pneumatic character of *sunsum*. Scholars who are not satisfied with this translation question whether there is any philosophical exactness between the Akan concept of *sunsum* and the Western conception of spirit. Wiredu and Gyekye battle this semantic inflection in the debate between the pneumatic character of *sunsum* and the philosophy of quasi-physicalism.

That said, as our studies progresses, we will encounter not only conceptual difficulties, but also philosophical interpretations and even more. Therefore, a historiographical approach is adopted here to investigate the

---

[47] (Rattray 1916: 9).

historical thinking of scholars studying the Akan concept of *sunsum*. Of significance, we will take into consideration the historical development of the meaning of *sunsum* and how scholars from different fields of study understood it and their impact on later scholars and socio-religious reforms. We will first begin by looking at one of the foremost scholars who studied Akan religions and culture in the early twentieth century with a particular emphasis on the *sunsum* concept, namely Robert Sutherland Rattray (1881-1938). Rattray, a Scotsman, worked in Ghana as a colonial official and anthropologist.[48] In doing so, I will review his ethnographical definition of *sunsum*. In the end, my purpose is to offer the best possible perspective of his characterization of *sunsum* and how such description has contributed to Akan literature and ideas.

4.1. Introduction to Akan Scholarship

The nineteenth century was a literary evolution for Akan studies. It became a period of scientific excavation of Akan traditional concepts for academic learning. The trajectories of that evolution can still be felt today. Indeed, the scientific method has had extensive coverage of studies that continue to stimulate academic interest and social reforms. It has also helped to shape the imaginations of many Ghanaians for the future. This present discussion of the concept of *sunsum* is one aspect that continues to shape Akan worldviews in the academic world and in several socio-religious sectors. While it is deemed fair to explore the various meanings of *sunsum*, it also requires a straightforward and constructive approach towards the development of a multidisciplinary and interdisciplinary scientific study.

4.1.1. Johann G. Christaller: A Precursor of Akan Scholarship

Akan scholarship is a significant area of research in the global academic sphere for reasons ranging from its extraordinary cultural richness to its pervasiveness in the Ghanaian socio-political and religious constructions. The genesis was an ethnographic big bang that for many years was going to change the way many Ghanaians live their lives. Its inception dates back

[48] Ghana used to be called Gold Coast until the introduction of the Ghana Independence Act in 1957.

to the early years of European presence in Ghana. Johann Gottlieb Christaller (1827-1895) was a German missionary, lexicographer, and philologist for the Basel Mission whose arrival in Ghana defined new methods of Christian missiology in the country, and who also gave great importance to the Twi language of the Akan (Figure 2). Christaller's primary mission was to engage Christian missions with the vernacular of the indigenous Akan people of Akuapem. It was also his intention to provide a structured language for both Europeans and indigenous missionaries working among the Akan. As far as Akan studies are concerned, he became the architect of Twi scholarship.

Christaller was sent to Ghana by the Basel Mission of Switzerland.[49] He arrived in Ghana in 1853. Before his arrival, the Twi language was only spoken, never written.[50] Twi scholarship mainly owes its origin to him. He transformed the oral traditions into literary scholarship which became the *modus operandi* of reaching the Akan indigenes in Ghana. Christaller believed the preservation of the Ghanaian vernacular could be useful knowledge for spiritual growth (Christaller 1888: 198). Some scholars think otherwise and suggest that Christaller had nationalistic motives to give preeminence to the Ghanaian language over English as a counter-culture to the European Enlightenment that gave superiority to Western civilization (Hauser-Renner 2009). This is true of a man of a philological caliber. Christaller is reported to have protested against attempts to publish the Basel Mission Akan/Twi periodical *Christian Messenger* in English. He is quoted saying, "I . . . beg all true patriots among our Gold Coast Christians to watch over the purity of their own vernacular language, their mother tongue, and to help to cultivate it to the benefit of their own nation" (Christaller 1888: 198). Christaller's passion to transform the oral culture of Akan people into literary history was the basis of his academic and spiritual contribution to the then Gold Coast. His most successful contribution

49 Ghana became the Basel Mission's first and most successful missionary field in Africa after their first operation in the Middle East, specifically in Iran, had failed.

50 Two other missionaries by the names Andreas Riis and his nephew H. N. Riis had already begun the development of the Twi grammar. Andreas Riis produced a dictionary of about 1200 Twi words which was later expanded by H. N. Riis and published in German in 1853 and again in English in 1854. What makes Christaller stand out was his significant contribution in publishing in the Twi language. He is remembered for his immense contribution to West African linguistics in general "because he analyzed the characteristic vowel harmony system and the tone system [...], their significance for the grammar" (Brown & Ogilvie 2009: 18).

to Akan literature and Ghana's nationalism was the translation of the Bible from the original Hebrew and Greek to the Akan Twi languages. Indeed, his works in the vernacular were "a manifesto of cultural nationalism" (Sanneh 1993: 83).

Christaller, in collaboration with an indigenous missionary, David Asante, and other Akan indigenes began translating the Gospels and Acts into Akuapem-Twi. The final draft was completed in Switzerland, where Christaller had withdrawn owing to ill health, and was published in 1859. The presence of David Asante in Switzerland facilitated the translation. Both returned to Ghana in 1862 where they began translating the Epistles (Ephesians, Philippians, Colossians, 1 and 2 Thessalonians). The Epistles of 1 Timothy, Philemon, and Hebrews were completed in 1863. With the help of other translators, Christaller and his team finished translating the New Testament in 1866, adding the Psalms and Proverbs. The complete edition of the entire Bible was published in 1871 by the British and Foreign Bible Societies (BFBS) (Worae 2016: 19, 20). The following inscription appears in big letters on the inside cover of the Bible: "The Holy Bible, translated from the original tongues into the Tshi (Chwee) language spoken by the tribes of Akuapem, Akem, Asante, Fante Etc., Gold Coast, Western Africa" (Figure 3). Here, we see the empowerment of the local dialects already at work as a vehicle for Christian civilization and nationalism in the Gold Coast.

Christaller's appreciation of the Twi language led him, with the assistance of both local and Western missionaries, to develop an English-Twi dictionary in 1874, Twi grammar of the Asante and Fante languages in 1875, and a dictionary of the Asante and Fante Language in 1881. He also compiled about 3,600 Akan proverbs in Twi in 1879. After his wife Christiane Emilie Ziegler died in 1868, Christaller left Ghana and never returned. He completed most of his significant works in the Twi language from Germany (Worae 2016: 19, 20). Christaller died on 16th December 1895 in Stuttgart, Germany. His work received little attention and was somewhat buried in obscurity for over thirty years until the Scottish anthropologist, Robert Sutherland Rattray, got permission from the Basel Mission to add English translation and notes to the *Ashanti Proverbs* (Rattray 1817: 7). As far as the history of Christianity in Ghana is concerned, Christaller remains one of the most influential missionaries, not only in the spread of the Christian message but also for his contribution to Akan Twi literature, scholarship, and modern Ghana nationalism.[51]

4.1.2. Christaller's Definition and Conception of *Sunsum*

Christaller discusses the concept of *sunsum* as a philologist rather than a conceptualist. He describes the meaning of *sunsum* in a dictionary-like framework, allowing for possible future conceptualization of the term. His interpretation of the *sunsum* comes to the fore in his seminal 1881 work, *Dictionary of the Asante And Fante Language Called Tshi (Twi)*. The book was widely regarded as the gold standard of Akan language in mainstream circles; an excellent translational text that fulfilled the theological mandate placed upon Christaller and his advisers. In this dictionary, Christaller established a strong platform for a constructive linguistic engagement between local Akan culture and the gospel.

Christaller identifies *sunsum* with the personality or distinctive character and quality that covers the essence of being. He made this clear through his study of the oral theology of the Akan people. While discussing the various traditional names for God, Christaller expounds on the Akan notion of Odomankoma (the Creator), who is known in the Akan world of experience as 'Nyankopɔn (God). Christaller relies on the Akan expression *Onyankopɔn onye Odomankoma Sunsum*, which he translates: "God is an Eternal Spirit," to describe how Akan people experience the Creator. Danquah later questioned Christaller's use of "spirit" to translate *sunsum* (Danquah 1944: 66). It was out of this linguistic conjecture that grew immense pneumatic concepts in determining the spirituality of *sunsum*. Nevertheless, Christaller brings to our understanding how the Creator is known and experienced by the Akan. 'Nyankopɔn as *sunsum* defines the personality of the Creator as "the boundless, infinite, interminable, immensely rich Being, or as the author, owner and donor of an inexhaustible abundance of things" (Christaller 1881: 89).

Christaller further translates the *sunsum* as soul, spirit, or ghost of man (1874: 112, 226; 1881: 464). The traditional notion given by the terms "soul" and "spirit" is the *'kra* of a person. In this regard, he clung to the impression created by and espoused by traditional Akan people about the

[51] Read more from (Sanneh 1993: 82-85).

survival of the soul, leading to Christaller's description of the *sunsum* also as a ghost. It is difficult to take this conclusion as applying to all Akan communities. Christaller's dictionary contains Twi-Fante vocabularies, hence, the designation of *sunsum* to a ghost may vary from one Akan cultural group to another. Among the Fantes, for instance, the phrase *Ne sunsum* (His soul/spirit) may differ in connotation to the Twi-speaking Akan who will refer to his *ɔkra*—the deathless part of a person that survives death to become a ghost or ancestor. There is no synonymity between *ɔkra* and *sunsum* among the Twi-speaking Akan. Going by Christaller's presumption that the *sunsum* is both spirit and ghost, it is safe to surmise that the English terms "spirit" and "soul" create ambiguity in Akan spiritual ontology.

Overall, Christaller's dictionary commands significant influence, especially because it was and still remains the go-to reference for scholars and practitioners that want to translate the gospel to the Akan dialect. The missionaries that collaborated with Christaller, for instance, used the text to spread and shape their message and delivery. Since the Akan dialect is generally underpinned by homogeneity, Christaller's definition of *sunsum* strikes a chord with the community in terms of comprehension and actualization of the gospel. Our encounter with Christaller does not end in this book. In my second book on contextual Akan Christian pneumatology, I have delved further into his work on Akan spirituality.

4.2. Robert Sutherland Rattray: A Precursor of Akan Anthropology

Rattray (popularly known as captain Rattray) is an important figure in Akan anthropology, and his name is almost synonymous with the discipline. His research focused on the customs and folklore of West Africans, specifically the Asante cultural group of the Akan in Ghana. Captain Rattray's contribution to scholarship is mostly related to the Asantes. As an anthropologist, he embarked on a wide range of studies in Asante social organization and law, art, and religion.[52]

Rattray was born in 1881 to Scottish parents in India where his father, Arthur Rattray, worked in the Indian Civil Service. He received his education from Stirling High School and Exeter College, Oxford, where he earned a diploma in anthropology as well as his doctorate (D.Sc.). He

52 "Captain R. S. Rattray, C.B.E." *Nature*, vol. 141, May 21, 1938, 928.

served the English colonial administration in different capacities. Before joining the Gold Coast colony in 1907, Rattray served as a trooper in the Boer War in South Africa and received the Queen's medal with five clasps.[53] Between 1902 and 1907 he was on the staff of the African Lakes Corporation in British Central Africa. From here, he published *Some Folk-lore Stories and Songs in Chinyanja with English Translation and Notes* (1907) which contains a collection of Chinyanja folklore and customs of Central Africa. Upon arrival in the Gold Coast in 1907, he served in the Customs Service. Later, he was transferred to the administrative department and became an Assistant District Commissioner in 1911, a District Commissioner in 1915, and acting Senior Assistant Colonial Secretary and Clerk to the Legislative Council in 1920 (E. W. S. 1938). As a government official, his task was to report colonial activities in the Gold Coast – specifically the customs of the Asantes.

The first anthropological department in Ghana was set up in the Asante region as part of the colonial exploration of practical administration among the indigenes of their colonies. The initial plan came from Charles Henry Harper, the then Civil Commissioner of Asante, and was later set up by the Governor, Sir Frederick D. Guggisberg in 1921 (Wilks 2000: 82). It was required of British officials serving the colonial administration to acquaint themselves with the customs and languages of the indigenes of the colony to effectively manage the relationship between the administration and indigenes. Regardless of its positive impact on Akan studies today, the newly created Anthropology Department served the colonial interest. It was more of an academic policy of the colonial administration than for the Akan people.

Rattray became the first head of department, and whatever he thought of this newly created department – with respect to preparing the Asantes for self-governance or preserving their customary integrity – it did not change its colonial agenda. This placed him at a more significant advantage, or responsibility, to begin a scientific inquiry into anthropological research within the Asante territories. Rattray himself recognized that he had two methodological options. The first, which he found nonproductive, was to make the Department the center of independent research where individual research would be reviewed, examined, and classified. However, he feared such an approach would create a greater collection of materials that may

53 Ibid, 928.

fail to receive proper scrutiny. The second approach was for him to take the work of research upon himself to investigate the beliefs and customs of the Asantes, which he did, producing a trilogy on Asante customs, arts, religion, laws, and constitution. The volumes became useful resources for all colonial officials and helped bring together the colonial administration in harmony with the Asantes.

How did Rattray obtain information? How accurate was his knowledge of the Asantes? Rattray considered the Asante territory to be terra incognita to the Europeans (Rattray 1915: 9). He believed that this area was devoid of Europeans' contamination of the indigenous customs (Rattray 1923: 5, 6). As a consequence, he saw a world of anthropological opportunities that could provide an epistemological legacy to successive generations. Rattray described how he sought information:

> It must be remembered that in Ashanti really valuable anthropological information is possessed by comparatively few of its inhabitants. Those who have accurate knowledge are the older men and women who have few dealings with the foreigner, live secluded lives in remote villages, and are ignorant of or indifferent to the social and religious changes brought about by the European (Rattray 1923: 7).

Rattray's discussants were the grey-headed Asantes. Why? There is information to be given here that will help in the understanding of the relationship between old age and knowledge or wisdom among the Akan. These details will bring to light the perception of aging among the Akan and how that perception is construed in Akan societies. I am convinced that this information is essential for individuals who regularly misinterpret or fail to grasp how age affects African politics.

There is a growing feeling of ageism among many world societies – even in Ghana and beyond.[54] Many aged persons live under the fear of rejection

---

54 Ageism is a word associated with prejudicing attitude towards people because of their advanced age. In many parts of the world, the term "old age" may carry "negative connotations of 'decrepit', 'decaying', 'worn out' and 'senile'" (Van der Geest 2002: 438). Ageism has risen to become a culturally embedded attitude among several African societies today. In Ghana, for instance, accusations of witchcraft are linked to old age (Van der Geest 2002), and this advertently causes panic among

and diverse stereotyping. Among the Akan, aging engenders positive feelings and it is a period of leadership and political power (Van der Geest 2002: 438). Even in today's complex societies, old age continues to hold high social standards in Akan societies. It is often associated with gerontocracy, a society governed by elders.

Traditionally, the Akan conception of knowledge is informal and closely related to the elderly. *Nana* or *ɔpayin* (elderly) are Akan terms for the aged and both express a degree of honor. The English term "old age" may not have a direct bearing on what majority of Akan people consider as aged since the English term "old," may somehow suggest expiring. *Nana* is a fundamental term that captures the ideology of respect especially in the Akan conception of God and ancestors. God is often assigned the title *Nana* 'Nyankopɔn, meaning the "Great Ancestor" or "The Ancient of Days." He is all-powerful and all-knowing. The same title is accorded to the ancestors (*Nananom*). Ancestors are a body of spiritual entities who were once among the living but are dead, and their spirits continue to live in the spiritual world. Because the Akan consider life as linear, meaning a journey, age and death are a journey towards perfection. Ancestors have attained spirituality to possess great power with which they can assist the living. Ancestors can provide visions and protect and respond when the living summon them. In Akan societies, it is the *Nana* (aged) with excellent social values who is revered as an ancestor. During the pouring of libation, the ancestors who form this band of spiritual elites are invoked and their presence duly recognized as such. For that reason, old age is considered a moment or stage in life where people reach their full potential to act in that respect as ancestors or guardians since they have now acquired wisdom and experience and can guide and protect the young to success (Van der Geest 2002: 438).

Akan people further believe age comes with experience and knowledge. The more one advances in years, the more knowledge, experience, and

---

the growing youth for fear of being killed or meeting with misfortunes in life. Material wealth, childbirth, good health, and manifold prosperous dimensions of life are said to be the targets of witchcraft. Consequently, being accused of practicing witchcraft is a crime. Witchcraft accusations are commonly the new form of ageism in Africa and several old people have to face death or mutilation as a result. Traditionally, old age was never an indication of witchcraft among the Akan. Witchcraft-ageism is a modern phenomenon and distortion of social customs. Further information about ageism among Akan people is found in the research work of Van der Geest (2002).

power the person acquires. This is a clear indication of why the power of performance is identified with gerontocracy in most Akan societies. For example, elders or older people who offer counseling relating to matters of kingship surround every king. Hence it is said, *Ohene a w'antie ne mpaninfoɔ asɛm no na ɔwe takraboa ɔnni ti*, literally, "A king who refuses to heed to advise from his elders eats a bird without a head." A bird without a head may somehow be a taboo bird supposed not to be eaten. There is another maxim that says, *Wo nni panyin wɔ wo fie a, due*, literally, "Woe to you if you do not have an elderly person in your house." The maxim describes the role of elderly persons in guiding the affairs of the next generation. A popular Akan adage also says, *Yɛn kɔ bisa aberewa*, meaning, "Let us consult the old woman." The proverbial saying is applied when a group of elders overseeing a case withdraws into seclusion to render the final verdict on a matter.[55] *Abrewa* is a symbol of progeny among the Akan people. This maxim stems from popular Akan myth in which an old woman exhibited extraordinary wisdom that eventually repented the heart of a vicious king. For her reward, the king built a house for her, and whenever the elders found it hard to judge a case, they would consult her for advice. Hence, the expression "Let us consult the old woman" came into use.[56] All these presuppose the importance of the elderly in Akan societies.

Now coming back to Captain Rattray, we have no difficulty concluding why he resolved to consult the elderly for information. If Rattray's work were to bear any credibility at all, it would be because of its direct reliance on his aged informants who were considered as people of great authority and honor in Akan societies, and not just abandoned, stereotyped, and a

---

55 An informant explained this thus: "This expression is used when the elders pronounce judgement over a case. The *ɔkyeame*, and a few important personalities who are trying the case, retire after the expression has been pronounced. They go to a secret, quiet place and decide what the judgement should be. After the decision, they come back and the group's spokesman pronounces the judgement thus: *Wie mpanyinfoɔ, yɛsoreeɛ sɛ yɛ rekɔbisa aberewa. Yɛkɔeɛ no na aberewa te awia mu reto awia.* 'Well, elders, we retired to consult the old lady. When we went, the old lady was sunning herself.' If it is evening, they will say, *Yɛkɔeɛ no na aberewa renom n'abua, bo, bo, bo.* 'When we went, the old lady was smoking her pipe – bo, bo, bo [the sound of her smoking]. When we related the case to her she said we did well to come and seek her advice. She listened and explained to us that if we hadn't consulted her we would have passed a wrong judgment" (Van der Geest 2002: 442; Twi corrected).

56 For an account of this folklore, see Van der Geest 2002: 442.

class of good-for-nothing persons suffering from societal seclusion. His interlocutors helped him to produce the following books for the Anthropology Department: *Ashanti* (1923, 1955), *Religion and Art in Ashanti* (1927, 1957), and *Ashanti Law and Constitution* (1929, 1956).[57]

In the *Ashanti*, Rattray set out the social ontology of the Asantes by taking stock of the social stratification system from the *ntorɔ* exogamy, festivals and ceremonies, and belief systems. His initial assignment was to investigate the legal and political life of the Asantes. However, he felt a proper understanding of the social organization would serve as a source of reference and background to future research in Asante politics (Rattray 1923: 7). Hence, he focused on the non-political, non-legal aspects of the Asantes (Herskovits 1939: 130). A further systematic inquiry led to the publication of *Religion and Art in Ashanti* (1927) which Rattray claimed was a continuation of the former. In this book, Rattray provided an ethnographic sketch of Asante religion by taking stock of the notion of God, pantheon deities (*Abosom*), and how religion pervades in the daily life of the Asantes. Rattray's final legacy to the Asante Anthropology Department was *Ashanti Law and Constitution*. This book was his initial assignment, but for the reasons given above, it became the last to be published. The book outlines the legal and political structure of the Asantes.

With this extraordinary ethnographical inquiry, Rattray became the foremost European specialist on Asante socio-religious culture. His magnanimous contribution to Akan studies has distinguished him as an outstanding anthropologist and authority on the native people of West Africa. Although his research works focused primarily on the Asante of the Akan people, he extended the study among the geographical affiliations to the Asante territories of the hinterlands. The result led to the production of two volumes on the Asante cultural group of the hinterlands in 1932. In 1933, he received the Rivers Memorial Medal from the Royal Anthropological Institute of Great Britain and Ireland for his contribution to the field of anthropology in the then Gold Coast (West Africa).

---

[57] Other books by Rattray are: Some Folk-lore Stories and Songs in Chinyanja with English Translation (1907), Hausa Folk-lore, Customs, Proverbs, etc. (2 vols.) (1913), Ashanti Proverbs, Translated from the Original with Grammatical and Anthropological Notes (1916), An Elementary Male Grammar, with a Vocabulary (1918), A Short Manual of the Gold Coast (British Empire Exposition) (1924), Akan-Ashanti Folk-tales (Text and Translation) (1930), The Tribes of the Ashanti Hinterland (2 vols.) (1932), The Leopard Priestess (1934).

Captain Rattray possessed high linguistic intelligence, had a humble personal demeanor and approached his discussants with the spirit of a seeker of truths (Rattray 1923: 11). As head of the newly established Anthropology Department, Rattray emerged as a positive influence and one with great importance to both the British and the Asantes. His roles as a scholar and colonial official came out of the British need to facilitate colonialism. Rattray's work stood at the heart of the colonial administration where anthropology became an imperial device to establish British conquest in Ghana. However, the necessity of the anthropological studies was primarily informed by the advancement of British interests and partly by academic progress of the Asantes. Rattray, therefore, became an instrument for extending British imperialism. His academic status in the colonial administration, coupled with great access to power (among colonial administrators and traditional rulers), made him successful in all aspects of his career in the colony. It is also noted that the range of his interest in research was unlimited as he could travel far and across the dense forest of the Asantes.

Having said that, there is no intention of exonerating Rattray from any form of criticism. Several criticisms have been leveled against Rattray, ranging from his accounts of historical facts to the accuracy of his information about the Asantes. Although I have discussed how age influences oral knowledge among the Akan and how it served as a source of information for Rattray's ethnography, it does not serve as a yardstick for accuracy. Tom C. McCaskie is an expert in Asante history, and his appraisal of Rattray's ethnography is a valuable source for studying the shortcomings of Rattray (McCaskie 1983). Nonetheless, for the sake of this present study we shall defer the criticism of Rattray's major works since his construction of the *sunsum* comes with many criticisms.

Generally, Rattray's work has had inevitable positive consequences on scholars – both past and present – studying Akan religions and culture. Besides his academic influence, Rattray set out a contextual framework upon which critical retrospection and constructive investigation of Akan realities permit interdisciplinary and multidisciplinary scholarship. Rattray retired in 1930 and died on May 14, 1938, while gliding as a pilot at Farmoor, near Oxford at the age of fifty-six years.

4.2.1. Rattray's Conception and Definition of *Sunsum*

Rattray's introduction to the *sunsum* concept appears in his trilogy on Asante customs, religion, and laws. Before these publications, the term was completely absent in his earlier translation and commentary on the *Ashanti Proverbs*, compiled by Johann Gottlieb Christaller in 1879. Two possible reasons can be given for this. First, Christaller did not use the term in the *Ashanti Proverbs* because *sunsum* is a rare term in Akan proverbs. Second, Rattray might not have been introduced to the term then, and even if he had had any knowledge about it at all, he might have preferred a substitutionary word instead.

There is enough reason to suggest that Rattray may not have had enough knowledge then about the *sunsum*. I will point out one instance in the *Ashanti Proverbs*. When speaking of the construction of Asante religion and how the traditional priest encountered the *Ɔbosom* (pantheon deity), Rattray writes: "If you ask what the 'it' is he captured, he cannot tell, but will probably say vaguely '*Onyankopon tumi*', or '*honhom*', that is, 'the power, spirit, or *mana* of Onyankopon'" (Rattray 1915: 22). Here in the *Ashanti Proverbs*, he uses *mana* four times to translate an impersonal power emanating from God, all linked to the essence of the *Abosom* (pantheon deities) whose nature is thought of as part of the power ascribed to God (Rattray 1915: 22, 30, 32). As to whether the terms he used were right or not, Rattray's use of *honhom* and *tumi*, herein for the *Abosom*, concerning the emanating force from 'Nyankopɔn establishes the first fact that Rattray never used the term *sunsum* to essentially denote God. It appears the identification of *sunsum* with God is completely absent in his writings as we will soon see. Again, one may deduce that the expression *Onyame Sunsum* was not preponderant during Rattray's ethnographic study. I found a similar trend in the writings of Christaller. The identification of *sunsum* with 'Nyankopɔn appeared in later scholarship – as I will show in the next chapter.

Now, let us turn our focus to Rattray's trilogy, *Ashanti* (1923), *Religion and Art in Ashanti* (1927), and *Ashanti Law and Constitution* (1929), where we encounter his ideas about the Akan *sunsum*.

4.2.1.1. The General Definition of *Sunsum* by Rattray

The pneumatic character of the *sunsum* first appeared in *Ashanti*, published eight years later after *Ashanti Proverbs*. In this book, Rattray, like Christaller, translated *sunsum* into English as "spirit," reinforcing its pneumatic character. The general definition of *sunsum* appears in Rattray as:

> "that spiritual element in a man or woman upon which depends – not life, i.e. breath, for that is the *okra* or *'kra* – but that force, personal magnetism, character, personality, power, soul, call it what you will, upon which depend health, wealth, worldly power, success in any venture, in fact, everything that makes life at all worth living" (Rattray 1923: 46).[58]

The definition given here by Rattray admittedly presents a wider scope of meaning that is multivalent and dynamic. We can only understand it when further analysis is conducted within the larger context of his writings. Therefore, I will focus on key conceptions in his definition.

4.2.1.2. *Sunsum* as "spiritual element"

Sunsum as a "spiritual element" in Akan worldview is basically a description of all objects that are conceived and perceived as physically nonconceptual. When Rattray used the term in connection with a human being, what did he mean? Is *sunsum* an astral component or a mysterious force? What is its origin? Rattray gives little information, but what is clear is that he brings out the dimension of a pneumatic character of the *sunsum* leading to the translation of it as "spirit" after Christaller.

I will not be quick here to think that there is a purported assertion by Rattray to characterize the *sunsum* as an entity – even if that is the case, there are few indications of that thesis. Rattray suggested somewhere that the tutelary deity called Bosomtwe is the child of the great Asante tutelary god Ta Kora of whom one of his informants, a priest to be precise, was

58 In one of her articles, "The Reality of Spirits? A Historiography of the Akan Concept of 'Mind'," Louise Müller misquoted Rattray by suggesting this was the definition he gave to the *ɔkra* (Müller 2008: 172).

introduced during a ritual at Bosomtwe as *Sunsum kɛseɛ a ɔwɔ baabi ara.*[59] Rattray translated the statement in English as "great spirit which is everywhere" (Rattray 1923: 195-6). In as much as such an idea of omnipresence may underline the statement, which is true based on the invocation of Ta Kora in the ritual, what the priest meant to say was "Ta Kora, the great god (*Bosomkɛseɛ*) who is everywhere."[60] Rattray had already used the expression "great god" to designate the same deity (Rattray 1923: 102, 117, 157, 175). Akan pantheon deities (*Abosom*) are considered *sunsum* in the sense of their mysterious essence or nature.[61]

A similar scenario is described by Rattray that purportedly characterizes *sunsum* as an intermediary spirit. At Tafo, near Kumasi, Rattray tells the story of an altar of *Nyame Dua* (God's tree) that was located on the bank of the river Santan.[62] Upon inquiry, the chief told him the altar was erected on behalf of one of his wives who was barren; after consulting a god, he was instructed "to set up the altar, in order that the *sunsum* (spirit) of the river might intercede for him to *Nyame* (the Sky God)" (1927: 305). Every well-informed Akan knows the expression "*sunsum* (spirit) of the river" was in reference to the *Ɔbosom* (god) of the river.[63] When Rattray further asked

---

59 Lake Bosomtwe is the largest natural lake in Africa, situated approximately 30km South-East from Kumasi in the Asante region. Scientifically, the lake was created by a chondrite meteorite. Legend says, according to an informant of Rattray, that "Lake Bosomtwe did not always lie in its present locality but was situated near the Bosomtwe Rock in Northern Ashanti." Rattray "was taken and shown a large natural depression, now perfectly dry and covered with trees and vegetation, which the local people say was in ancient times the site of this lake, but owing to it not being able to get on with 'his brother' Tano it departed from here and went and made its home where it is now found." (Rattray 1923: 195)

60 In Akan thought '*ɔwɔ baabi ara*', in reference to lesser divinities, refers to most or many places. Akan people do not attribute omnipresence to lesser divinities. They are regarded as creatures of God and limited in their activities.

61 *See* (Ephirim-Donkor 2016).

62 Tafo is a sub-region of the Kumasi Metropolitan District area in the Asante region. It was a village during the time of Rattray's research and was notable for its crafts in pottery. There is a belief that the first potter came from Tafo. Her name was Osra Abogyo and legend says she learnt the art from the eternal God called *Odomankoma* (Rattray 1927: 301).

63 Rivers, although they can be considered sacred, are not in essence spiritual as one can fetch water and drink, but rivers may host or possess a spiritual agent. This relationship between water and spirits can be confusing, but it seems clear to the

whether the river had a *sunsum*, the chief replied, "not only had it a spirit [*sunsum*], but that the whole village of Taffo belonged to it and owed its origin to the river" (1927: 305-6).[64] Unless *sunsum*, in this context, is in reference to an entity it cannot intercede for the chief or become a progenitor of the village. The allusion here reminds us of the roles the *Abosom* play as progenitors of children by the transmission of the *ntorɔ* through a male agent. This is one reason why Rattray often confused *sunsum* with *ntorɔ*. His use of *sunsum* for the river gods in the two scenarios is exactly the conventional description of the *Abosom* by the Akan people. The nature of Ta Kora and the other deities is interpreted synonymously as *sunsum*. The attribution of "great" and "everywhere" to Ta Kora defines the essential quality of the deity as *sunsum*.[65] Therefore, *sunsum* becomes an alternative term to describe the nature of the deities.

4.2.1.3. *Sunsum* "in a man or woman"

Rattray grapples with an important dimension of the *sunsum*, i.e. its anthropological connection.[66] The definition given above by Rattray is anthropological. As already stated, Akan anthropology suggests that every human being possesses an immaterial substance called *sunsum*. The central idea here presents *sunsum* as a vital component of the human being. The human being is only a subject of its operational experience but the *sunsum* is never indispensable from the body. Rattray underlined this assertion with several experiences of the *sunsum* in the human being. A person's *sunsum* can take sleep peregrination, and it can get knocked about by other *sunsum*, after whence the person may fall sick and die. For these reasons, Rattray identified the *sunsum* with volatility of the *'kra*. The *sunsum* is an advanced guard that protects a person (Rattray 1923: 152; 1927: 154). Among the Akan, only males transmit the *sunsum* just like the *ntorɔ*. Rattray supports this

---

Akan that rivers are quintessentially deities and once the river dries, it will suggest the deity is departed.

64 There is no trace of the Santan River today since Tafo is now populated with houses and lies in the center of the city. Urbanization in most parts of the country has affected the ecological integrity of river bodies and the Santan River may be a victim.

65 Further analysis will reveal the difference between a thing called *sunsum* and a thing that possesses *sunsum*.

66 The anthropological aspect of *sunsum* is mostly talked about because it occupies a central place in understanding the concept of a person.

assumption with a popular saying among the Asantes that *Ɔbaa nni sunsum*, literally, "A woman has no *sunsum*." Further details given by Rattray imply that "a woman has no real soul (of this kind) of her own; it is true, they say, that she has 'a small kind' of *sunsum* which her father gave to her, but for all practical purposes she is nevertheless soulless, because she cannot transmit any kind of *sunsum*, but only her blood" (Rattray 1927: 318).[67] Given the account by Rattray, the *sunsum* of a person cannot be said to be divine, neither is it feminine. It is exclusively a physiological and spiritual element coming from the father.

4.2.1.4. *Sunsum* as "force" and "power"

The character of the *sunsum* appears in Rattray's understanding as force and power. There is no equivalent word in the Akan Twi for "force" other than *sunsum*.[68] Power may be rendered in Akan Twi as "*tumi,*" which is also equivalent to "authority." *Tumi* may capture the intrinsic power of the *sunsum,* but it is never synonymous with it. Therefore, Rattray's use of "force" should be understood as an emanating power or mysterious aura, even though sometimes he will use "spirit" to translate such notions. An informant recounted to him that in the event of a divorce, the children will always return to their father, without opposition from the mother or her clan because the mother is afraid of the father's *sunsum* (spirit) (Rattray 1929: 9).[69] Rattray elucidates the idea of the father's *sunsum* seizing the wife in the event of adultery: "If a man's wife is unfaithful, it is his *'kra* which will inform his *Ɔbosom* (*ntorɔ*), which will then let his *sunsum* know, and this last will seize the woman so that she may become ill and die" (Rattray 1927:

---

67 Ephirim-Donkor later expounded on this notion by taking it beyond the lesser deities to God as the supreme *Sunsum* who transmits His *sunsum* to activate the *mogya* (blood) of the female to become active, thus making conception possible. Hence, God becomes the progenitor or Father (*Agya*, meaning "Father") of creation (Ephirim-Donkor 2016: 78). In theory, the all-encompassing nature of *sunsum* as divine never appeared in Rattray, neither did he give any clue of that except our own deductive reasoning of the Abosom whose essence is thought of as *sunsum* and are said to be children of God.

68 The usage of "force" here is not the application of pressure on an object to cause motion or an act which in the Akan language is "*ɔhyɛ*" (to force against one's will).

69 Rattray shortly nuanced this statement with a different meaning when instead of using the term *sunsum* used *nton* (totem) to speak of same statement (Rattray 1929: 11).

154). This hypothesis has been given an entitative interpretation to think of the *sunsum* as a spiritual. Rattray did not give further details beyond the statement. Neither did he mention any relative conception of that assumption. If we take it for the sake of argument that *ɔkra*, *ntorɔ*, and *sunsum* are spiritual entities, would that not suggest tripartite entities forming the human being instead of them being substances? Akan anthropology describes substances (genetic spiritual elements) and not entities. For all practical purposes, Rattray defined *ɔkra* as the life principle, *ntorɔ* as a physiological principle, and *sunsum* as a spiritual element. An exception is given here to the *ɔkra*, whose nature presupposes properties of an entity, but this idea will occupy later discussions. Rattray described the *ntorɔ* as "the male totemic spirit which every child, male or female, inherits from its father. Like all supernatural elements it is powerful" (Rattray 1929: 8). Most Akan will not say that the *ɔkra* is powerful; such a character belongs to the *sunsum*. For Rattray, the relationship between the *ntorɔ* and *sunsum* is mutual, and both are forces without too much differing character (Rattray 1927: 154-5). In the case of the above illustration discussed, logically, it is the *Ɔbosom* (*ntorɔ*) of the father that seizes the woman by its *sunsum* in the man. The *sunsum* remains the pervasive force that protects, acts, and experiences.

Further, Rattray talks about *sunsum* and witchcraft. Is the *sunsum* always protective? The answer lies in its moral character. Rattray says: "One's *sunsum* may be an *obayifo* (witch)'" (Rattray 1927: 155).[70] The mystical allusion here refers to the dynamic nature of the *sunsum* in becoming something else. The question as to how one's *sunsum* becomes a witch is enigmatic, since witchcraft is not a possession by a foreign spiritual agent as understood by the Akan, rather, it is the use of one's *sunsum* for such evil supernatural activities. In fact, the *sunsum* is only an instrument and a power for achieving the ends of witchcraft. Witchcraft is a mysterious force and a power that can manifest its supernatural abilities all day long.[71] This de-

---

[70] Prior to and during the advent of the Europeans, witchcraft ranked as one of the anti-social crimes. In most cases the penalty was excommunication or the culprit "was smeared all over with palm oil and cast into a fire, or clubbed or strangled or drowned" (Rattray 1929: 313). Most Akan communities continue to eschew witchcraft and victims often have to face brutalities from perpetrators if a quick intervention by rescuers does not take place.

[71] It is unclear which spirits empower a witch. Our earlier discussion referred to *Sasabonsam* as the chief agent of evil and master of dwarfs and witches but there is

scription adds to the popular assertion that witchcraft is a nocturnal peregrination. An informant named Yao Adawua described to Captain Rattray how a witch was known: "The conclusive evidence that any person is a witch is, he said, the discovery of her *bayikukuo* (witchcraft pot)" (1927: 30). Witchcraft pots or cauldrons are mostly made of clay and may contain several amulets or ritual artifacts from whence the powers of the witch are derived. They are mostly kept out of reach, under a person's bed, beneath the earth, or under a tree. The pot, just like a shrine, is transferable, making witchcraft inheritable.[72] In cases where the cauldron is discovered and destroyed, the person will lose the spell of witchcraft. This makes the connection between witchcraft and one's *sunsum* accidental rather than ontological. Adawua further told Rattray of how "he could tell a witch practically at sight" and when Rattray asked how, "he replied he could 'see red smoke coming out of their heads'" (1927: 30). Adawua finally told Rattray about his ability to "cure people of being witches without having to kill them, provided that once he had treated them they did not resort again to their evil practices; if they did so, they would die" (Rattray 1927: 30). The power of witchcraft, according to Rattray, is a practice in relation to which a person's *sunsum* becomes vulnerable to carrying out such evil activities.

4.2.1.5. *Sunsum* as "personal magnetism," "character," "personality"

A key feature of Rattray's interpretation of the Akan *sunsum* is its operational force or determining principle for experience. The *sunsum* is responsible for the moral and psychological qualities of an individual. The human being is the subject of physicality and the projector of several psychosocial experiences. Rattray underlined this with specific descriptions such as "personal magnetism," "character," and "personality." These aspects of a human being in the Akan worldviews are not interpreted in abstract terms; instead, they are the qualities of a human being and a person's spiritual and

---

no apparent evidence that witchcraft is a product of the power of *Sasabonsam*. Asare Opoku thinks the power of witchcraft stems from mysterious forces in the universe that manifest themselves as witchcraft, magic, and sorcery. Read further from Asare Opoku 1978: 140-147. At one point, Rattray did mention *sunsum bɔne* (bad spirit), but it is not clear what he meant by that statement (Rattray 1929: 213).

72 That transfer has no boundaries like the *ntorɔ* and *sunsum*, of which only males are said to be transmitters.

social experience. Personal magnetism is the power of attraction and influence that a person exerts in society with valuable results of commendation. Rattray talks of degrees of *sunsum* as strong, weak and evil: *Me sunsum edu* (My *sunsum* is heavy), *Me sunsum yɛ den* (My *sunsum* is strong), *Me sunsum gyina m'akyi* (My *sunsum* stands at my back) (1923: 198; 1927: 154).[73] In the same way, personality varies from one individual to another. Thus, the *sunsum* remains a versatile force differing from one person to another. *Suban* "character," according to the Akan, is a spiritual phenomenon of both inner and outward dimensions.[74] The inner being is the real element, which is called *sunsum*, and the outward is the peripheral (*suban*). A person's *sunsum* is the operational force for the formation of character and the art of being, which is personality. It is a person's *sunsum* which interacts and operates on various aspects of personality and social interaction. The evil *sunsum* is the witch or wizard discussed above.

4.2.1.6. *Sunsum* as the "soul"

Rattray gives us a conceptual dualism about the soul. In his *Religion and Arts in Ashanti*, Rattray suggested that *ɔkra* is best rendered by the word "soul," i.e. the soul of a man from God (1927: 153). Then shortly afterwards he wrote: "'In life the *'kra* is considered partly as the soul or spirit of a person (cf. *sunsum*, *honhom*), partly as a separate being, distinct from the person, who protects him" (1927: 153).[75] Having said this, he then purports to assert that the *'kra* and *sunsum* are both souls: "It is very difficult sometimes to distinguish between the *'kra* and the next kind of soul, the *sunsum*"

---

73 The evil *sunsum* is not only exclusive to human beings but also to trees (Rattray 1923: 258).

74 *Suban* is one of the closest words supposed to have derived from *sunsum* with the *su* (nature) being the prefix and short form of *sunsum*, whiles the *ban* means character or nature. Hence, *suban* would mean the expression of a person's *sunsum* in life. Ephirim-Donkor defines the *su* as the raw essence of the *Ɔbosom* materialized in the corporeal world as a driven force in human beings. *Su* therefore corresponds with the intangible *sunsum* of the *Ɔbosom* manifested as character and experience of physicality. Ephirim-Donkor emphasized that "the Su is raw essence and basis for all character traits and ethical principles...The Su develops into the Suban (essential character formation) when a child first develops awareness of itself as a child or *self*" (Ephirim-Donkor 2016: 89-92).

75 A citation by Rattray (1927: 153) from Christaller's *Dictionary of the Asante and Fante Language*, 254-5.

(1927: 154). Rattray's identification of the *'kra* as a divine soul, and *sunsum* as man's soul, creates a dual polymorphism of the term "soul." In effect, a human being consists of a bipartite soul. We can see how the English term "soul" might be used to describe two distinct Akan realities here. The idea put forth here suggests that Rattray confused the use of the terms "soul" and "spirit" in reference to Akan spirituality. Rattray accepted his difficulty in finding the right English word to define the concept of *sunsum* when he wrote, "'the *sunsum* is the soul, or power, or whatever we like to call it" (1923: 293). This linguistic ambiguity did not stem from what the Akan meant by *ɔkra* and *sunsum*, but rather from Rattray's limitations in finding appropriate English words to characterize them. What Rattray does here with the *sunsum* is a description of *how* it operates but not *what* it is. How a thing expresses itself and what that thing is can vary.

Still on *sunsum* as the "soul," it is important to underline an aspect of Rattray's understanding of *sunsum* as innate *anima* in creation: "In the animistic creed of Ashanti everything in nature, animate or inanimate, has its *sunsum* (soul or spirit), and the *osese* tree is no exception" (1923: 296).[76] The possession of *sunsum* by trees was the reason behind the interest in sacred arboricultural traditions among the Akan. Rattray did not pay much attention to the source of this innate power in creation. However, two propositions have emerged after him. First, there is the theory of panentheism, which suggests that the *sunsum* is the activating principle from God, a principle which is present in natural objects (Danquah 1967; Gyekye 1998). Panentheism presents the view that there is an unconscious divine presence that regulates matter to produce its natural and spiritual experiences. This theory is central in the pneumatic conception of the *sunsum*. The second is the proposal that the essence of the *Abosom* (tutelary deities) is water that permeates and interpenetrates through natural objects as water is present in living things (Ephirim-Donkor 2016). This may be the reason why sacrifices are performed to the *sunsum* of a natural object in the same manner as to a pantheon deity.[77] Further in this belief are the shrines of groves, rocks,

---

76 Reference to *sunsum* of trees can be found also in Rattray 1927: 3.

77 Most of the rituals performed to the sacred trees follow such rituals performed to the deities. The protective *sunsum* of the trees are nothing but in loco the essence of the *Abosom*. Under the *osese* tree, Rattray records these ritual incantations: "*'Osese gye 'kosua di, Aburokyire 'Hene 'ba a ɔrekɔ awadeɛ no, sɛ ɔtena wo so a, ma no nkyɛ, mma dade ntwa me.*'" Translated, "*Osese* tree, accept this egg and eat, and when the child of the English King sits upon you let her have long life. May the

caves, and mountains venerated as residence of the lesser deities. The offering of sacrifices to the *sunsum* of a tree agrees with sacrifices offered to a lesser deity, making this *sunsum* nothing but *sunsum* of the gods.

4.2.1.7. The collective *sunsum* "soul" of the Asantes

Here again, it is necessary to revisit our discussion of the sacred *Sika Dwa Kofi* (Golden Stool) already underlined as containing the *sunsum* of the Asantes. It remains the most fascinating discovery of Captain Rattray. In his description, he saw the Golden Stool as exclusively religious and something that through hallowed custom and belief engendered the objective and consensual virtues of obedience, respect, and great loyalty, as well as being a symbol of power, health, bravery, welfare, and the shrine of the *sunsum* of Asante nationality (Rattray 1923: 287-93; McCaskie 1983: 197).[78] In this

---

knife not cut me.'" (Rattray 1923: 296) [*Twi text corrected by me*]. These offerings are not made as to *'Nyankopɔn* but to a lesser spirit. The ritual prayer follows a similar prayer of propitiation offered to Bosomtwe: "'*Kwesi Bosomtwe, wadaworoma; wo se ne Ta Kora, sunsum kɛseɛ a ɔwɔ baabi ara, ɔno na yɛ frɛ no ɛsono. Na Oboroni abɛ hwɛ nanim mu, na ɔse ɔrebɛ sene akɔhwɛ asuom', na wo Bosomtwe nso ɔntumi nsan wo ho nkɔ, na me nso me ntumi mfa m'ani hunu me nhwɛ wo. Me kura me nsam kosua de rema wo. Me srɛ wo nkyerɛ; me srɛ wo nkwa: me srɛ wo akwahosan; gye o!*' Translated, 'Bosomtwe, (whose day of service is a Sunday), by your favour; your father is Ta Kora, that great spirit which is everywhere, it is he we call elephant. The white man has come and looked upon his face, and he tells you he is passing to go and look upon the water (the Tano), but you, Bosomtwe, he cannot pass by on his way (ungreeted), and I also cannot come and look upon you with my eyes alone, so I hold in my hand an egg to give you. I beg of you long life; I beg of you health; I beg of you continuing strength (and throwing the egg against the rock); receive!'" [*Twi text improved by me*] (Rattray 1923: 295-6). However, I noted one occasion where Rattray talks about the *sunsum* of a tree being distinct from the *Ɔbosom* that resided in the roots of the tree. When he inquired from the priest how the two co-exist, the priest said to him, "'I do not ever give offerings to the *sunsum* (soul) of the *Akata*' (the Ashanti name of the tree)" (Rattray 1927: 3).

78 The sacrality of the Golden Stool is very much ambiguous because it also engenders political power as it is a symbol of right to rule. MacCaskie's review of the Golden Stool saw it as an emblem that "propagated and fertilized dreams of power" (MacCaskie 1983: 198). He further underlined how it has been used as a political weapon to command authority for power and governance. He writes, "the Golden Stool was a sacred object, but its very sacrality ensured that it was a potent weapon in the strictly secular disputes of powerful – and often unscrupulously ambitious – men" (MacCaskie 1983: 198). He supports this statement with the following remarks: "In

sacred object rested the historical past, present, and future of the united independent state of the Asantes.

Rattray's investigation of the Golden Stool emerged out of curiosity of a supposed desecration or destruction of it in 1921. The news had thrown the Asante people into national disarray, while within the circles of the British government in Kumasi there was fear of war (Rattray 1923: 287). The communal uproar at the hint of a possible desecration of the Golden Stool expresses the intrapsychic effects it brings, much in the same way a person's *sunsum* can fret to become ill. Therefore, the sacrality of the Golden Stool engenders greater force for the welfare and unity of the Asantes, while an attack against it signifies a national decline. Rattray derived from this notion of the national *sunsum* an intra-relational intervention theory for peaceful cooperation between the British and Asantes – a contribution he is celebrated for because of his Anthropology Department and knowledge concerning the Golden Stool, which proved how knowledge and politics were indispensable qualities for peaceful intervention.[79]

Besides the knowledge provided to the British, Rattray's own interpretation of the collective *sunsum* enshrined in the stool was that of a transcending process upon which depended "an unfolding map of predictable development" that can forge successful socio-economic and political future of the Asantes.[80] Rattray makes the connection thus:

---

ca. 1800, Osei Kwame (1777-1803), in conflict with Asantehemaa Kwaadu Yaadom, seized the Golden Stool and the royal regalia and fled to exile in Dwaben, where he attempted to establish an alternative government... in 1823, Osei Yaw Akoto took possession of the Golden Stool and, fleeing to the south, used it to secure the army's support for his ambitions, thereby nullifying the claims of his rival Fredua Agyeman to be the successor of Osei Tutu Kwame... in August 1883, Akyempemhene Oheneba Owusu Koko (1820-1884), sponsor of the youthful royal Agyeman Kofi, threatened to destroy the Golden Stool rather than let it fall into the hands of his client's dynastic rival, the deposed Kofi Kakari" (MacCaskie 1983: 198).

79 It is necessary to reiterate how Rattray processed raw knowledge from the Asante customs to sustain the colonial administration in the Asante region. Knowledge and colonialism were like a single unit during the British presence in the Gold Coast. Rattray's knowledge of Asante customs and laws helped to forge a decisive alliance between Asante natives and the British and averted many possible wars.

80 Borrowed phrase from (McCaskie 1983).

> "I have told them that they will become better and finer men and women by remaining true Ashanti and retaining a certain pride in their past, and that their greatest hope lies in the future, if they will follow and build upon lines with which the national *sunsum* or *soul* has been familiar since first they were a people." (Rattray 1923: 12. Italics are my emphasis).

A closer look at the above statement reveals his earlier notion of the Akan *sunsum* as the reason for health, wealth, power, success in any venture, and everything that makes life at all worth living. Rattray consistently understood that *sunsum* was the operational force for the welfare of its constituent agency. The *sunsum* in all its characteristics appears as a dynamic vanguard or as Rattray himself puts it an advance guard which often sits at the door (1927: 154).

The *Sika Dwa Kofi* brings out some of these significant idioms about the *sunsum* into the memory of the Asantes. The Golden Stool itself is not the *sunsum*; it is a repository or, more specifically, the shrine of the *sunsum* of the Asante state (Rattray 1923: 292). There are two main thoughts identified in this understanding. The first is in the semantics, where the collective *sunsum* is spoken of in the singular, i.e. the *sunsum* of the Asantes. Whatever character this *sunsum* is given, it has a communal bond of strength. The single representation of *sunsum* of the nation exemplifies the unification agenda of the Asante nation as one body. The second idea is the linguistic tradition of the fact that the *sunsum* pertains to the people, not to a deity. Although the Golden Stool descended from the sky – a sign from Nyankopɔn – there is no direct reference of its *sunsum* deriving from Nyankopɔn; neither did Rattray offer any details beyond that.

There are a few more questions to ask. From where derived the *sunsum* in the *Sika Dwa Kofi*? Why did Rattray refer to the Golden Stool as a shrine?

The question of the nature of the *sunsum* in this national symbol of the Golden Stool is a paradox since it deviates from the usual cosmological understanding of *sunsum* and turns into an artistic object that is entirely different from the iconic representation of the *Abosom*. We could, perhaps, make a connection between the Golden Stool and the sacrality of the ancestral stools – which is believed to contain the *sunsum* of the ancestors. That connection is possible since the *Sika Dwa Kofi* is the single most sacred stool which contains the *sunsum* of the Asantes. If that is the case, it will mean the spiritual energy or *sunsum* of the Golden Stool is that of the ancestors. Rattray's definition of it as a shrine agrees with this hypothesis and further shows the source of *sunsum* of the Golden Stool.

The term shrine is often associated with a place of sacred meeting. Its root comes from the Latin *scrinium*, which means "case or box for keeping papers." Rattray did not justify his use of "shrine" for the Golden Stool, but the Latin root may be equivalent to the Akan word *suman*. *Suman* is any consecrated object by a priest or spiritual agent that has the potency to empower or create protection against evil. *Suman* means "world of," implying that it is an object that hosts spiritual energy.[81] On the accounts of the coming down of the Golden Stool, Rattray reported how Ɔkomfo Anɔkye "caused the King and every Ashanti chief and all the Queen Mothers to take a few hairs from the head and pubes, and a piece of the nail from the forefinger. These were made into a powder and mixed with 'medicine', and some was drunk and some poured or smeared on the stool" (1923: 289). The consecration ritual initiated the spiritual bond between the Golden Stool and the Asante nation, here represented by their chiefs and queen mothers. The Golden Stool, therefore, is a symbol of protection, making it a shrine or *suman* for the Asante nation. That means it possesses an intrinsic power from Nyankopɔn to enable it to contain the *sunsum* of the people. And since the *sunsum* of the Asantes and their ancestors reside in it, the Golden Stool is not supposed to be sat on.[82]

What if the Golden Stool gets stolen or destroyed? Will the Asante nation fall? The shreds of evidence we have gathered so far suggest the destruction of the Golden Stool will lead to the fall of Asante as a nation. We recall Ɔkomfo Anɔkye's charge to the chiefs and queen mothers to keep the stool from destruction or from being stolen, else "as a man sickens and dies whose *sunsum* during life has wandered away or has been injured by some other *sunsum*, so would the Ashanti nation sicken and lose its vitality and

81 More details about *suman* will be dealt later.

82 In March 1900, the Asantes besieged Kumasi, then occupied by the British, following a request by Sir Frederic Hodgson, then governor of the Gold Coast, to sit on the Golden Stool. The Asantes, seeing his request as open defiance of the sacred stool, declared war against the British, led by the then Ejisu queen mother Yaa Asantewaa. The war lasted for six months resulting in fatalities on both sides. Queen mother Yaa Asantewaa was captured alongside with other traditional leaders and was exiled to the Seychelles Islands where she died. This war marked the last conflict between the Asantes and the British. A peace treaty was made and the Asantes maintained their independent state though working under British rule.

power" (Rattray 1923: 289, 290). Besides the security measures to ensure the safety of the Golden Stool, Ɔkomfo Anɔkye made further provisions, should every measure fail. Rattray gives an account of a sacred stone at Kokofu known as *Ahantan Bo* (The proud stone).[83] It is believed Ɔkomfo Anɔkye sanctified the stone with the rest of the portion used in sanctifying the Golden Stool including other ritual elements. The stone stands as an alternative shrine should the Golden Stool be stolen. Ɔkomfo Anɔkye "stated that this stone must stand for a symbol of the Golden Stool, and if that emblem were ever lost or stolen, the *sunsum* (spirit) of the Nation would enter this rock" (Rattray 1929: 218). The stone was not supposed to be stepped on because it embodies the same sacrality accorded to the Golden Stool, and periodic rituals are associated with it. The various rituals related to the preservation of the national *sunsum* signify its supreme importance and the place the concept occupies in the overall Asante traditional system. I have no doubt Captain Rattray understood this to the fullest.

4.2.2. An Overall Critique

In this section, I will offer an overall evaluation of Rattray's conception of the *sunsum*. The purpose here is to underline some of the methodological problems that confronted Rattray which have directly or indirectly affected the *sunsum* discourse over time and how they form part of the contemporary criticism of the nature of the *sunsum*.

First, there is the problem of language. Rattray's use of the English language to describe Akan realities was inevitable, but it led to problematic interpretations. Language embodies the essential elements of a people's culture, and through it a person is introduced or oriented into the depths of a given cultural worldview. Rattray used the terms "spirit" and "soul" to

---

[83] Among the people of Kokofu, the stone is widely known as Anokye *boɔ* (The stone of Anokye). An informant from Kokofu explained to me why it came to be called *Ahantan boɔ*. The stone was given to the then chief of Kokofu to carry it from his palace and walk a distance through the streets. Wherever he will drop the stone will become the center of the town. It is said that the chief, because of pride, carried the stone for a short distance from his palace and dropped it and to date, that spot has become the center of Kokofu. The stone has been fenced and considered sacred up to date.

translate anything non-conceptual as matter or bearing spiritual properties.[84] For example, *ɔkra*, *ntorɔ*, *sunsum*, and the Abosom were often translated as "spirit" or "soul." In most instances, the two English terms "spirit" and "soul" were used variably – if not interchangeably – to translate one concept. An example relates to the nature of the *sunsum*, which Rattray saw as both polymorphic and polysemic. He translated *sunsum* interchangeably as "spirit," or "soul," and sometimes both (Rattray 1923: 12, 46, 195-6, 258, 289, 292-3, 296). Rattray further maintained *ntorɔ* as a "spirit" and wrote of the *ntorɔ* as a term best translated by "spirit" (1923: 45-6, 202).[85] Whatever Rattray meant by the term "spirit" is up to future generations to figure out. The most obvious thing here is that his understanding of what a spirit is did not stem from the Akan context, but instead from his background as a European.

Second, we encounter the problem of description of Asante realities. Rattray's work has been reviewed as descriptive and non-theoretical (Müller 2008: 167). He sought to undertake a comprehensive survey of Akan customs and religion. In the preface to *Religion and Arts in Ashanti*, he wrote: "I have striven throughout this volume and in *Ashanti* to make them as purely objective as the subject and scope seem to demand" (Rattray 1927: v). However, the description was not always "purely objective" as he encountered difficulty in distinguishing the relationship between *ɔkra*, *sunsum*, and *ntorɔ*. He wrote: "I have stated that *ntorɔ* may perhaps be translated by 'spirit.' Indeed, it appears to be used at times synonymously with *sunsum*" (Rattray 1923: 46). Again, in his attempt to explain the Asante concept of *Akowuakra*, meaning "when you die, you bid farewell," Rattray said: "before death, the *sunsum* or *ntorɔ* or *spirit*, about to quit the body for ever, flits from wherever the dying man or woman may be… and says 'good-bye'" (1923: 55). Indeed, there is a relationship between *ntorɔ* and *sunsum*, but the two are not synonymous. Also, an informant seems to have told him that *ɔkra* and *sunsum* are the same (1927: 155). The complex dialectical relationship between *ɔkra*, *sunsum* and *ntorɔ* was not only a conceptual problem for Rattray, but a difficulty that has been transmitted

---

[84] Spirit and soul are two confusing words, both in Western philosophical and theological thinking. Chapter five of this study will take into consideration the need to expound on the meaning of the two terms in Western thought and why the quasi-physicalist objects its usage in dealing with traditional Akan thought forms.

[85] Rattray maintained a consistent use of *ntorɔ* without an English translation in most of his writings.

through subsequent scholarship, where both *ɔkra* and *sunsum* are often translated as "soul" (Meyerowitz 1951; Busia 1954; Müller 2013).

Third, it is evident that Rattray did not use the expression, "God's *sunsum*," or "God's spirit." Neither did he associate the *sunsum* with God. His discussion of the *sunsum* was more limited: it was limited to the pantheon deities, and so did not pertain to God. In speaking of the pantheon gods as the spark of God's power, Rattray used terms like '*Onyankopon tumi*,' or '*honhon*,' that is, "'the power, spirit, or *mana* of God" (Rattray 1915: 22). Unlike the *ɔkra* that is indisputably from God, the possible source of *sunsum* for Rattray was from the pantheon deities who transmit their *ntorɔ* and *sunsum* through Akan males; this is another reason which led Rattray to confuse *ntorɔ* with *sunsum*. *Sunsum* then appears in his writings as an emanating pantheon force that protects an individual.

Fourth, there is the question of the nature of the *sunsum*. There is no clue from Rattray that the *sunsum* is an astral personality or double of the person. If anything of that sort is inferred from his writings, it will be nothing more than a linguistic conundrum of his translation of *sunsum* in the English language as both "soul" and "spirit." Even though Rattray tried to be candid and report what he saw and heard, his English background inevitably determined the various interpretations he gave of the Akan worldviews. This led to the repeated difficulty he encountered in distinguishing between the *ɔkra*, *sunsum*, and *ntorɔ*.

Finally, Rattray gives us an idea of the Akan *sunsum* as signifying a personal presence of an emanating force or spiritual agent. *Sunsum* will always imply, or refer to, the presence of an agent. Examples include *sunsum* of a person, *sunsum* of Ta Kora, *sunsum* of a river, *sunsum* of the Asantes, *sunsum* of a tree, etc. When Rattray asked whether a particular river had a *sunsum*, the answer given to him was an emphatic "yes," reaffirming the Akan view that all rivers are deities and therefore contain emanating force.

4.3. Summary

The rise of Akan studies is the bedrock for a historiographical quest to investigate the nature of the *sunsum*. The lexicography and writings of Christaller set the stage for subsequent research into Akan religions and culture. Another significant figure was Captain Rattray, who remains an important figure in the evolution of Akan scholarship as well as in his role as an anthropologist for the British colonial administration in the then Gold Coast. We know Rattray as an anthropologist rather than a historian because of his ethnographical sketch of Asante customs and religion, and as head of the then newly created Anthropology Department in Asante. He was an ethnographer rather than an ethnologist: he embarked on a descriptive study of Akan religions rather than doing a comparative study between two or more ethnic groups.

Rattray remains influential, and the most cited scholar in Akan scholarship. His contribution to the meaning of the Akan *sunsum*, with its various dimensions as force, personal magnetism, character, personality, power – upon which depend health, wealth, worldly power, success in any venture, and everything that makes life at all worth living – agrees with most scholars studying the *sunsum* concept. The only exception is his characterization of the *sunsum* as "spirit" which my research seeks to critically engage. In the following chapter, I will continue my historiographical investigation into the nature of the *sunsum* by considering the contributions of succeeding scholars studying Akan religions.

5. Later Scholars and the *Sunsum* Construction

> *"Onyankopon's value for life is any active value, a working value, the value for activity, of how best man should carry himself in conduct. Goodness implies value of something done. Onyankopon's doing is good. Onyankopon is good, is in fact the Supreme Good, the Akan God of Beneficence, practical content of the moral life. Why should he not be worshipped?"*— Joseph Boakye Danquah.[86]

This chapter is a continuation of our historiographical investigation into the nature of the Akan *sunsum*. In the previous chapter, we introduced the conception of Captain Rattray in his study of the *sunsum* among the Asante of the Akan ethnic group. Rattray's work has been adjudged descriptive rather than theoretical in the sense that he wrote from an observer's point of view. His work was more useful to the colonial empire than to the Asantes (Müller 2013: 167). Again, *sunsum* was not a subject of study for Rattray. Hence, little inquiry went into it – unlike his attitude towards the *ntorɔ* exogamy. Later scholars who studied Akan religions built their research around Rattray but with some theoretical divergences.

This chapter brings to the forefront some of these divergent views that have had impact on Akan religious practice and scholarship. The interlocutors in this chapter are chosen chronologically and geographically rather than according to a classification of Western and non-Western views. The reason is to ascertain the systematic evolution of the meaning of *sunsum* over time and to understand how the geographical backgrounds (or fields of study) shaped their perception about the *sunsum*.[87] The following historiographical investigation focuses on the works of Joseph Boakye Danquah (1944), Eva Lewin-Richter Meyerowitz (1951), Kofi Abrefa Busia (1954), Heleine K. Minkus (1980), and Anthony Ephirim-Donkor (1997, 2016).

---

86 Danquah (1968: 152).

87 Although Akan people share common cultural traditions and languages, the meanings and application of certain terminologies may differ from one group to the other.

These scholars are chosen not necessarily for their academic contribution, but also for their conceptual contribution to the study of *sunsum*.

5.1. Theological Encounter with Philosophy in J. B. Danquah

Following Rattray was the Ghanaian nationalist and theological philosopher Joseph Boakye Danquah, who pioneered a critical inquiry into the *sunsum* concept. Danquah hails from the Akyem group of the Akan ethnicity, from where his religious knowledge about the Akan was shaped. He authored the book *The Akan Doctrine of God* (1944, 1968), which was published twenty-one years after Rattray's *Ashanti*, and six years after Rattray's death. The book describes Akan theology of God and religio-cultural practices, with a focus on two major areas.

First, Danquah contends that in most human societies, God is self-evident. However, God is known by various shades of varied degrees as well as numerous vernacular names. The concept of God reveals a set of knowledge about God and how that knowledge affects humans' perceptions of what it means to live a meaningful life. In spite of this, the reality of God is not always a simple notion, especially when what is meant by the term "God" can be subjective. This is because the question "what or who is God?" still exists today. Danquah tackles the question of the reality of God and the revelation of God in the context of human societies. The strength of this approach is in his view that each society has discovered the supernatural, and among the Akan, "there is a 'native' or seed-quality about their name for God, which is evidence that they had, of themselves, found God" (Danquah 1968: 1).

In Danquah's opinion, the Akan religions recognize only one God, and the depths of that understand underline the framework of the spiritual and social construction of the Akan. Danquah's first task was to diminish the former missionaries' teaching of a Supreme or High God who they thought of as contrary to the God of African traditional religions. The West conjured up the term fetish to weaken the spiritual substance of African traditional religions, thereby giving way to the superiority of the Western God over that of Africans. The fetish cult, according to Danquah, is nothing more than a blend of superstition and individuals' private quest for material fulfillment and should not be confused with the Akan religious conception of one God (1968: 39). The gods are not fetish either, and their spiritual representation in material objects does not define their essential qualities and should not be taken as such (1968: 7, 8). The Akan use images as symbols of their religious beliefs. Danquah argues that God is not an imported product of the West; neither is God to be identified with fetishism.

That polemical assumption drove Danquah's desire to expound on Akan theology with greater emphasis and appreciation of his own traditional religious realities. Danquah argues in favor of his native religion which over the years has shaped his personality and worldview and which continues to shape the spirituality of most Akan citizens. As a staunch Christian, Danquah remains one of the foremost African scholars who took a particular interest in dealing with the Akan traditional religion as worthy of study.

The second principal aspect of Danquah's *The Akan Doctrine of God* is an investigation of the Akan religious system and the deity Onyame. Danquah makes nine postulates about Akan religions, which are classified into three classes by Kwesi Dickson (Danquah 1968: xxiii): (1) Individual Postulates: these are concerned with the life process of the individual and include *E-su*, *Sunsum*, and *Honhom*; (2) Social Postulates: this involves the ethical or moral aspect of life and comprise *Ɔkra*, *Ɔbosom*, and Nana; (3) Theological Postulates: these deal with the concept of God among the Akan. Here in the third postulate, Danquah pursues a tripartite conception of the Akan names for God, i.e., Onyame, Onyankopɔn, and Odomankoma. Onyame is the general idea of the deity.[88] Onyankopɔn is the personality behind Onyame, i.e., a personal religious God, the Supreme Being. Odomankoma is the interminable or infinite being (Danquah 1968: 30). To the well-informed reader of Akan religions, Danquah has philosophically expounded on the concepts in ways that make them relevant to Western thought; still, some think of his postulates as neither Western nor consistent with Akan religions, but as his own ratiocination (Welbourn 1965; Basden 1944). There could be several questions concerning Danquah's doctrine, but our concern now is how he conceived his ideas about the Akan concept of *sunsum*.

[88] Danquah capitalizes the first letters of *Sunsum* and *Honhom* in sentences to refer to God or the Spirit of God.

5.1.1. Danquah's Conception of *Sunsum*

In order to understand Danquah's construction of the *sunsum*, there is the need to state right from the start that it is not very simple to read Danquah's works. Reviewers of *The Akan Doctrine of God* have reacted negatively to his style of writing. G. T. Basden sees the language and terms used by Danquah as highly academic. He further observes the whole production of his work as more after the style of a degree thesis rather than a normal book (1944: 283). Edwin W. Smith compares the complicated writing style of Danquah to that of Hegel (1944: 186). Besides the complexities in his writing style, Danquah's astute scholarship, combined with his first-hand knowledge of Akan religions and experience as a researcher in Western philosophy, gave him the skills to express his thoughts in a highly scholastic thinking. So, as we reveal his valuable contribution to the concept of *sunsum*, we will also keep in mind his philosophical interpretation of Akan realities.

Danquah's interpretation of *sunsum* differs from Rattray's anthropological view. For Danquah, our understanding of *sunsum* should begin with God. His first task was to dismiss the pneumatic character of the *sunsum* by analyzing the Akan maxim, "*Onyankopon ye Odomankoma Sunsum,*" translated by Danquah as, "God (*Onyankopon*) is the Infinite God's (*Odomankoma's*) Personality (*Sunsum*)" (1968: 66). The translation of *sunsum* as "personality" was Danquah's way of brushing off earlier pneumatic translations of *sunsum* in the maxim as "spirit." He says, "the notion which corresponds to the Akan 'Sunsum,' namely, not 'spirit' as such but the personality which covers the relation of the 'Body' to the 'Soul' (Okara)" (1968: 66).[89] The justification for this is given in the wider view of Danquah's definition of reality. *Sunsum* as "personality" makes it an experience where personal endeavors are realized in life. Nevertheless, Danquah has more to say about the relationship between personality and experience.

---

[89] Ephirim-Donkor classifies Danquah among the Akan scholars who followed Rattray in defining the *sunsum* as spirit (Ephirim-Donkor 2016: 40). I am not convinced this is accurate. Even though Danquah seemed to postulate the ontology of the *sunsum* as an immaterial element, he never used the term "spirit" for the *sunsum*. It is the *ɔkra* that is accorded with spirituality in Danquah's doctrine. But this happens only after a metamorphism, in which the *e-su* has become *sunsum*, and *sunsum* has become *ɔkra*, and *ɔkra* "become a *honhom*, a fully developed spirit or mind" (Danquah 1968: 113).

The application of *sunsum* to personality is pivotal to understanding reality. Experience defines reality in the sense that every experience is subject to reality. Danquah thinks *sunsum* is an experience of reality. He brings that notion to bear when he thinks of Onyankopɔn, the Akan name for the Supreme Being, as the ultimate source of experience whose nature corresponds to *sunsum*. Onyankopɔn is the reality that portrays the personality, that is, the nature of the deity Onyame (Danquah 1968: 41, 67). In other words, Onyankopɔn is ascribed the principle of experience, the *Sunsum* (Personality) of God. It is Onyankopɔn who is known to the Akan as the ultimate reality through whom the Akan worship *Odomankoma*. Onyankopɔn is just an image of *Odomankoma* as Danquah concludes, saying, "Odomankoma is best known to man in Nyankopon, in the domain or "house" of experience (Sunsum)" (1968: 68). From this background, we can better understand Danquah's postulation of Onyankopɔn being *Sunsum* as only the appearance of the nature of the infinite (Odomankoma), and this *Sunsum* is what is known to the Akan as the personality of Odomankoma. Danquah makes a typological case in support of this assumption:

> Odomankoma is conceived as the Okara of which Nyankopon is the Sunsum or Experience, and the idea to be fulfilled is the evolved and completely realized Honhom or Spirit of the Thing. In other words, just as an individual personality has a *sunsum* for experience, so, too, the Thing [Odomankoma] has a Sunsum for experience (1968: 68).

We can determine how Danquah uses the typology of *ɔkra* and *sunsum* to shape his pneumatology. Odomankoma as *Ɔkra* is the infinite Creator, better known in the world of experience as Onyankopɔn (*Sunsum*) through whom the Akan experience the creative power which Danquah assumes is the final fulfillment or realization of Odomankoma's *Honhom*.

We may find it challenging to grasp the full meaning of Danquah's thesis, but two things are quite evident in this typology. The first has to do with the relationship between *ɔkra* and *sunsum*: he assumes the latter is the reflection of the former. The second is how he draws our attention to the difference between *sunsum* and *honhom*; *sunsum* being personality, and *honhom* being the Spirit. These two are relevant to our study and need to be given further elaboration in the context of Danquah's pneumatology and anthropology.

Danquah says *sunsum* is the ideal of a prototype called *e-su* (*phusis*; 'nature' in English), which "provides the possibility of the incipient individual's appearance in Nyankopon's presence… to obtain his *nkrabea*, destiny or intelligence, his 'message' to earth, to realize the essence or capacity of his particular soul (okara)" (1968: 66, 67). The Akan term *e-su*, which means nature, designates the nature of an object that appears in experience. *Suban* (character) is an example of the *e-su* of a person. All personality traits are characterized by *e-su*. It is the distinctive quality of being and the definition of the degree of being. Danquah postulated that "*e-su* represents the fundamental bio-physical nature of man" (1968: 111). The nature of being can be characterized as "the distinctive capacities of a truly human being with a corresponding responsibility to realize those capacities" (1968: 111). Consequently, Danquah was right to see *e-su* as comparable to the Greek *phusis* (nature) since it is the exclusive constitution of power that defines an individual. For example, it is the *e-su* that makes a person human. The *e-su* can be an animal, a thing, etc. In the origin of human beings, Danquah believes "the Akan took it to be the primitive root of being" (1968: 111).

In an attempt to offer further elaboration, Danquah explains that *e-su* (nature) is the "prime genetic basis for the origin of the social subject, i.e., man" (1968: 111). The *e-su* is a spark from Odomankoma, the source of race and humanity. In life, *esu* is known to the Akan as *sunsum*, the subject of experience of the *ɔkra*, making the two divine and counterpart. Here, we encounter one of the most difficult aspects of Danquah's anthropology, which is his concept of the origin of the human being and the relationship between *ɔkra* and *sunsum*. Most scholars of Akan religions think it is the *ɔkra*, instead of *e-su* or *sunsum*, that takes leave before God. Given the difficulty, I will examine Danquah's interpretation of *e-su* in relation to *ɔkra* more closely to show how he understood and interpreted Akan anthropology. How does the relation between *okra* and *sunsum* work together?

Danquah seems to have answered this question in his attempt to outline the main argument for that postulate. The origin of the human being is an evolutionary process. *E-su* appears before Onyankopɔn for *nkrabea* (destiny) or purpose decree, thereby acquiring *hyɛbea*, the *e-su*'s soul or *ɔkra*. The *ɔkra*, being the bearer of that destiny, then comes to inhere in the human being to realize that purposed decree. The *e-su* does not disappear after acquiring a soul or becoming a human being. It is carried into the mundane world of experience, "where it is known under the term *sunsum*, the counterpart of the spiritual, of the okara" (1968: 112).[90] The finality of the process makes *e-su* a determinant principle for personality (*sunsum*).

There is a further note on the relationship between *e-su* and *ɔkra*; the connection is ontologically inseparable. The *ɔkra* bears a composite principle of destiny that can only be realized by the *e-su*, "the bearer of conscious experience, the unconscious or subliminal self remaining over as the *okara* or soul, which the primitive *e-su* has to realize in its individual being" (Danquah, 1968: 112). The *sunsum* appears in Danquah's doctrine as a panentheistic element or an "ideal archetype pre-existing in Nyankopon as the Sunsum of Odomankoma" (1968: 113). The operational force of the *sunsum* as a conscious counterpart of the *ɔkra* is to prepare for the destiny to be made good and the message (*nkrabea*) to be carried out (Danquah 1968: 115). This preliminary theory by Danquah will suggest that destiny (*ɔkra*), being inactive in itself, could be brought to activity or fulfillment by the *sunsum*.

The whole evolutionary process of the origin of the human being could be summed up thus: "*E-su* gets its *okara* or soul from Nyankopon. *E-su* is also the matter of experience, of being in the world of the living. It is the basis of the *sunsum* of man. Likewise, Nyankopon is the *Sunsum* of Odomankoma" (Danquah 1968: 112, 113). So, "from *e-su* to *sunsum*, and from *sunsum* to *okara*, this *okara* becomes a *honhom*, a fully developed spirit or mind" (Danquah 1968: 113). Odomankoma (*Ɔkra*) is the source of life (*ɔkra*) of the human being, while Nyankopon (Sunsum) is the experiencing deity who emerges as the *sunsum* in life. Hence, a person's *sunsum* is the act of experience of the *ɔkra*, which when it is fully experienced, earns participation in divine immortality where it becomes part of God, i.e., one in substance and being as spirit (*honhom*).

In this context, Danquah provides the theological basis for two of the Akan concepts of the *ɔkra*. First, the departure of the *ɔkra* at the point of dying is proverbially referred to among Akan people as *Ne honhom kɔ*, "His breath or spirit is gone," to signal the death of the person. I will return to this in subsequent chapters. The second supports the notion of the immortality of the *ɔkra*, and indeed a majority of Akan people view the *'kra* as deathless. This explains the belief in ancestral spirits.

---

90 This conception underlines Kwame Gyekye's philosophical theory of an *ontic* unity of the *ɔkra* and *sunsum*. More details in the next chapter.

The foregoing anthropological analysis may hardly correspond to the ordinary Akan thinker's understanding of the origin of human beings. Indeed, we may get the same difficulty when we compare Danquah's anthropology to that of Rattray's. What we appreciate in Danquah is how he provides new possibilities to examine Akan realities. He offers a philosophical and theological reinterpretation of Akan religions towards a new self-definition of how Akan people should regard their history as a people.

Danquah presents the nature of *sunsum* as responsible for personality in the world of experience. Its divine origin and role as the basis for conscious experience is stated with more specific emphasis on its non-pneumatic character. Danquah did not apply the English term "spirit" to *sunsum*. *E-su*, known in the individual's world of experience as *sunsum*, is "personality," but not "spirit." The definition he gives to a "spirit" refers to an immaterial psycho-dimensional object synonymous with the mind or the *ɔkra*. Both *ɔkra* and *sunsum* are spoken of in psychological terms, and on several occasions Danquah equates the *ɔkra* to the mind, which is spiritual (*honhom*) and a fully developed individual.

Danquah's reading of Akan religions has been adjudged nonindigenous and fused with Christian theological thoughts (Müller 2008: 173). He was also a victim of his own polemics against Western commentaries on Akan religions, as he attempted to convince his readers that Akan religious concepts are compatible with Western ideas, which does not appear to be the case.

5.2. *Sunsum* as the Personal Soul in Eva L. R. Meyerowitz

Eva Lewin-Richter Meyerowitz (1899-1994) is another European anthropologist whose competence in and contribution to Akan anthropology is highly praised. She was born in Berlin, Germany, and was married to sculptor Herbert Vladimir Meyerowitz in 1925. Both spent some time in South Africa where Herbert taught at the University of Cape Town and opened an art school. Their interest in arts and crafts brought them to Ghana where both became supervisors of arts and crafts at Achimota College in Accra. Herbert suffered manic depressive cyclothymia in 1945 and died that same year from suicide in London (Cardew 2002). Mrs. Meyerowitz spent forty years among the Bono cultural group of the Akan people of Ghana and was made queen mother in 1950 in Tekyiman. Her contribution to Akan literature and ethnohistory is considerable.

Meyerowitz's introduction to Akan studies began in 1943 while serving as art supervisor at the Achimota College. The quest for artistic interest in gold ornaments turned into lifelong research into the study of Akan history and ethnology. That turnaround in her career mirrored the heightened interest in Akan studies around the mid-twentieth century. Since 1943, she contributed significantly to Akan literature and remains one of the most cited authorities in Akan studies. The range of her interests in Akan studies covered areas in Akan nationalism, history, religion, and politics. Her books include *The Sacred State of the Akan* (1951), *Akan Traditions of Origin* (1952), *The Akan of Ghana* (1958), and *The Divine Kingship in Ghana and Ancient Egypt* (1960). Her research primarily focused on Akan settlement and migration.

Meyerowitz's ethnohistorical research delved into the origins of primitive Akan beliefs. She relied partly on Danquah for interpretation and reinterpretation of Akan religio-cultural categories. Their paths sometimes even crossed. While she proved that the Akan had a great past, she stimulated their memory to envision a future that encompasses the whole of that history. Meyerowitz's contribution met the approval of Danquah who recommended her work as inspiring a living future hitched to a history embedded in the beginning of things (Danquah 1952: 366). Readers appreciate Meyerowitz for her ambitious independent attitude towards the reconstruction of Akan history, although she was not competent in the Twi language like Rattray and Danquah. This lack of linguistic mastery might have contributed to her historical speculations in the attempt to connect the Akan people to ancient Egypt. As we review her contribution to Akan anthropology, we shall keep in mind some of these gross misrepresentations.

Meyerowitz's views on Akan spirituality appeared in *Africa: Journal of the International African Institute* under the title, "Concepts of the Soul among the Akan of the Gold Coast" (1951a), and also in her book, *The Sacred State of the Akan* (1951b). These materials express in detail the depths of her understanding of Akan spirituality.

At first glance, one may question whether Meyerowitz is treating the Akan as a homogenous group. There are little indications of the Akan subgroups she is dealing with. Akan ethnicity is a complex reality with several sociological divergences from one cultural group to another. Meyerowitz's work focused on the Northern sector of the Ashanti, precisely among the

Bonos of the Akan ethnicity. On few occasions, she made references to fieldwork among the Akan people in the South.

5.2.1. The Concept of God Among the Akan

The premise given by Meyerowitz in speaking of Akan spirituality stems from her conception of the Akan God. Onyankopɔn, a "bi-sexual deity of the cosmos Nyame Amowia, visible as the Moon, gave birth to the Sun god, she gave him her *kra*, her eternal soul or life-giving power; hence his name, the Only Great Nyame (*Nyame*; *ko-* only; *pɔn-* great) generally drawn together as Nyankopɔn" (1951a: 24). Thus, the theory postulates a moon cult which in her writings seems to compel for a good ground to interpret Akan anthropology with a specific emphasis on the matrilineal and patrilineal systems. It further serves as the grounds for interpreting Akan political structure where the queen mother, represented as the Moon, enstools the king representing the Sun.

Danquah had earlier brushed off any connection of Onyankopɔn to the celestial bodies; thus, Onyankopɔn is "a personality that must be something divorced from the impersonal sky or the firmament" (Danquah 1968: 39). Nonetheless, in a review of Meyerowitz, Danquah appears to agree with her connection of the Akan deity to the celestial bodies, but only as a typology that corresponds to some Akan realities (Danquah 1956: 362, 363).[91]

Rattray did not say much about a moon cult, except on the accounts of some mural designs he saw on the wall of Ta Kora's temple, where he described the arts of celestial bodies as depicted "in connexion with the Supreme God, 'Nyame'" (Rattray 1923: 173). Besides this remark, there is no deification of the moon and sun in Rattray's conception of Onyankopɔn. We will, therefore, read Meyerowitz's understanding of God in relation to the celestial bodies as only a personification rather than deification. More details on this concept of God can be found in her book, *The Sacred State of the Akan* (1951).

---

91 The typology deduced by Danquah from the moon cult of Meyerowitz represents the celestial triad of Onyame, Onyankopɔn, and Odomankoma. This becomes the basis for the matrilineal triad of mother, son, and uncle, representing the terrestrial triad of queen-mother, king, and ancestor.

5.2.2. The Construction of the *Sunsum*

In connection with the foregoing interpretation, Meyerowitz assumes that the Akan matrilineal system is a representation of the Moon (Nyame). She writes: "a matrilineal ancestor, as representative of Nyame, endows a child with a *kra*, the child to be born and still without a *kra*, receives the *sunsum* from the hands of a patrilineal ancestor, also as representative of Nyame, in the *samandow* or nether world" (1951a: 26).[92] The *ɔkra* is an activation of the mother's blood capacity to bring about life.

To understand the connection to the moon cult, we are here introduced to the female as the symbol of life. Besides the *ɔkra*, the child is further endowed with the personal soul called *sunsum*, and a paternal spirit called *ntorɔ* from a patrilineal ancestor (Meyerowitz 1951a: 24, 25).[93] Rather than God and the pantheon deities, it is the ancestors who play vital roles in the spiritual and physical formation of the human being. As already mentioned, the Akan community involves the living and the ancestors, and with Meyerowitz's conception of birth, the relational idea is strengthened even more. The role the ancestors play, as representatives of God (Nyame) in procreation, displaces the pantheon deities (*Abosom*) as progenitors of children as theorized by Rattray and other scholars. If the ancestors are capable of endowing these vital properties, then they are powerful just like the pantheon deities. However, the available evidence does not support Meyerowitz's conception of the birth of the human being, even if the attribution fits perfectly with Akan realities.

How did Meyerowitz understand the *ɔkra*? To her, the *ɔkra* is not just a principle of life, but the twin or double of the individual. It is a spiritual being that reproduces itself in the physical dimension as a human being. Meyerowitz speaks of the *ɔkra* thus:

> "The *kra* then is life itself; it is man's vital force, the source of his energy, his great reservoir of strength and sustenance. It is, further, a divine spirit, and inspirations, dreams, visions, and

---

92 Meyerowitz tells another account of the *sunsum* as what a father passes on to his child during sexual intercourse. The father kisses the mother and lets his saliva mingle with hers (1951a: 27).

93 Later scholarship referred to the *ɔkra* as life-soul, and *sunsum* as the personality-soul (Akesson 1965: 286).

> phantasies are attributed to it. It is also regarded as a man's instinct, which protects him and may save him from danger, and hence it is also called man's guardian spirit" (Meyerowitz 1951a: 24).

There are divergent views here as to whether *ɔkra* is the double of the human being. A majority of scholars favor *sunsum* as the image or double of the individual that wanders in sleep (Rattray 1923; Asare Opoku 1978; Gyekye 1987). Despite this, Meyerowitz makes a strong argument in support of her assertion by referring to the Akan maxim, *Ne 'kra n'edii n'akyi ntira anka w'awu*, meaning, "But for his *ɔkra* that followed him, he would have died." The maxim presupposes two characteristics of the *ɔkra*; first, as an astral "spirit," and second, as a person's companion. The strength of Meyerowitz's conception of the *ɔkra* as the double of the individual rests upon this fact. I will respond to this theory in the next chapter. But for now, similar statements in Akan purport to support her assumption. These include, *Wo reku me 'kra*, meaning "You are killing/hurting my *ɔkra,*" and *Me 'kra redi awerehoɔ*, meaning "My *ɔkra* is aggrieving." These anthropomorphic sentiments are often attributed to the *ɔkra* as though it is an astral being that can suffer some form of physical experiences. However, the statements above do not define the ontological properties of the *ɔkra*. Proverbs are metaphors; they are not to be taken literally. *Ɔkra* is a principle of a life-force. Anything that diminishes life, for example, as in grieving, pain, and death, are attributed to the *ɔkra*. After all, Akan people believe the *ɔkra* cannot die; how then can one's '*kra* be aggrieved to death if not in a figurative sense? Hence, the statements should be understood metaphorically rather than literal.

Meyerowitz seems, in part, to offer a solution to Rattray's contradiction of the *ɔkra* and *sunsum* by translating both terms as "soul." She wrote, "the *kra* is a divine, impersonal soul, the *sunsum* is regarded as the personal soul" (Meyerowitz 1951a: 26).[94] The impersonal soul (*ɔkra*) is compared to Sigmund Freud's Id, i.e., the unconscious and instinctual part of the personality; on the other hand, the personal soul (*sunsum*), is compared to the Ego, the conscious and principle of reality. The *ɔkra* is the uncoordinated drive

---

[94] The *ɔkra* as divine is not a contradiction of Meyerowitz' reference to the ancestress as responsible for the *'kra*. The ancestress represents Nyame in the nether world where she receives the *'kra* from Nyame.

or the unconscious impulses, the psychological disposition that is seeking fulfillment (1951a: 27).

Meyerowitz uses a Freudian analogy of the ego for the *sunsum* to convey the manner that the individual wishes to express itself in life, and the plans the person desires to put into action in the world (1951: 26, 27). Akan people refer to this life disposition as *nkrabea* (destiny), which Meyerowitz attributes to the *sunsum* – what Rattray said of as "upon which depend health, wealth, worldly power, success in any venture, in fact everything that makes life at all worth living" (Rattray 1923: 46).

Both Meyerowitz and Danquah believe the *sunsum* is the bearer of *nkrabea* (destiny), although they disagree on the process. Danquah thinks it is the *e-su* (thing) that appears before Onyankopɔn to receive its *hyebea* (*ɔkra*) and destiny (*sunsum*). Consequently, in Danquah, the *sunsum* and *ɔkra* have ontological unity where the *sunsum* is the intelligence of the spiritual being, the *ɔkra*. Danquah further wrote: "In *nkrabea*, destiny or intelligence, both the *sunsum*, and the *okara* are immeasurably involved" (1968: 68). Meyerowitz, on the other hand, thinks the *sunsum* is given by a patrilineal ancestor from Asamando (the spirit world of the dead), but the *nkrabea* (destiny) is pronounced by 'Nyame. The only message given to the *ɔkra* was a command "to be a good human being, and to do good deeds during his lifetime." This is what Meyerowitz calls *hyɛbea* (*hye* – command, commandment; *bea* – type of) (Meyerowitz 1951a: 24). In this sense, both *ɔkra* and *sunsum* are bearers of distinct messages.

According to Meyerowitz, the *sunsum* is the conscious structure that puts the unconscious pleasures of the *ɔkra* (Id) into real balance or, to use Danquah's words, "to live the objective and destined life" (1968: 67). Meyerowitz's assumption agrees with the general conception among Akan people that the *sunsum* is the operational force for personality and the subject of experience. This is besides her perception of *sunsum* as the bearer of *nkrabea* – a majority of Akan people believe *nkrabea* is dependent upon the *ɔkra* as the derivation of the term *nkrabea* (*nkra* + *bea*) suggests.[95]

Whereas it may appear that the *ɔkra* and *sunsum* are two separate entities, Meyerowitz sees them as two elements of one soul (1951a: 27). The *ɔkra* and *sunsum* form a compound unity. This agrees directly with Rattray's characterization of the *sunsum* as the volatile part of the *ɔkra*, as well as the counterpart of the *ɔkra* in Danquah (Rattray 1957: 154; Danquah

---

95 See explanation on chapter two.

1968: 112). The unanimous agreement among scholars on the relationship of the *ɔkra-sunsum* ontological unity lays the foundation for the idea that as the body cannot exist without an *ɔkra*, so *ɔkra* cannot function in the mundane world without a *sunsum*. According to Meyerowitz, the two elements are not one and same; however, they have essential unity in their operation, making them co-existent.

Meyerowitz emphasizes the separation of *ɔkra* and *sunsum* at death. In her anthropology, there is disembodiment of the human being at death when the *ɔkra* returns to God and "the *sunsum* becomes a ghost or spirit (*saman*) in the image of the deceased and returns to the *samandow,* the realm of the spirits" (1951a: 27). She further alludes to the fact that the *sunsum* of the wicked individuals "are not wanted there and are condemned, after judgment in heaven, to live to eternity in the *abronsamgyam*, the place of wickedness or hell" (1951a: 27).[96] I cannot think of any conception of heaven, judgment, and hell in Akan religions except in Christian doctrines that have found their way within the Akan culture. But given the benefit of the doubt, we are interested in her thoughts about what becomes of the *sunsum* after death. If *sunsum* survives death and can become a ghost, or is judged to spend eternity in hell, could it then be thought of as entitative? It appears to me as such, even though Meyerowitz had earlier rejected the nature of the *sunsum* as not divine but "only a shadow, which lives as long as a person can throw a shadow, and can therefore not be reincarnated" (1951a: 26). If that is the case, would it not be logical for one to assume that *sunsum* perishes at death or it does not go to *Asamando*, let alone suffer hellfire since a dead person cannot throw a shadow? Other scholars discuss the postmortem reality of *sunsum*, which we are going to look at in the next discussion after Meyerowitz.

To sum up everything that Meyerowitz had to say on *sunsum* and Akan anthropology, we come to the following observations. Meyerowitz differs widely from both Rattray and Danquah on the notion of *ɔkra* and *sunsum*.

---

96 Meyerowitz absorbs Christian doctrines of "heaven," "judgement," and "hell" into Akan realities which I think nuances a comprehensive view of Akan religions. In Akan belief, the good ones qualify to join the ancestors and those who could not make it roam about in the spiritual world (occasionally revealing themselves to people) until Onyame gives them the chance to be reborn, i.e., reincarnation. The Akan believe that no one is ultimately doomed and hell, if it is to be applied to the Akan reality, is only a temporary excommunication from the ancestral world.

Whereas Rattray believes the *ɔkra* is the bearer of *nkrabea* (destiny), Meyerowitz attributes the bearer of destiny to the *sunsum*. And whereas Danquah presents a metamorphic evolution of *e-su* to *sunsum* to *ɔkra* and finally to *honhom*, Meyerowitz considers the former three as separate soul components whereby the *ɔkra* is divine, coming from Onyankopɔn, and *sunsum* is an ancestral spirit rather than divine. Meyerowitz believes *sunsum* is a patrilineal spirit, unlike Rattray who linked it to the *Ɔbosom* (*ntorɔ*) of the father.

There is an entitative conception of the *sunsum* in the account of Meyerowitz, which is related to the notion that it survives death and eventually becomes a ghost, a fully developed spiritual being. The question, then, is how was the *sunsum* apotheosized as a living spiritual entity (*saman*/ghost) without the life force, i.e., *ɔkra*? In our next chapter, we will show how Kwame Gyekye seeks to solve this dilemma. But before that, let us consider several scholars who have something to say about the *sunsum*.

5.3. *Sunsum* as a Paternal Biogenetic in Kofi Abrefa Busia

So far, the idea of a transmission of *sunsum* through males has been recurrent in the study – with the exception of Danquah. *Sunsum* is a male-line biogenetic predisposition, not a female-line predisposition (Rattray 1923; Meyerowitz 1951). More elaboration is given by one of the most important authors of Akan anthropology and a Ghanaian statesman, namely Kofi Abrefa Busia (1913–1978). Busia was born into a royal family at Wenchi in the Bono-Ahafo region (then Western Asante) of Ghana. He is best known for his intellectual career rather than as a politician. Educated at Wenchi Methodist School, Mfantsipim School in Cape Coast, and then at Wesley College, Kumasi (all in Ghana), Busia started as a teacher at Achimota Secondary School in 1935, where he won the Achimota Council Scholarship, as well as for his degree in medieval and modern history at the University of London as an external degree student. Another scholarship from the Achimota School sent him to Oxford University. As the first Black student at Oxford, Busia became the first African to receive a Bachelor of Arts degree in philosophy, politics, and economics. In 1942, he became the first of two Africans appointed to serve as district commissioners by the British. The only book he published, *The Position of the Chief in the Mod-*

ern Political System of Ashanti, was from a dissertation for his doctoral degree in Social Anthropology (D. Phil.) at Oxford. Busia was appointed as the first African professor at the University College of the Gold Coast in 1949; later, in 1954, the University of Leiden in Holland conferred a professorship on him, making him become the first African professor. From 1962 to 1969, he was a professor of Sociology and senior member at St. Antony's College, Oxford (Roberts 2013).

Busia became the Prime Minister of Ghana in 1969 until 1972 when he was ousted in a military coup d'état while on medical checkups in England. He died there while in exile in 1978. The legacy of Busia largely rests on his theories in African nationalism and cultural transcendence. Several authors revere his intellectual contribution, and he is considered one of Africa's most influential scholars. His academic and political career was shaped by his remarkable ardency to shape the socio-cultural climate of the people of Africa and establish the principles of democratic rule (Roberts 2013).[97]

Busia's anthropology focused on the Asante cultural group of the Akan group where he showed great interest in the socio-cultural aspects of Asante traditional politics, religious concepts, and cultural evolutions. Busia pointed out how individuals' lives and community are directly affected or reflected by their traditional orientations such as belief in an inspirited universe, the role of man and society, the establishment of political institutions, and also how their evolution over time possesses absorptive capacities to embrace (not replace) new ideas.

Busia's anthropology is an advanced exposition on some aspects of Rattray's anthropology on the Asantes. He shows great appreciation for Rattray by making some crucial references to him. The admiration is even more striking when one considers what Busia said of Rattray: "But the most intimate and accurate knowledge of the Ashanti we owe to Captain R. S. Rattray whose books *Ashanti*, *Ashanti Law and Constitution*, *Religion and Art in Ashanti*, and *Ashanti Proverbs* have covered in an admirable way different aspects of Ashanti culture" (Busia 1954: 190). As a consequence, Busia shares many common ideas with Rattray, especially in the conception of *sunsum* as it relates to the human being and the entire universe.

---

[97] See also, "Busia, Kofi Abrefa." *The Columbia Encyclopedia, 6th ed.* Encyclopedia.com. (June 19, 2018). http://www.encyclopedia.com/reference/encyclopedias-almanacs-transcripts-and-maps/busia-kofi-abrefa. Last visited June 22, 2022.

5.3.1. Busia's Anthropology and his Conception of the *Sunsum*

The conception of the human being is a duality of biological and spiritual components. First, the biological nature consists of the *mogya* from the mother that creates the matriclan (*abusua*) affinity. The *mogya* gives the child status and membership within the lineage, the clan, and the community, as well as the child's rights and obligations as a citizen. The *mogya* ideology forms the basis of the matriclan, the concept of the life hereafter, and the consequent ancestral cult that provides the religious link and unbroken continuity with the individual's kin (Busia 1954: 199, 200). Second is the spiritual, the *ntorɔ*, which is received through the father from a tutelary spirit. The *mogya* and *ntorɔ* determine the social organization of the Asantes where an individual's genealogical connection links the person with kinsmen, fellow citizens, and society (Busia 1954: 196, 197). Besides the *mogya* and *ntorɔ*, the Akan child receives two other distinct spiritual gifts, i.e., *sunsum* and *ɔkra*. The two are not synonymous and identical, according to Busia. The *sunsum* is transmitted from the father to the child to mold the child's psychological and spiritual disposition or distinctive character. Every male child possesses this "personal power, or cast of countenance" from the father (1954: 197).[98] The expected result is that the child will uphold moral qualities commendable to shape the accepted social values that hold the community together.

Busia further asserts, like Meyerowitz, that the *sunsum* is not divine, but perishes with the person at death. It is not clear what Busia meant by the perishability of the *sunsum*. Meyerowitz's interpretation of that assumption alluded to the disembodiment of the *sunsum* from the body, which ultimately becomes the ghost after death. Rattray had asserted repatriation of the *sunsum* to its source, thus a return to the tutelary deity (Rattray 1923: 55). Danquah did not talk about the perishability of *sunsum* since it is only a personality and has ontological unity with the *ɔkra*. Busia did not give further details about the posthumous state of the *sunsum*; rather, he seems to say that there is no experience in a dead person since the *sunsum* is departed. In speaking of the *ɔkra*, Busia considered it to be the life force, a spark of the Creator that lives in every person's body. The *ɔkra* is deathless, the bearer of destiny and the part that returns to God after the individual dies (Busia 1954: 197).

---

98 See also (Akesson 1965: 286).

To look further into the nature of the *sunsum*, Busia characterizes it using pneumatic terminologies, although he does not seem to call it a "spirit" categorically. He technically calls it "spiritual gift" from the father that binds the child to him. He writes: "*Sunsum* is that which you take with you to go to the side of the woman and lie with her; and then the *Onyankopon*, the Great One, will take his *kra* and bless your union. You give your *sunsum* to the child, not your *kra*" (Busia 1954: 197).[99] The relationship between the child and the father is a spiritual bond. Rattray had already stated the pervasive force of the father's *sunsum* over his wife and children (Rattray 1927: 154; 1929: 9). Busia integrates that idea into his understanding to reinforce the father's role in the transmission of the *sunsum*. He sees the *sunsum* as a biogenetic component, a paternal spiritual gift transmitted during the act of sexual intercourse. The character of the *sunsum* as "spiritual" is here used by Busia in a felicitous manner to ontologically designate it as something intangible, not necessary a spirit-being or an astral entity. How does Busia trace the origin of the *sunsum*?

It has already been indicated that Busia directly relies on Rattray's ideas, making them a pedagogical basis for his anthropology. He contributes to it as an indigenous scholar whose cultural background is shaped by those ideas. That reliance supported Rattray's work in a pervasive manner as Busia clarifies most of the terminological nuances, especially the relationship between the *sunsum* and *ntorɔ*. Busia's conception of the *ntorɔ* indirectly answers to the question of the origin of *sunsum*. He believed it is the *ntorɔ* that is technically transmitted by the father to his child, although many Asantes gravitate toward *sunsum* instead. An "Ashanti will say that a man transmits his *ntoro* (spirit) to his child" (Busia 1954: 197). Busia continues to assert the fact that "*ntorɔ* is the generic term of which *sunsum* is a specific instance" (1954: 197).[100] In this sense, Busia says the two terms are used synonymously but in a different context. This means *sunsum* has an innate affinity to the *ntorɔ*, even though the two are not the same. *Ntorɔ* is the carrier of the *sunsum* and forms a part of the whole *ntorɔ* spirituality.[101]

---

99 This belief demonstrates the authority of the Akan father over both his family. Consequently, Asantes believe a child cannot thrive if his father's *sunsum* is alienated or may fall ill if the father's own *sunsum* is aggrieved (Busia, 1954: 197).

100 The *ntorɔ* as a generic term was earlier used by Captain Rattray (1923: 45).

101 This conceptualization forms the premise for a later designation of the *sunsum* as a counterpart of the *ntorɔ* transmitted to a child at conception (Wiredu 1987: 161;

That conclusion brings to mind Rattray's statement on the symbiotic relationship of the *ntorɔ* and *sunsum* (Rattray 1923: 46).

Like Rattray, Busia affirms *ntorɔ* as a tutelary spirit or under the aegis of a god (Ɔbosom). These gods, widely considered among Akan people as representatives of God, share in his spiritual nature. Busia continues to add that "the *Ntoro* are children of the rivers from whom they derive their spirits; and in the same way that the *Ntoro* is a child of the river, so the *sunsum* of a man is a child of the *Ntoro* and shares its nature" (1954: 198). The affinity between the *ntorɔ* and *sunsum* is ontological. We arrive at a conclusion to view the intrinsic vitality of *sunsum* as coming from the tutelary deities (*Abosom*/*Ntorɔ*). Once again, we find in both Rattray and Busia the same conclusion concerning the *sunsum* as an emanating force from the *Abosom* who transmit their *ntorɔ* through the father to the child. Busia, like many Akan, knew all too well that "all spiritual power derives from the Supreme Being," and therefore *sunsum* is indirectly a divine essence (1954: 198, 200).

To sum up, the question of the nature of the *sunsum* appears in Busia's conception as a personality, personal power, and a spiritual bond between the father and child. It is not a spiritual being that can live independently of the person. *Sunsum* as an individual's double did not appear in Busia's anthropology, and neither did he make any reference to any sleep peregrination. These omissions do not prove that he doubted such experiences. Busia's overall assessment of the *sunsum* makes it only a personality, a form of charisma. It is not just a concept, but an ontological reality that comes with the *ntorɔ* from the Abosom. The father who transmits it is only an instrument in the same way that the gods serve God as intermediaries for humanity (Busia 1954: 198, 200). So, even though the Akan will say of the *sunsum* that it is the father's "spirit," it derives in essence from the Abosom. Reference to the habitation of the Abosom in natural objects such as rivers, trees, stones, mountains, etc. help understand the pervasive nature of *sunsum* in natural objects.

The attribution of mortality to the *sunsum* directly challenges the pneumatic nature theory since the spiritual is imperishable. The use of *spiritual* by Busia makes the *sunsum* an intangible force, rather than a living entity.

Ephirim-Donkor 2008: 57). The *ntorɔ* denotes character resemblance and gives general characteristics to the group of which the father belongs. The twelve chief characteristics of *ntorɔ* are listed in chapter four and chapter eight of this dissertation. Further studies on the *ntorɔ* can be found in Rattray (1923) and Busia (1954).

When he spoke of it as mortal, he referred to its disembodiment at death, not necessarily to its destruction. After all, most Akan people believe the *ntorɔ* is inheritable; the same is true of the *sunsum* (Asare Opoku 1978: 98).

5.4. The Exclusively Spiritual (*Ye Sunsum*) and the Inspirited (*Wo Sunsum*) in Helaine K. Minkus

The various descriptions given to the *sunsum* find a wider rational expansion in Helaine K. Minkus, an American international cultural anthropologist who spent two years in Akropong in Ghana from 1969 to 1971. She learned the Akan Twi language and researched the traditional concepts of the Akwapim people of the Akan group. She was born in Chicago, Illinois, on November 28, 1943, and died on July 16, 2015, in Charleston, South Carolina. Her research in Ghana formed part of her Ph.D. dissertation, which she completed at Northwestern University (Evanston) in 1974.

Minkus contributed to Akan literature through her detailed understanding of Akan spirituality and causality. Two of her articles, "The Concept of Spirit in Akwapim Akan Philosophy" (1980) and "Causal Theory in Akwapim Akan Philosophy" (1984), are regularly cited in Akan studies. Minkus was an Associate Professor of Anthropology at the University of Wisconsin-Eau Claire from where she lectured and retired. We may not have much to say about her biography and scholarship, but she is known among Ghanaian academics because of her literary connection with the Akan people. Her thorough ethnographic sketch on Akan pneumatology advanced the *sunsum* historiography and contributed to its constructive evolution.

5.4.1. Ontological Definition of *Sunsum*

Minkus' commentary described the concept of *sunsum* as a major premise in Akan philosophy. It forms the basis of several categories such as ontology, psychology, epistemology, and theory of causality (Minkus 1980: 182). She may be considered the foremost scholar to have investigated the ontology of the *sunsum* in a much broader sense, and her work may also be seen as a sound representation of contemporary Akan cosmology. In a few words, Minkus defined the *sunsum* thus: "The *sunsum*, so necessary to existence, is not conceived as an indwelling spirit foreign to the object in which it resides. Rather the *sunsum* is the essence of the being or object, its intrinsic activating principle" (Minkus 1980: 182). This statement from Minkus forms the basis of my discussion of her work.

Minkus believes the Akan universe is not a duality of spiritual and material worlds, but one inspirited universe. There is no exclusive material world with its material objects, distinct as it were from a spiritual realm of spiritual existents. As she wrote, all that exists is inspirited or active (Minkus 1980: 182). This assumption stems from her understanding of the *sunsum* as an essence of natural objects and the principle of intrinsic activation. Without an innate vitality, life ceases to exist. She writes: "In Akwapim Akan thought, anything which exists in its natural state has *sunsum*. It is the *sunsum* which enables the being or object to exercise power and to function in its characteristic manner" (1980: 182). Hence, the world and its natural objects are active because of the *sunsum*, and because of *sunsum* they are capable of possessing power and vitality in themselves. This indication explains the idea of animism among the Akan.

Animism presupposes that natural objects (both animate and inanimate) possess souls or consciousness in themselves. Although Minkus did not use the term animism, the notion of an inspirited universe yields the tendency of animistic conception. There are several reasons to justify this assumption, particularly from Minkus' insistence that there is no matter without awareness or action. She also seems to come to the same conclusion with Rattray who saw *sunsum* to be an innate *anima* in creation. Rattray wrote: "In the animistic creed of Ashanti everything in nature, animate or inanimate, has its *sunsum* (soul or spirit)" (Rattray 1923: 296). Instead of thinking of *sunsum* as separate from the object, we are led to think of it as the essence of the object. The all-pervading spirituality of *sunsum* is a spiritual substance rather than an indwelling spirit (entity) foreign to the object. All these give support to Minkus' view of the unitary nature of the universe.

When we look at the source of *sunsum*, Minkus comes to the same conclusion as Busia that all spiritual powers or *sunsum* are indirectly from God. Minkus refers more specifically to *sunsum* as proceeding directly from the Supreme Being, the Creator and source of all existence (Minkus 1980: 182). But whereas Busia talked of intermediaries in the transmission of *sunsum*, Minkus links the activities of *sunsum* directly to God, creating an intimate connection between creation and God. We have here the reason why Akan religions are panentheistic, and not pantheistic. God is not immanent in person as nature, but God's *sunsum* is absorptive in the universe, making God immanent.

Minkus' divine association of *sunsum* with God strongly aligns with Danquah's thesis that Onyankopɔn is the personality (*sunsum*) of Odomankoma, and therefore the universe itself is Onyankopɔn's universe, making it capable to be experienced. Their point of departure, however, consists in the nature of *sunsum*. With Danquah, *sunsum* is only a personality. Even though Minkus agrees with Danquah's assessment of *sunsum* as partly a force for personality, she thinks *sunsum* is a generic description of spiritual existents and forces, and a spiritual force for activity in the universe. These are the bases for her pneumatological background of Akan religions.

Minkus explores the concept of *sunsum* as the essence of existents that are observable on two categories. The first is the exclusively spiritual (*yɛ sunsum*). This may comprise entities conceived of as spiritual beings, e.g., God, gods, dwarfs, ghosts, and other spirits named in the Akan cosmology. Here, we can see a radical evolution of the nature of *sunsum*, from an emanating force to the very essence of being. That means *sunsum* has become a generic term for beings and objects that are nonphysical or spiritual. In other words, there are, on one hand, objects that are non-conceptual as physical, i.e., beyond the reach of human perception and senses (Minkus 1980: 183). On the other hand, there are objects that are inspirited, i.e., those that have *sunsum* (*wɔ sunsum*), e.g., human beings, animals, plants, stones, rivers, etc. *Sunsum* is required for the exercise of their essential qualities. These two categories represent the definition of the *sunsum* in Minkus' pneumatology. Further details will throw more light on these two categories.

5.4.2. The Exclusively Spiritual (*Yɛ Sunsum*)

Minkus classifies God, the deities, the ancestral spirits, and personalized talismans as *sunsum* because their substance and whole being is *sunsum* (Minkus 1980: 183).[102] Akan religions recognize myriads of entities that are exclusively force-beings. These are part of the world but outside the reach

[102] It will be appropriate if we classify talismans as part of the inspirited objects rather than the exclusively spiritual objects. Talismans are materials made to absorb spiritual powers and do not seem to qualify to be called exclusively spiritual.

of physical contact. An exception is given to God, whose nature and existence transcend this world although it is not without God's presence. Exclusively spiritual objects are described to be *sunsum* because their mode of operation is not open to ordinary perception but requires extraordinary or spiritual means to determine their existence (Minkus 1980: 187). Spiritual existents can, according to Minkus, "sometimes materialize and appear to have a spiritual analogue to physical form which may be perceived by certain people with special powers" (1980: 183).[103] The observation is true but needs further clarification to avoid confusion with other Akan realities.

Spiritual entities may choose, on rare occasions, to reveal themselves in physical forms to people. In such transfiguration, it does not always require any extrasensory abilities to recognize them. Akan people are made aware of the presence or influence of spiritual forces in the physical world, and this is the reason why the community involves unseen existents. Spiritual agencies like gods, ghosts, and others, are capable of materializing themselves and entering into communication with human beings. Ephirim-Donkor writes: "the unseen, the spiritual, will, from time to time, materialize just enough to remind people that they are still around, like when people claim to see the dead momentarily" (Ephirim-Donkor 2016: 3). The ancestors, herein referred to as the dead by Ephirim-Donkor, possess the spiritual qualities that make them capable of entering the physical world to exercise physical contact. Their nature in the temporary manifestation or physicality is not "an intrinsic or defining aspect of their nature" (Minkus 1980: 183). Apart from God, who no one claims to have seen or heard among the Akan,

---

[103] The acquisition of extraordinary powers to perceive the unseen is further detailed by Minkus as: "Persons with exceptional power to see and hear in spiritual ways (described *as ohu n'ani so ade* and *ote n'aso so ade*) are able to see the spiritual forms of the deities, personalized talismans and spirits of the dead, and to hear what ordinary persons cannot. Such persons can determine the causes of illness, misfortune and death, can detect witches, and are able to foresee future events. The power of special vision and audition is acquired through the application of an herbal concoction, or as a gift from God, or, according to some informants, may be inborn. Any person who applies the medicine to his eyes and ears will thereby be enabled to see and hear in an extraordinary manner. The medicine is employed principally by medium-priests but can be taken by any individual who can persuade someone who knows how to make it to give it to him. However, the ability to see and hear in extraordinary ways is potentially dangerous. A person who does not have a strong *sunsum* will be frightened by the strange sights and sounds he encounters and may become mad" (Minkus 1980: 184).

all the spiritual existents can make themselves known or take upon themselves appearances of physical properties.

Coming back to the discussion of what is exclusively spiritual, Minkus establishes that people with special spiritual abilities may perceive spiritual existents. She writes: "individuals with special powers, innate or gained through the application of medicine or by divine gift, are believed capable of perceiving what is not ordinarily perceivable" (1980: 183). In as much as this is true of Akan religions, in some rare cases non-clairvoyants are capable of perceiving spiritual existents especially when the spiritual agent desires to be seen. Now, in order not to confuse what is essentially *sunsum* with what is *spiritual* in the general sense, it is better we give further explanation.

The underlying problem in the contemporary argument of the nature of the *sunsum* is the question of whether *sunsum* should be rendered as "spirit." That is the idea we get from Minkus, who follows Rattray and translates *sunsum* as "spirit." Should anything that cannot be perceived with the naked eyes or be felt by the natural senses be rendered as *sunsum* or spiritual? In my analysis above, and also according to Minkus, "the designation 'spiritual'" ought to be "reserved for extraordinary perception" (Minkus 1980: 184). Extraordinary perception defines what is spiritual, which the Akan calls *sunsum*. For the sake of argument, we shall take the *ɔkra* as an aspect of spirituality, since Minkus calls it "another spiritual component" (1980: 184). In general, Akan people believe "highly developed medicine men are claimed to be able to enter into communication with an 'okra,' and those that have eyes with medicinally heightened perception are said to be capable of seeing such things" (Wiredu 1987: 161). Does that characterize its essence as spiritual such that we might think of it as *sunsum* (*ye sunsum*)? I do not think so. Busia refers to the *ɔkra* as a spiritual gift, but never did he, or any Akan scholar, call its essence *sunsum*. To call it *sunsum* would engender much confusion in the Akan worldview, especially when the two terms have distinct religious connotations. Even scholars who think that the *ɔkra* and *sunsum* have ontological unity would never describe the nature of the *ɔkra* as *sunsum*. Therefore, it should be clear that not anything rendered *spiritual* in the English language can be translated as *sunsum* in Akan languages. And when Akan people use the term "spirit," they refer to what is describable, as Minkus rightly noted, and not merely something which is abstract (Minkus 1980: 182). On the other hand, Akan people talk of *sunsum mu nsɛm* (mystical matters) to describe the mysterious part of the world. They employ the term *sunsum* to define the unseen of which aspects may qualify the *ɔkra*. An example is the act of entering into communication with the *ɔkra*. Akan people will consider the process as *sunsum mu nsɛm* (mystical) because the passage is not done through the ordinary world. In every practical sense, the essence of the *ɔkra* may be best described in the Akan language as *honhom*, i.e., breath, as I will attempt to show later in my second book.[104]

5.4.3. The Inspirited (*Wɔ Sunsum*)

The second category in Minkus' description is the inspirited or what possesses *sunsum* (*wɔ sunsum*). Here, she presents *sunsum* as an essential component of experience in everything that exists in its natural state in contrast to spiritual objects. Human beings, animals, plants, rocks, bodies of water and other objects that exist in their natural state possess *sunsum* as their intrinsic activation. Minkus says their entire being cannot be said to be *sunsum*, and yet it can only exist when their constituents are inspirited with *sunsum* (1980: 183). Life constitutes in itself the vitality of *sunsum*; without it several aspects of experience may not be achieved. The expression given here has been the framework upon which several Akan scholars have dealt with the *sunsum*, either as the principle of animation or of experience.

Minkus reconciles with Danquah, Meyerowitz, and Busia to designate *wɔ sunsum* as personality (ego) or character, although she is more inclined to side with Danquah, who at one point talked of *sunsum* as "the power that sustains a person's character or individuality" (Danquah 1945: 22).[105] Minkus likewise thinks of it as "the power which underlies and enables the manifestation of those activities and traits which mark a person as both a human being and an individual" (Minkus 1980: 185). A person's *sunsum* is the force for higher intelligence and those things that pertain to being human in the sense of functioning as a human being. The character disposition in daily choices to realize one's destiny is all dependent on the *sunsum*. Minkus description of the *sunsum* reminds us of Rattray's definition of *sunsum* as "everything that makes life at all worth living" (Rattray 1923: 46). There is a far-reaching experience of being inspirited by *sunsum*.

---

[104] Further discussion in my second book will reveal how Gyekye identifies the *ɔkra* as *honhom* or the breath of life.

[105] Cited by Minkus (1980: 185).

There are many aspects of the *wɔ sunsum* that Minkus articulates in agreement with other scholars. Minkus believes *sunsum* is primarily an enabling power, "an intrinsic source of spiritual strength and resistance to attack through spiritual mean" (1980: 185-6). The statement is made in reference to the dynamic nature of *sunsum*. There are individuals with strong *sunsum*, meaning they are high-spirited. Akan people have the adage: *Ne sunsum mu ye duru*, i.e., "his *sunsum* is heavy." Others are said to have weak *sunsum*, e.g., *Ne sunsum mu yɛ hare*, meaning: "he has a weak *sunsum*," or "he is a coward" (Minkus 1980: 187; Rattray 1955: 198; 1957: 154). These varying degrees of vitality define an individual's charisma and how one can protect and withstand danger. Someone with strong *sunsum*, according to Minkus, "can repel evil spiritual agents and forces, can safely take the medicine for special visions and auditions, and is viewed by others as an imposing and influential figure" (1980: 186). This is not the case for those with weak *sunsum*.

Like her predecessors, Minkus links *sunsum* to males. We have already established that Akan people perceive the *sunsum* to be a patriarchal substance that runs through the father's lineage. Minkus underlines this about the maxim, *Ɔbaa nni sunsum*, which means: "A woman does not have *sunsum*." She explains this in the following way: "a woman is not as strong spiritually as a man and cannot transmit her *sunsum* to her children" (1980: 186). The Akan do recognize the *sunsum* of women (Rattray 1927: 318). The maxim implies that the woman transmits only her blood, a physical bond, and the basis of Akan social organization. This is equally important, just like the father's *sunsum* that establishes the spiritual bond with his offspring. If there is any gender "inequality" among Akan people, it is not so much determined by the agency of *sunsum* than to other social factors. The dynamic nature of *sunsum* makes each person prone to being weak or strong. For this reason, one cannot entirely regard the maxim as ontological – universally – than a biopsychological diversity. When one examines the differences in the psychology of males and females, particularly variegated in personality, we come to the conclusion that the Akan have found some key answers to gender identity in their social framework.

Minkus stresses the strong influence of the father's *sunsum* as a mystic bond between him and his offspring. It is thought that the *sunsum* of the father protects his children, "especially during childhood when the child's own *sunsum* is weak" (Minkus 1980: 186). In case of divorce, the mother of a sick child will take the child to the father for spiritual reinforcement to heal the child.[106] In cases where the man feels alienated by his offspring, Minkus says the man can spiritually take revenge to harm the children (1980: 186). The spiritual bond is unbreakable as long as it is a mystical definition of personhood.

There are other qualities of *wo sunsum* mentioned by Minkus. She sees *sunsum* as the basis of moral qualities. Persons who commit morally commendable acts are thought to possess good *sunsum* (*sunsum pa*), or their *sunsum* is good (*ne sunsum yɛ*). These are individuals who uphold commendable moral qualities. The opposite is individuals with bad or evil *sunsum* (*sunsum bɔne*). An evil *sunsum* will seek to damage or kill others (Minkus 1980: 186).

In most cases, Akan people associate *sunsum bɔne* with witchcraft. Witches are not spiritual beings.[107] They are humans who use supernatural methods to assume their operations. Witchcraft is the development of the evil *sunsum* that makes the witch proficient in the exercise of witchcraft power (Minkus 1980: 186).[108] Minkus' comments agree with Rattray's understanding of the relationship between one's *sunsum* and witchcraft (1927: 155). The *sunsum* of the witch is separated from the body during nightly peregrination. This brings Minkus to the same conclusion with Rattray that the *sunsum* is the volatile soul or spiritual element of the *ɔkra* (Minkus 1980: 186; Rattray 1927: 93, 154, 192). The evil *sunsum* must not always

---

106 In one of her ethno-psychiatry studies in Ghana, Margaret Joyce Field, a clinical psychiatrist working with the British in then Gold Coast administration, observed this traditional belief in an occasion of a sick child who was brought to the shrine for treatment. She writes: "One ailing child whose parents were on bad terms and whose father was seldom at home was pronounced by the priest to be 'getting no *sunsum* from its father.' I was surprised, at my weekly clinic at Mframaso, to see how often it was the fathers and not mothers who brought children for treatment. The small child regards its father as its natural worshipper" (Field 1960: 27-28; Cited in Ephirim-Donkor 1997:15).

107 The idea that witches can be hunted and trapped by witch hunters suggest that they are not spirits but can perform spiritual activities analogous to spiritual beings.

108 We can be cautious here not to think of the *sunsum* as being the witch. It is the contamination of the *sunsum* that makes witchcraft possible. Witchcraft is a supernatural practice that is made possible by a willing *sunsum*. When one's *sunsum* is not willing, the person cannot become a witch. This explains why individuals can be cured of being witches (Rattray 1927: 30).

be a witch in order to carry out evil actions. Acts of violence, dehumanization, and felony are attributed to an evil *sunsum* since they threaten the social order.

What happens to *sunsum* after death? Minkus says *sunsum* does not go to the netherworld with the deceased and neither is it transformed into a ghost (1980: 186). To sustain that assumption, she relied on her informant who said, "it is the *sunsum* of the dead chief, not his 'ghost' (*ɔsaman*), which is thought to enter the ancestral stool when invoked during ceremonies" (1980: 186). Minkus appears to distinguish the *sunsum* of the deceased from the person's ghost (*ɔsaman*). Since she did not give further details to this, we are led to believe that an ancestral spirit is not subject to the character traits of *sunsum*.

Why then does she classify the ancestors as part of the exclusively spiritual (*yɛ sunsum*) dimension? The only reason given is because they are spirit-beings, whose nature is not subject to physical constraints. The *ɔsaman* is nonphysical but not in essence *sunsum*. Ephirim-Donkor contrasts the world of "spirits" from the ancestral world (Asamando/Asamandzie) by looking at two aspects of the spiritual realm. He says, "the Samanadzie is different from the realm of Àsunsum (spirits)... the Abosom – who are incapable of death – do not enter the realm of the Samanadzie because the Samanadzie is reserved for only those who have tasted death and been resurrected as Nananom Nsamanfo or just Nsamanfo (spiritual or abstract personalities)" (Ephirim-Donkor 2016: 2). Thus, our historiographical review establishes the premise that *sunsum* proceeds from a spirit-being whose very essence is *sunsum*.

Minkus again points out the influence of an ancestor's *sunsum* in child naming. Akan names are significant in meaning. There are at least three dimensions of it, namely the *kradin* (natal names or soul names), family names (*Ntorɔ*/paternal spirit names), and affectionate names (after an important personality, ancestor or event). When an affectionate name is given after an ancestor, the child "may exhibit some of the behavioral traits which were characteristic of the person" (Minkus 1980: 186). In this instance, the character of *sunsum* seems more likely as a spiritual element rather than an entity.

In summary, Minkus' contribution to Akan literature comes with a categorization of spiritual realities according to the Akan people of Akwapim. She adopts this approach of reconstructing reality to examine the notion that spirits are definable or describable, unlike the *spiritual* among the Akan.

The most significant aspect of her contribution is the generic, instead of a specific, use of *sunsum* to describe all spiritual existents. There are spirits in the universe that are unperceivable by human senses unless through extrasensory means. These immaterial beings or forces do not operate from another world to exert their influence and manipulation in the ordinary world, but they form part of a single inspirited universe.

Given all this, she deals with the concept of *sunsum* from the various categories given to it, i.e., what is exclusively spiritual (*yɛ sunsum*), and what is inspirited or have *sunsum* (*wɔ sunsum*). Minkus believe these two categories provide the lens through which Akan ontology, epistemology, psychology, and the theory of causality can be explained.

5.5. *Sunsum* As the Ɔbosom in Anthony Ephirim-Donkor

Anthony Ephirim-Donkor is a significant scholar in Akan scholarship. He hails from the Fante cultural group of the Akan group. There are two Akan subgroups, namely, the Twi-speaking Akan, and the Fante-speaking Akan. The Fantes are predominantly found in the South (mainly on the coastal areas). There is a large extent of shared similarities between the Fantes and the other Twi Akan subgroups. Ephirim-Donkor's recent contribution to Akan literature from his Fante background has been well received and commented. He remains an authority in Akan spirituality and personality, especially on his studies of the concept of *sunsum*.

Besides his academic credentials, Ephirim-Donkor has been an ardent practitioner of the Akan traditional religions as a local chief working with traditional priests and other religious officers in Ghana. The chieftaincy, with its associated religious rituals, brought him closer to the Abosom (pantheon deities). He claims experiential knowledge of the Abosom through divinations and other ways (2016: xi). As an informed Akan who had witnessed divinations in my own local town, I have no doubt of the claims of Ephirim-Donkor. Two of his significant books on the study of *sunsum* are *African Spirituality: On Becoming Ancestors* (1997) and *African Personality and Spirituality: The Role of Abosom and Human Essence* (2016). Both books provide detailed information about the meaning of *sunsum* from both previous and contemporary scholars. However, I find the latter more insightful on the meaning of *sunsum* from his own conception and construction of Akan religions.

5.5.1. The Meaning of *Sunsum* by Ephirim-Donkor

The notion of *sunsum* appears in Ephirim-Donkor's understanding as a determining principle for Akan spirituality and personality. Through this view, he argues that *sunsum* is an essential quality known to the Akan as a shadow, image, or double of the individual. It is the self, the spiritual aspect of an individual. Ephirim-Donkor adds that *sunsum* also defines anything intangible or unseen, and as a result, he translates *sunsum* as "spirit" to capture the idea of it being a non-human, unseen, and independent agency (Ephirim-Donkor 1997: 20; 2016: 35, 40). In its anthropological conception, *sunsum* is an essential part of the human being that is capable of influencing objectivity and the bases for achieving personality and spirituality. Of greater significance is his treatment of *sunsum* to characterize God, the Abosom (pantheon gods), and all other spirits as the locus of religio-spiritual reflection on Akan cosmological realities. For God to be exceptional, God should be differentiated from the Abosom (gods) who are primeval offspring of God. That means, God is not an Ɔbosom, but the single most supremely powerful, incomparable *Sunsum* of all *sunsum* (Ephirim-Donkor 2016: 40). How does the essence of the divinities as *sunsum* affect the overall understanding of *sunsum* in Ephirim-Donkor's writings?

5.5.2. The Role of the Abosom in Akan Anthropology

Much of what to expect from Ephirim-Donkor on the notion of *sunsum* is dependent on his understanding of the *Abosom*. To him, the *Abosom* are "spirits of God… unseen primeval forces of incredibly immense might," and possessing power and intelligence, "with the capability of materialization and transformation into anything they desire" (Ephirim-Donkor 2016: 43, 44). He further explains that the Akan classify them as gods because the essential qualities of the *Abosom* and God are the same. Nevertheless, "God is the ultimate combined spirit of all the Abosom, and so to speak of the Abosom is to speak of God because the Abosom are on earth at God's behest" (Ephirim-Donkor 2016: 44). This conception agrees with the Akan general notion of the *Abosom* as children of God. The relationship between human beings and the Abosom is indirectly with God. Therefore, the Akan rendition of worship to the Abosom does not cause any contradiction of allegiance to God, instead, it is a normal worship procedure at the superintendence of God as long as the role of the Abosom is *in loco dei*.

Ephirim-Donkor continues to argue that it is the essence of the Abosom, i.e., water, fire, air, and blood that defines the basis of human nature because the essence of the human being is the Ɔbosom incarnate. This conclusion follows his analysis of the Akan maxim, *Nnipa nyinaa yɛ 'Nyame mma, obi ara nyɛ asaase ba*, i.e., "Human beings are the progenitors of God and none is a child of the earth." The interpretation given to this maxim by Ephirim-Donkor connects human beings directly to the deities and not the Earth. It is necessary for such an anthropological definition of personhood to give reasons why "God's offspring must also be of the same spiritual substance or essence as God, without material properties, as the Abosom" (Ephirim-Donkor 2016: 78). The implication for all this is that human beings have divine origin other than the Earth, and the rationale behind human beings' capacity to continue to live after death among the Akan. On the contrary, if human beings were of the Earth, Ephirim-Donkor explains, "then there will be no afterlife because when people die that will be the end… But since human beings are children of God, it means that there is life after death because the Sunsum survives death and the basis for ancestor worship proved" (2016: 78). The relationship between God and the universe, hence, is established by the *sunsum*. How do human beings, qua material, share the same essential qualities with the Abosom, who are purely spiritual beings?

Ephirim-Donkor draws from the divine origin of *sunsum* as the basis to define the spiritual part of human beings. His assumption defeats any belief that relates the spiritual part of the human being to the physical body. The physical part, instead, depends on the spiritual. This advances the notion that *sunsum* is not just an abstract reality but a "spirit" in a material body. The *nipadua* (body) is only material and subject to perish contrary to the real, which is spiritual and immortal because the human being is a direct product of the divinities or the divinities themselves. Ephirim-Donkor affirms the latter by linking the origin of human beings to the Abosom instead of directly to God. Human beings are Abosom incarnate; hence, every person is an Ɔbosom *ba* (child of a deity or Ɔbosom). Ephirim-Donkor explains that "before an Ɔbosom becomes a human being, the head, or father, of an Abosom Kuu (group, pack, family) selects or appoints the Ɔbosom to relocate to the corporeal" (Ephirim-Donkor 2016: 80). This statement is in support of his belief that human beings are willed directly by the Abosom, not God. The doctrine of incarnation is quite observable in Ephirim-Donkor's definition of the human being, which shows the capability of the Abosom to put on the conditions of the human being. Apparently, this rational argument implies that *sunsum* is an indwelling "spirit," an entitative object herein discussed as the Ɔbosom in corporeality.

At this point, the difficult question, also raised by Ephirim-Donkor, is: how is it possible for an Ɔbosom to turn into a human being? The question is important because any explanation given to this mode of transition should be coherent with the essence and purpose of life. Again, if spirits can take the form of physicality, then it means their mode of transformation would call for a mysterious metamorphosis even if such transformation would also require some sort of physical means. As to how an Ɔbosom becomes a human being, Ephirim-Donkor answers that the "Abosom intrinsically take hold of material subjects conjugationally resulting in deposition of active essential attributes in living things which ultimately becomes the basis for ethical living" (Ephirim-Donkor 2016: 77). The Abosom infiltrate their essence through the act of conjugation and copulation between a male and female.

It so happens that the dynamic and corporeal adaptation of the Abosom is through a human agency. The act of "copulation – or rather semen (*huaba*/*ntoro*) – then becomes the means, mode of delivery of an Ɔbosom" (Ephirim-Donkor 2016: 82). Or, "an Ɔbosom, as Sunsum (spirit) is transmitted through a father's semen (*huaba/ntoro*) during a sexual act… the Sunsum triggers an activity that transforms an otherwise inactive *Mogya* (blood) or egg of a female into what becomes a human being" (Ephirim-Donkor 2016: 83). The symbiotic relationship between the *ntorɔ* and *sunsum* in Busia's anthropology is once again established here by Ephirim-Donkor. However, unlike Busia who thought of the *ntorɔ* as the Ɔbosom, and *sunsum* as child of the *ntorɔ*, Ephirim-Donkor defines *sunsum* as the Ɔbosom (Ephirim-Donkor 2016: 83). Ultimately, the human being, the Ɔbosom incarnate, is of both spiritual and physical nature, which in fact allows for the possibilities of achieving the highest goals in life and beyond.

Ephirim-Donkor further affirms some aspects of the *sunsum* in agreement with the majority of Akan scholars. He affirms the masculinity of *sunsum* as a paternal spirit, hence, transmitted by males only to a child. The rationale is that the "Abosom are masculine agencies" explains Ephirim-Donkor: "It happens that what they transmit retains their masculine essential attributes in terms of activity" (Ephirim-Donkor 2016: 83). He emphatically states: "Men then transmit an active agency called Sunsum" (Ephirim-Donkor 2016: 84). Children exercise their power from a male progenitor. Therefore, it is said in Fante language, *Agya ni sunsum hata biribiara do*, meaning, "the Sunsum of a father hovers over all things physical as well as spiritual" (Ephirim-Donkor 2016: 86). *Sunsum* establishes the basis of male influence because everything that comes under the aegis of the father is protected by his *sunsum*. So, *sunsum* qua Ɔbosom, also has an emanative effect.

We can now determine the origin and essence of *sunsum* underlining the conception of Ephirim-Donkor's pneumatology. *Sunsum* is a spirit, herein identified as an Ɔbosom (pantheon deity), also incarnated as the human being. Observation of the nature of the human being now becomes the Ɔbosom in corporeality. Hence, the concept of both Ɔbosom and *sunsum* together are the bases for exploring an objective approach to defining the nature and mystery of human existence.

Of particular emphasis, the notion of *sunsum* as Ɔbosom may form the basis of the inspirited universe of the Akan. There is nothing at the moment to suggest that there is a kind of *sunsum* that exists independently without the Abosom. *Sunsum* is either entitative or emanative. So, the idea that the universe is populated by varying degrees of spiritual entities and forces shapes Ephirim-Donkor's understanding of the Abosom (pantheon deities) and the role they play in human procreation and Akan cosmology.

Ephirim-Donkor has answered the question of the origin and nature of *sunsum* by looking at the role the Abosom play in Akan cosmology. By so doing, he entered into difficult expositions on Akan worldviews and perhaps raised some more controversial questions about Akan anthropology. For example, the description given to *sunsum* and *ɔkra* calls for a more avid clarification to avoid incoherencies and varying interpretations of Akan realities. Ephirim-Donkor believes *sunsum* survives death; either it is reincarnated in some circumstances or returns to join the phylogenetic Abosom (Ephirim-Donkor 2016: 80, 156). The *ɔkra*, on the other hand, though coming from God as a life principle, does not travel to *Samanadzie/ Asamando* (land of the departed spirits), but returns to God (2016: 108).[109] Neither is

[109] Ephirim-Donkor gives elaborative accounts of the *ɔkra* which the current researcher finds strange or new. He states the *ɔkra* is inhaled at birth – outside the womb – as the first breath of the neonate. The *ɔkra* is feminine. He further states the *ɔkra* resides on the shoulders of the body. Finally, the *ɔkra* returns to God (See also Ephirim-Donkor 1997: 72). Although he gives extensive explanation to support all these assertions, the current researcher is not convinced, and the majority of Akan scholars would contest this characteristic nature of the *ɔkra*. On the other hand, these

the *ɔkra* the part of the human being that becomes an ancestor. To him, the *ɔsaman* (ancestor) is an abstract personality that emerges spiritually from the *sunsum*, *mogya* and *ɔkra* (Ephirim-Donkor 2016: 156). He emphatically says "the Ɔsaman does not need the original Ɔkra… no longer has needs for the Sunsum that enabled it to be active" (Ephirim-Donkor 2016: 156). Although Ephirim-Donkor seems to assert that "the Ɔsaman is the same as the Sunsum," in reality, he meant to say that the *ɔsaman* is an abstract creation, "an imprint of its creator, the Ɔbosom that became a human being" (2016: 156). That means, in the end, none of the core essences of the human being, namely *ɔkra*, *sunsum*, *ntorɔ*, and *mogya* goes to Asamando. This construction disagrees with the majority of scholars who accept the *ɔkra* incarnate as *ɔkrateasefo* (a human being) and with a strong emphasis on the survival of the *ɔkra* as an ancestor.

5.6. Summary

The purpose of this chapter was to look further into the historiographical development of the meaning and nature of *sunsum* after Captain Rattray's pioneering ethnographic literature. The largest proportion of their findings were emic studies, i.e., a description of the internal elements of the Akan religions. This approach made their findings static or objective, with the exception of Danquah, whose approach was a subjective philosophical analysis of Akan religions as a theological framework. Danquah, Busia, and Ephirim-Donkor are indigenous scholars of Akan religions, unlike Meyerowitz and Minkus who were Western scholars studying Akan religions. The general definition of the *sunsum* is not as much about their background as the context from which they gathered their information. Unlike Rattray who engaged in gathering raw information among the Asantes, these scholars more or less relied heavily on literature available to them, even when they seemed ethnographic.

The study of the *sunsum* did not end with these scholars. In the next part of this research, I will look in more detail how the conclusions of these scholars underpin contemporary academic debate about the nature of *sunsum*. In the following chapter, we will encounter a critical, subjective, and

characteristics do affirm the reality of the *ɔkra* and may be that the Fante people perceive it differently from the Twi people.

theoretical interpretation of the nature of *sunsum*. The bone of contention for discussion is whether *sunsum* is "really" a spirit.

The table in the next page shows a summary of the various interpretations given in this chapter concerning the *sunsum*. From the table, we can deduce specific claims. For example, there is almost a unanimous agreement on the masculine transmission of *sunsum* to an individual. Most scholars also agree on the perishability of the *sunsum* at death. It is also obvious to see how the indigenous scholars, namely Danquah and Busia, did not translate *sunsum* into English as either "soul" or "spirit," unlike their foreign counterparts. For the indigenous scholars, *sunsum* is only a personality or the power behind the personality. Danquah and Busia indirectly connected *sunsum* to God. Ephirim-Donkor thinks *sunsum* is synonymous to the Abosom and all other unseen realities, although he calls God the incomparable *Sunsum* of all *sunsum*.

Rattray (Asante)	That spiritual Element (force, personal magnetism, character, personality, power, soul) upon which depend health, wealth,	Soul, spirit	matic	Abosom Father		Repatriation to its source
Danquah (Akyem)	It is only an experience and not outrightly "spirit."			*Esu*, Go		
(Bono)	the personal soul.		Ego, bearer of destiny	ancestor		becomes a ghost
Busia (Asante)	It is a spiritual gift that serves as the personal power or cast of countenance from the father.		Ego, spiritual gift	Abosom Father (indirectly from Go		Perishes
Minkus (Akwapim)	It is the essence of the being or object, its intrinsic activating principle.	Spirit		God, Father	Yes	Returns to the family
Donkor (Fante)	double of the individual. It is the self, the spiritual aspect of an individual. It also defines anything intangible or unseen, non-human agency and unseen as independent.		Spirit, Sha-	indirectly		or returns to the Abosom

PART III

CONTEMPORARY CRITICS AND APOLOGETICS OF THE NATURE OF *SUNSUM*

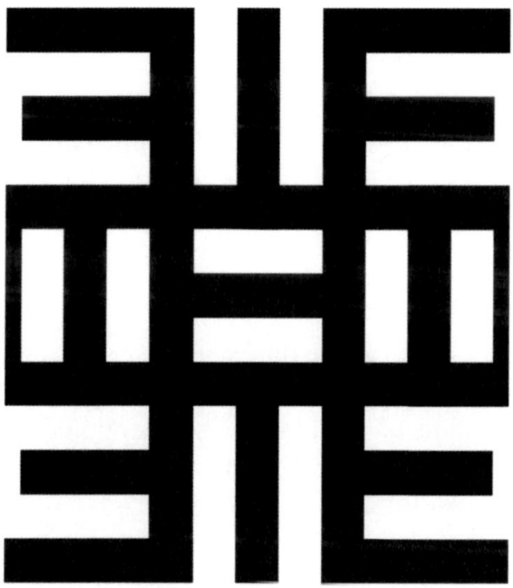

NEA ONNIM NO, SUA A OHU
"He who does not know can know from learning"
A symbol of knowledge, life-long education, and continued quest for knowledge.

6. Towards a Philosophical Decolonization and Deconstruction

"Let me begin by defining what I mean by decolonization in African philosophy. By decolonization, I mean divesting African philosophical thinking of all undue influences emanating from our colonial past. The crucial word in this formulation is "undue". Obviously, it would not be rational to try to reject everything of a colonial ancestry. Conceivably, a thought or a mode of inquiry spearheaded by our erstwhile colonizers may be valid or in some way beneficial to humankind. Are we called upon to reject or ignore it? That would be a madness having neither rhyme nor reason." – Kwasi Wiredu.[110]

The previous chapters focused on divergent views of *sunsum* from scholars studying Akan religions. For the most part, their approach was objective, i.e., descriptive accounts on hard facts. The adoption of a historiographical approach brought out the different perspectives on the nature and meaning of *sunsum* to lay down the fundamental framework for further theoretical analysis.

This chapter will focus on the contribution of contemporary philosophers studying the *sunsum* concept. Contemporary philosophers are more critical and analytical than their predecessors. They employ a subjective approach to treat Akan religions as a dynamic structure of ideas that is capable of transformation, and capable of philosophical discourse. Instead of treating *sunsum* within the spectrum of static ethnography, contemporary philosophers treat *sunsum* as a philosophical concept that has its own presuppositions for defining the principles of being within the larger context of Akan livelihood.

---

[110] Wiredu (1998: 17).

What are the issues that Akan philosophers grapple with as they consider the *sunsum*? The dilemma revolves around the nature of *sunsum*, particularly its translation into English as "spirit." As I will point out, contemporary scholarship focuses mainly on analytical critique. For this reason, I will begin to examine how the contemporary scholarly approach is linked to the ethnographic approach, and why contemporary scholars seem to question the nature of the *sunsum*. The discussion will focus on two significant Akan philosophers, namely Kwasi Wiredu and Kwame Gyekye. The two contemporary philosophers have significantly contributed to Akan scholarship by way of their philosophical interpretation of Akan religions.

Kwasi Wiredu criticizes several African concepts as being ostensibly contaminated by Western colonial scholarship. He attributes this to the English medium of instruction. Wiredu identifies two major problems pertaining to how these colonial modes of conceptualization find expression in African studies (Wiredu 1998: 17). The first is foreign conceptual influence, and the second is the problem of indigenous susceptibility to embrace Western philosophies (Wiredu 1998: 18–20). The two problems convinced him to see the task of deconstructing the African pedagogy as technically a philosophical decolonization and necessarily a conceptual enterprise (Wiredu 1998: 18).[111] His philosophical ideas revolve around this conceptual agenda. As further details will reveal, Wiredu thinks the nature of the *ɔkra* is not spiritual but quasi-physical. So, it is with the *sunsum* – it is not pneumatic but quasi-material. This manner of defining Akan worldview is the meaning of his philosophy of quasi-physicalism. I intend to give more details about these terminologies in subsequent sections.

Kwame Gyekye, on the other hand, disagrees with Wiredu and argues in favor of *sunsum* as indeed pneumatic, which means a "spirit." He disregards the philosophy of quasi-physicalism as running counter to Akan belief in disembodied survival or life after death (Gyekye 1987: 86). Gyekye is among the few contemporary Akan philosophers whose work has influenced modern African philosophy. He focuses on personhood and community as ontologically inseparable, i.e., an individual's identity stems from the community. He borrows from philosophers and thinkers before him, as well as from contemporary traditional thinkers. A great deal of his argument

---

[111] Wiredu does not singularize Africa's complex conceptual diversities. He uses the term "African" in the context of his paper to articulate a phenomenon common in most of Africa's socio-cultural pedagogy. Meanwhile, he focuses strictly on the Akan community of West Africa as a subject of discussion (Wiredu 1987: 153).

stems from Danquah, but he also manages to bring forth a comprehensive and coherent construction of the Akan philosophical agenda. In my view, Gyekye comes across as pro-Danquah, in the sense of his designation of *sunsum* as a divine essence and experience (Gyekye 1987: 102). In Danquah's philosophy, *sunsum* is a divine essence.

Gyekye crosses paths with Wiredu on what Akan people consider to be spiritual. Wiredu believes the Akan worldview is not strictly spiritual but quasi-physical. Gyekye will not accept that but defends the dominant pneumatic worldview. Their main point of departure is based on the nature of the *ɔkra* and *sunsum*, which essentially is the question that occupies this chapter and the whole of this research.

In the subsequent sections, we will look at the emergence of the philosophy of quasi-physicalism, its background, and how the quasi-physicalist characterizes the *sunsum*. We will also explore how Gyekye argues in favor of the pneumatic nature of *sunsum* against the philosophy of quasi-physicalism, and how he makes a strong argument in redefining Akan cosmology.

6.1. The Emergence of the Philosophy of Quasi-physicalism

The philosophy of quasi-physicalism may sound new to many people. Nevertheless, it has been around for almost three decades, and many contemporary writers around the world are engaging with it. Some notable scholars who have studied the theory include Kwame Gyekye (Gyekye 1987), Kwame Safro (Safro 1992) Mohammed Majeed (Majeed 2013), Louise Müller (Müller 2008), among others. The philosophy is Wiredu's creation and marks his attempt to speak of certain aspects of Akan metaphysics and philosophical conceptions. I find the theory very essential to my research based on two reasons. First, it questions the nature of the *sunsum* as not pneumatic, and second, it is a resourceful philosophical concept for the study of Akan religions. It is emphatically stated here that Wiredu became the first Akan scholar to question the English translation of *sunsum* as "spirit" and its pneumatic character. He dismisses the English description of *sunsum* as "spirit" and neither does he characterize it with any property of physicality (Wiredu 1987: 162, 163). It, therefore, becomes essentially expedient to discuss Wiredu in any pneumatological discourse in Akan studies, and even beyond.

I will also mention that not many scholars identify themselves with quasi-physicalism. However, there is one passionate quasi-physicalist in the person of Kwame Safro. He is an Akan philosopher whose research areas cover African philosophy and the philosophy of computers. He currently lectures at Lincoln University in Pennsylvania. Safro has embraced and formalized in detail the philosophy of quasi-physicalism in his articles, "Why I Am Not A Physicalist" (1992), and "Quasi-Materialism: A Contemporary African Philosophy of Mind" (2004). So, what are the details in quasi-physicalism?

6.1.1. The Meaning of Quasi-Physicalism?

What is considered quasi-physical, according to Kwame Safro, are those objects that belong "to a category between the realms of the obviously physical, i.e., those objects that obey the known laws of physics, and the realm of the so-called spiritual or completely immaterial objects that do not obey all the known laws of physics" (Safro 1992: 193). The quasi-physicalist imagines a realm that supposedly lies between the physical and spiritual. Safro does not believe in a spiritual world like the ordinary Akan do. It is the reason why he uses the phrase, "so-called spiritual." He feels more comfortable using the term quasi-physical for existents like God, ghosts, *ɔkra*, etc. (Safro 2004). In other words, the realm of these objects is beyond the physical or human physical senses but can be reached through extrasensory perception or what he presupposes could be subject to scientific verification in the future. In all practical sense, quasi-physical is not synonymous to a spiritual realm. If you ask a quasi-physicalist to describe electromagnetic waves, whether they are physical, spiritual, or quasi-physical, the answer to expect will be that they are "physical" since electromatic waves react to the laws of physics. That means the theory of quasi-physicalism is not about what cannot be seen, but rather what is beyond the confines of the laws of physics, yet not characterized as spiritual. With this background, we are now in a better position to read Wiredu.

6.1.2. Wiredu's Akan Anthropology

Wiredu lists five components of the human being, namely *nipadua* (body), *ɔkra* (life-giving entity), *sunsum* (that which gives a person's personality its force), *mogya* (literally blood and the basis of clan identity), and finally *ntorɔ*, which is the basis of membership in a patrilineal group. Wiredu claims the doctrine of *mogya* and *ntorɔ* is bound up with some rudimentary genetics (1987: 161). His definitions open a wide curiosity of scientific, philosophical, and ontological inquiry into Akan religions. Of particular interest is how Wiredu provides a logical framework for interpreting Akan religious ideas. His anthropology largely follows the fundamental definition of the human being. However, he seems to have more to say about the nature of the *ɔkra* and *sunsum*.

Wiredu thinks the *ɔkra* is not spiritual but quasi-physical. He says this to prove that it has no spiritual properties to be characterized as such. And this is not only about the *ɔkra*, but the *sunsum* as well. Wiredu perceives them as seemly possessing entitative qualities with physical properties. However, they are not entities in the usual sense of the word (Wiredu 1987: 161). If we are to even think of them as entities, then they are not spiritual. Wiredu comes to terms with Danquah who had earlier hinted at what could be termed as "concrete personified entities" for the *ɔkra*, *sunsum*, and *honhom* (Danquah 1968: 146). Wiredu's quasi-physicalism designates the *sunsum* and *ɔkra* as mere personified entities but not outrightly spiritual or physical. The rejection of the *spiritual* is directly related to his conceptual decolonization agenda to free "African frameworks of thought from colonial impositions" (Wiredu 1998: 44). As I will discuss in the next section, Wiredu gives more details on the necessity of decolonizing African conceptual thoughts to set the context for the philosophy of quasi-physicalism.

6.1.3. Quasi-Physicalism as a Philosophical Decolonization

Wiredu is a reconstructivist and who thinks Akan beliefs can be studied in a better logical framework that is distinct from Western philosophies, that is, within the Akan conceptual realities. Quasi-physicalism is one of his rational approaches to interpreting Akan realities. I will at this point look further into the rationale behind his rejection of the pneumatic nature of the *ɔkra* and *sunsum*, and how his interpretation of these concepts is construed. As we saw earlier, Akan scholarship emerged largely as a product of Western colonialism. The English language, which was (and still is) the medium of exploring knowledge, determined most of the meanings we ascribe to Akan realities. An example is the translation of the Akan term *ɔkra* into English as "soul." Language embodies the expressions of essential thoughts that define the worldview of a group of people. Wiredu knew this very well and thought some Western terms could not correctly define Akan realities, and one of them is the "soul" (Wiredu 1996: 137). He bases his suspicion on the definition of the soul in Western thought as a "purely immaterial entity that somehow inhabits the body" (Wiredu 1987: 161). In our previous historiography, we saw how Rattray, Meyerowitz, and Minkus translated *ɔkra* as "soul" or identified it with the Western concept of the soul. Wiredu thinks it is entirely misleading and quite definitely wrong (Wiredu 1987: 161). He believes the Akan understanding of the *ɔkra* and the Western conception of the "soul" are two entirely different things to identify one with the other. The contrast he draws between the two terms is based on their inherent conceptions.

Wiredu's definition of the soul is akin to Homer's view of the soul. There are two main distinctive usages of *psuche* (soul) in Homer's poems. First, the soul is something that a person risks in battle and loses in death (Lorenz 2009). The second conception of the soul is its departure from the person's limbs at death to travel to the underworld, a place of relief from pain. The two ideas have the same connotation. One can risk and lose one's soul and, after death, it endures as a shade in the underworld. Homer's view of the soul is related to life and specifically, the life of a human being. There is no life without the soul, and it is the soul that distinguishes the living human body from a corpse. The soul, according to Homer, is only a life entity and nothing more (Lorenz 2009).

In subsequent years, at the end of the fifth century BCE, the Greeks came to identify the soul with "a wide variety of activities and responses, cognitive as well as emotional, and to think of it as the bearer of such virtues as courage, temperance and justice" (Lorenz 2009). Socrates, Plato, and Aristotle saw the soul as imperishable, i.e., it survives death. It was also viewed in terms of cognition and intelligence. For both Socrates and Plato, the soul became the essence of the human being. To Plato, the body is perishable and the soul imperishable. Socrates believed the soul to be responsible for vitality. The soul is deathless or immortal (Lorenz 2009).

All other subsequent philosophies of the soul have been interpreted upon these fundamental conceptions until the turn of the modern era, when Western philosophers began to understand the concept of the soul as part of an individual's intuition and transcendence. In Emmanuel Kant's transcendental philosophy, transcendental knowledge is considered to be the activity of the soul (Bishop 2000: 262-267). Ralph Waldo Emerson views the soul as the source of self-transcendence in a human being and that it is connected to the Spirit of God (Emerson 2009).

Wiredu sees the *ɔkra*, by contrast, as quasi-physical. It is not a physical object; neither is it fully subject to spatial constraints. The human eye cannot perceive it. However, highly developed medicine men and those with extrasensory abilities are capable of communicating with the *ɔkra*.[112] Therefore, Wiredu claims to credit the *ɔkra* with paraphysical properties, not strictly a spiritual entity because its conception is redolent of/with material analogies (Wiredu 1987: 161, 163).

Additionally, everyone possesses a unique *'kra* as the proverb says, *Obi rekra ne Nyame no, na obi nnyina ho*, literally, "When one was taking leave of God (before birth), no one was there." The proverb means the *ɔkra* or *nkrabea* received from God varies from person to person. From this account arises the reason why Akan people believe a particular *ɔkra* may be allergic to certain taboo foods while the same taboo foods may be nutritious to another *ɔkra*. In the event where such taboos are violated, Wiredu says, "the okra may need to be pacified with offerings of appropriate food and drinks" (Wiredu 1987: 161). The Akan concept of *ɔkra* is obviously not the same as the Western concept of the soul.

Wiredu continues to defend the non-identical conception of the *ɔkra* and "soul" with more evidence. He advances to a controversial aspect of the notion of the *ɔkra* as the double of the individual.[113] It is "conceived in his material image complete with a head, hands, legs, and all" and can at times go its separate way from the body (Wiredu 1987: 161). This may seem not too far from the classical definition of the soul in Western thought as given above. However, Wiredu sees differently and argues that the fact that the *ɔkra* is a principle of life and at the same time a separate entity that can go its own way from the body is evidence that the *ɔkra* and "soul" are non-identical concepts (Wiredu 1987: 162).

---

112 In some traditional accounts, medicine men could only sense or read the intentions and actions of the *ɔkra*. There seem to be no traditional Akan expressions to suggest that medicine men communicate with *ɔkra* as in the case of the ancestors. The ancestors express their wishes and grievances to the traditional priests and medicine men in a dream and other means.

113 We encountered this conception in Meyerowitz' anthropology, even though Wiredu cites from a later account in Asare Opoku (1978: 96). According to the amount of evidence presented in my present research, some Akan believe that it is the *sunsum*, rather than the *ɔkra*, that roams about in nightly peregrination.

Wiredu's most convincing argument comes as a result of the difference he draws between the *ɔkra* and "soul", namely that "the 'okra' is very distinctly, indeed categorically, different from 'adwene' (mind)," whereas "the soul seems to be regarded as being the same as the mind" (Wiredu 1987: 162). The concept of the mind as immaterial and non-substantial apart from the body is one of Wiredu's important contributions to Akan philosophy. "Mind" and "soul" are analogous in English philosophy, but the application of such an analog among the Akan would be, as Wiredu says, "the veriest babble" (Wiredu 1987: 162). He argues that the mind, which in Akan is *adwene* (the verb form is *dwen* "think"), is not ontologically a material component, neither is it identical with the *ɔkra* or *sunsum*. Wiredu thinks the mind is non-substantial, not an object but only "a logical construction out of actual and potential thoughts" (Wiredu 1987: 159). This explains why Akan people do not list it as a constituent of a human being (Wiredu 1987: 163).

Wiredu further associates the mind with thoughts. Thus, *adwene* produces thought, which is not conceived as an entity, "neither material nor immaterial, physical nor nonphysical" (Wiredu 1987: 169). Therefore, *adwene* cannot be an entity (Wiredu 1987: 163-164). Whereas *adwene* is an abstract capacity in charge of an individual's thoughts, *ɔkra* is a living entity, which may possess *adwene* according to Wiredu. Akan people believe the *ɔkra* had a pre-existence, and before its entrance into the mundane world, it appeared before God to take its message, that is, *nkrabea* (destiny). Wiredu thinks it is logical to conclude that *ɔkra* "must have the capacity to understand a message or transmit one" (Wiredu 1987: 162). Here, we see a clear point of divergence between the preexistence of the *ɔkra*, which is not the same for the soul in certain quarters of modern Western philosophies. As a consequence, Wiredu prefers to define the *ɔkra* as "that whose presence in the body means life and whose absence means death and which also receives the individual's destiny from God" (Wiredu 1987: 162).

Wiredu says little about the nature of the *ɔkra* after death. The Akan belief postulates the *ɔkra* as becoming an ancestor after death. The living summons ancestors through the performance of rituals such as the pouring of libation and offerings, but this does not seem to be the same for the "soul" in Western philosophies. For conceptual reasons, Wiredu is right to leave *ɔkra* untranslated, especially when conceptual blunders already exist between the English translation of terms such as *ɔkra* and *sunsum*.

So, on the part of Wiredu, the linguistic distortion is not only a form of colonization, but an undermining mechanism for understanding Akan spiritual world views.

6.1.4. Spiritual or Quasi-Physical?

How do we differentiate the spiritual from the quasi-physical? The definition of what is spiritual as nonphysical, according to Wiredu, is too superficial to capture the whole idea of the meaning of the term. He is not convinced and argues that the word "spiritual," understood in the sense of "nonphysical," is for him "very far from a determinate idea," and he "cannot see that there is anything in Akan language corresponding to it" (Wiredu 1987: 163). He does not seem to deny the existence of "spirits," since it is a fundamental belief in African traditional religions, and since several religious beliefs and rituals are associated with it. In spite of this, he contends that "these 'spirits' are not conceived of as *spiritual* entities" (Wiredu 2007: 30). Wiredu's definition of a spiritual being is "an entity that is non-extended, non-spatial, immaterial, as opposed to extended, spatial, material" (Wiredu 2007: 30). The definition does not come as a description of the Akan understanding of a spiritual being, but a Cartesian rationality of what is spiritual. The separation of the immaterial from the material (mind-body dualism) is credited to Descartes. The dualistic notion presents the spiritual as an independent essence that is capable of consciousness, and the material as a mechanical object of the spiritual. Wiredu does not consider this definition applicable to Akan realities of spirits.

In the case of the ancestors, Wiredu says they were not always spirits. Ancestors are extended beings because they once lived as human beings. He cites the philosopher Okot p'Bitek from Uganda, and the British anthropologist Kenneth Little, who researched among the Mende of Sierra Leone, to buttress this point.[114] Both talk about the anthropomorphic character of

[114] Okot p'Bitek says the ancestors "were not spirits but the ancestors as they were known before death; their voices could be 'recognised' as they spoke through the diviner, they 'felt' hungry and cold, and 'understood' and 'enjoyed' jokes and being teased, etc. They were thought of as whole beings, not dismembered parts of man, i.e., spirits" (p'Bitek 1970: 104).

the ancestors as extended beings.[115] In comparison with the Akan view of ancestors, Wiredu comes to this conclusion:

> The ancestors are, in terms of imagery, like mortal persons, but they are not perceivable to the naked eye and are conceived to be exempt from the ordinary law of motion. Ontologically, all the entities or forces referred to above as spirits are of this kind: they are physical in image, but not subject to all the laws of the ordinary world. Let us call them, for convenience, quasi-physical. Then it would follow from our earlier considerations that spirits are admissible in an African ontology only in a quasi-physical sense. The place of the dead would thus be a quasi-physical environment (Wiredu 2007: 31).

Wiredu uses this argument to advance his quasi-physicalism to assume that, instead of a "spiritual" realm and of "spiritual" objects, Akan people should start speaking of a quasi-physical realm and quasi-physical objects. If there is any validity in quasi-physicalism, it is centered on the above statement. With this description of the ancestral world, Wiredu seeks to dislodge the idea of a spiritual worldview or the notion of spirits possessing spiritual properties. This would seem to suggest at least two levels of realms, namely a quasi-physical and a physical realm.

6.2. Critical Assessment of Quasi-Physicalism

My critique follows that, first, the Supreme deity, lesser deities, and the ancestors are correctly spiritual beings, even if they are spoken of in quasi-physical terms. Second, the *ɔkra* and the phenomenon of sleep peregrina-

---

115 Likewise, Kenneth Little came to a similar conclusion that in the ancestral world, "the conditions of this world are apparently continued in the hereafter, and the life led by the ancestral spirits seems to be similar in many respects to that of the people on earth. Some informants described them as cultivating rice farms, building towns, etc. It also seems that the spirits retain an anthropomorphic character and much of their earthly temperament and disposition" (Little 1954: 116).

tion of the *sunsum* may conveniently be qualified with quasi-physical properties. Third, ordinary perceptible objects that follow the laws of physics form the physical realm.[116] These three realms need further clarification.

A quasi-physical realm sits well with the Akan worldview, but not in the way Wiredu speaks of it, especially his view that spirits are not spiritual. The emerging problem is how a spirit-being cannot be spiritual. It is particularly useful to state that Akan people have their unique way of describing their worldviews. Even in the West, what is a spirit or spiritual has different meanings. In Western idealist philosophy, the spiritual is the ideal in its absolute form, e.g., God, spirits, soul, etc. I mentioned in this chapter that the spiritual in the Cartesian school of thought is a conscious substance, while Hegel defines it as consciousness in activity. The different ways of describing the spiritual also follow for the Akan people. Minkus came to the conclusion that the Akan people describe spirits but not necessarily what is spiritual. Existence is real because it can be described. These descriptions carry expressions familiar to the Akan worldview. If you ask an Akan whether ghosts do exist, the response is always, *saman wɔ hɔ*, meaning, "ghosts are there (real)." The phrase "*wɔ hɔ*" is used to express existence. Wiredu explains the *hɔ* (there) as spatial or locative – at some place (Wiredu 2004: 10).

Spirits exist, and although these immaterial existents are unseen, Akan people have formulated their ideas to relate to them. One such idea is the nature of the pantheon deities, which since time immemorial Akan people have represented in visual arts and carved objects. A widespread misconception is that the object itself is the deity; in actuality, it only serves as the abode for the spiritual agent, making it a localized deity. Early Europeans

[116] Minkus comes to the same conclusion by identifying a three-pronged mode of perception among the Akan. Although she did not used the term quasi-physical, she seemed to have hinted at the existence of quasi-physical objects. Her analysis follows like this: "In general, what cannot be seen using the ordinary faculty of vision can also not be perceived through the other senses. Exceptions are wind, cold and heat, which may be felt but not seen. The kind of seeing referred to in the above dichotomy is the ordinary perception of normal, living persons. Certain individuals with special powers, innate or gained through the application of medicine or by divine gift, are believed capable of perceiving what is not ordinarily perceivable. No one, however, would claim to see or hear the Supreme Being. The twofold division is actually a threefold one: the unperceivable, the extraordinarily perceivable and the ordinarily perceivable" (Minkus, 1981: 183).

misunderstood these physical representations of the deities and characterized Akan religions as fetish. The essential point here, however, is that the material representation (artistic objects) of spirits do not represent their real essence. Even if they do represent their being, they cannot purely and simply be identified with their essence. Similarly, the anthropomorphic descriptions of spiritual beings, and the ascription to them of physical properties reflect the whole system of the Akan religions, where the spiritual is perceived through the known (material), or when spiritual beliefs tend to take the form of physical expressions. This mode of description pervades all world religions and is frequently the catalyst for the emergence of idolatry.

Wiredu seems to have overlooked this connection by taking the physical descriptions in human terms as reality or as ontological. In this context, the argument for quasi-physicalism fails, in my opinion. The world of spirits, including the resting place of the ancestors, cannot be said to be quasi-physical. However, if the argument for quasi-physical objects does hold, that will not contradict the overall Akan worldview. Quasi-physicalism, it seemed to me, should be accepted as a descriptive principle for Akan spirituality rather than a reality principle. My argument follows that spirits are dynamic beings that possess the quality of interpenetrating the various realms of the Akan world. Spirits are spiritual beings not because they are unseen, but because they represent the ideal forms of being supernatural. Quasi-physical objects, as understood from the discussion, are found in a quasi-physical realm where extraordinary perception can discern their reality.

And finally, natural objects belong to the natural world of experience where everything is perceptible with the naked eyes. The approach of quasi-physicalism is a Cartesian philosophy, even though it seemingly postures itself as a direct opposition to Western philosophies.

6.2.1. Definition of *Sunsum* by Wiredu

The core principles of the philosophy of quasi-physicalism take away the spirituality of *sunsum* – the reason why my research has to deal with this philosophy. Wiredu denies the spirituality of the *sunsum* in the same way he denies the spirituality of the *ɔkra*. In principle, he thinks the *sunsum* also calls for a similarly circuitous translation (Wiredu 1987: 162). To translate *sunsum* as spirit or soul will characterize it pneumatically. Wiredu avoids the English translation as he proposes that the term should not be translated, but rather understood as "'that which is responsible for the total effect communicated by an 'individual's personality'" (Wiredu 1987: 162). If so, per Wiredu's conception, it becomes certain that *sunsum* is not spiritual at all, but only a force for personality. The definition does not follow the overall understanding of the concept of *sunsum*, but instead an anthropological definition. Wiredu's overall conclusion is as follows:

> As for the 'sunsum', it is not altogether clear that it is unambiguously conceived of as a kind of entity. But even if we assume that it is thought of in this way, it still cannot be called 'spiritual' in the present sense; for, apart from anything else, the 'sunsum' is believed by the Akans to perish at death, whereas spiritual beings are supposed to be immortal by nature (Wiredu 1987: 163).[117]

Wiredu is pro-Busia in the sense that the significant point he draws about *sunsum* from the above statement is referenced to Busia. He succeeds in bringing together the anthropological ideas of Busia about the *sunsum* into a philosophical school of thought. Busia saw the *sunsum* as a spiritual gift (charisma), a child of the *ntorɔ*, a spiritual substance passed from the father to his offspring, and that which perishes at death. Wiredu does not see any characteristic of a "spirit" in the description of *sunsum* by Busia. Hence, the *sunsum* is neither spiritual nor material but quasi-material. In referring to dream peregrination of the *sunsum*, Wiredu thinks the dreamland is not a spiritual realm but quasi-physical, and if it is to be considered a spiritual world, the *sunsum* does not belong there, as it will always return to the individual. In other words, the entity in the dream is limited by space and time. On the contrary, the fact that it can travel through space means it is not entirely material (Müller 2008: 173). Consequently, Wiredu sees the *sunsum* as quasi-material.

---

[117] I have already explained what some of the Akan thinkers meant when they used the phrase "to perish" for the *sunsum*. It simply means *sunsum* does not go to *Asamando* (ancestral world) with the *ɔkra* because it goes back to its source.

6.3. The Argument Against Quasi-physicalism

In following Wiredu's critique of the *ɔkra* and *sunsum* as strictly not spiritual, two Ghanaian philosophers, Kwame Gyekye and Mohammed Majeed, have sought to refute the philosophy of quasi-physicalism (Gyekye 1987; Majeed 2013). Gyekye, for instance, thinks such a philosophy is "completely wrong" and "runs counter to the belief of most Akan people" (Gyekye 1987: 86). Majeed follows with a similar critique that "aspects of the doctrine of quasi-physicalism itself are utterly inconsistent with some basic Akan beliefs" (Majeed 2013: 24). He argues that such a theory is philosophically indefensible. Gyekye and Majeed remain strong opponents of the philosophy of quasi-physicalism. Their arguments are brought here as well as their philosophical conception of the *ɔkra* and *sunsum*. The late Malawian philosopher Didier Njirayamanda has observed the disagreement between Gyekye and Wiredu as "not so much on the existence of the *okra* as a constituent of a person, as on its nature" (Wiredu 2004: 333). There are three ontological concepts which underline the critique of Gyekye and Majeed. First, it is correct to translate *ɔkra* into English as "soul." Second, the philosophy of quasi-physicalism is mistaken. Third, *sunsum* is better translated "spirit" and is, therefore, pneumatic.

6.3.1. *Ɔkra* as Soul?

Gyekye defines *ɔkra* as "that which constitutes the innermost self, the essence, of the individual person…the individual's life…the embodiment and transmitter of the individual's destiny (fate: *nkrabea*) …a spark of the Supreme Being (Onyame) in man. It is thus described as divine and as having an antemundane existence with the Supreme Being" (Gyekye 1987: 86). Akan people often refer to the human being as *ɔkrateasefo* (a living soul). Gyekye makes the connection that the expression identifies *ɔkra* with life; that makes it a vital element upon which rest activity as well as a determinant for life and death. The nature of *ɔkra* as an essence of God makes it capable of surviving death and defining the rationality behind life after death or immortality of the soul. The ancestors are departed *akra* (plural form of *ɔkra*). Gyekye sees that as a good reason to characterize the *ɔkra* with spirituality, and more importantly "as the equivalent of the concept of the soul in other metaphysical systems. Hence, it is correct to translate okra into English as soul" (Gyekye 1987:85). Majeed supports Gyekye's assumption that "although not necessarily Cartesian, is ultimately dualistic; and I am more inclined toward it than toward Wiredu's and Kwame's [Safro's]" (Majeed 2013: 25).

Another point of departure between Gyekye and Wiredu is their analysis of Western philosophical thought on the meaning of the soul, especially in Descartes. Wiredu concludes that the mind-soul concept in Descartes is essentially "thought" and not entitative. He writes: "When Descartes says that the soul is a thinking substance (*res cogitans*) he does not merely mean that it is a substance which can think; he means that it is a substance whose whole essence is thought" (Wiredu 1987: 171). The only place for the *ɔkra* in Western metaphysics is in "pre-Cartesian notion of the soul as the principle of life" according to Wiredu (1987: 171). Gyekye thinks Wiredu's use of "thought" is in the ratiocinative or cognitive sense and that it is too narrow to capture the full essence of the soul in Cartesian philosophy (Gyekye 1987: 87). Gyekye thinks "what Descartes means by mind or thought is consciousness" and that "consciousness, which is equivalent to the soul or mind in Descartes, can be a translation of okra" (Gyekye 1987: 87). Gyekye draws this conclusion to support his view that "thought (*adwen*) in the narrow sense is in Akan philosophy an activity of the *sunsum*," which he interprets "as a part of the soul (okra)" (Gyekye 1987: 87). He finally concludes that the mind is appropriately *sunsum*. In other words, *sunsum* produces thought.

However, the problem arises for the *'kra* as consciousness. To think of consciousness as synonymous to *'kra* will imply that consciousness is a life-principle. The Cartesian consciousness is a cognitive process, whereas the Akan concept of *ɔkra* is a life entity. We know unconsciousness may occur without losing the *'kra*. Losing the latter will lead to death. Again, the synonymity of *ɔkra* and soul (*consciousness*) runs counter to the entitative nature of the *'kra* in Gyekye's own conceptualization. How can the *ɔkra*, being entitative, having the capacity to travel through space, as the bearer of destiny, and its extension as a ghost after death, be equal to the Cartesian notion of the soul as consciousness? The analogy is philosophically incongruent since the concept of *'kra* among Akan people "seems to be born out of hypostasis" (Wiredu 1987: 172). As already mentioned, for linguistic convenience, the *'kra* may be translated into English as "soul," but conceptually, both have different meanings, and this is how scholars over the years have treated it.

6.3.2. Against the Philosophy of Quasi-physicalism

Gyekye thinks the philosophy of quasi-physicalism is contrary to the already established Akan conceptual position on spiritual objects. He sees it as completely wrong. Gyekye agrees with Wiredu that highly traditional medicine men "or people with extrasensory (or medicinally heightened) perception in Akan communities are said to be capable of seeing and communicating with the okra" (Gyekye 1987: 86). Wiredu thinks this phenomenon of extraordinary perception proves the fact that the *ɔkra* has spatial constraints, and by empirical methodologies, one can see it. Therefore, it is better be rendered as quasi-physical. Gyekye rebuts the views by stating, "these phenomena do not take place in the ordinary spatial world; otherwise anyone would be able to see or communicate with the okra (soul)" and "the fact that the okra can be seen by such people does not make it physical or quasi-physical (whatever that expression means), since this act or mode of seeing is not at the physical or spatial level" (Gyekye 1987: 86). Majeed argues in favor of Gyekye by theorizing that since "a person's *'kra* is believed to be linked or subsumed with his body, and the person lives in a world which is both physical and spiritual, he or she is possibly not prevented in the physical realm from reaching to the nonphysical side" (Majeed 2013: 26). Gyekye and Majeed believe a cross-realm effect or interaction is possible between the material and immaterial. They hold this view to support their view of the *'kra* as a spiritual property instead of quasi-physical.

The rejection of the philosophy of quasi-physicalism by Gyekye and others renders the theory not only indefensible but needless. Safro notes that Gyekye and others reject the philosophy of quasi-physicalism because "they ignore the category of the quasi-physical and, hence, have no other choice once they acknowledge that traditional Akans believe in entities that are not completely materialistic in the classic sense" (Safro 2013: 347). The quasi-physicalist holds the view that a spiritual entity is non-spatial, non-extended, and immaterial. Wiredu and Safro do not see the *'kra* as possessing these qualities. The *'kra* is only a life-entity subsumed to a person's body to give life. If correctly understood, we may call it a prisoner of the body, released at death. The *'kra* cannot go its separate way from the body since that will result in the death of the individual.

The most vital question in the debate is not whether the *'kra* can continue to exist after death or not; both Gyekye and Wiredu agree to that fact.

The question is how then does a life entity become an ancestor, complete with anthropomorphic character, and called upon in the rituals of the living? The question is important because it determines the strength and weakness of each side of the debate. Does the *'kra* flit out of the body as a "living soul" or as a transfigured object? It is not so difficult for dualists like Gyekye and others to accept the former. Akan worldview suggests both a linear and cyclical view of life. The linear view means the *'kra* survives death and continues to live on as an entity in an immaterial world of ancestors. And the cyclical view means the *'kra* can be reincarnated into the material world under certain circumstances. Gyekye thinks a quasi-physical object that is "seemingly physical," or "almost physical" cannot achieve such spiritual degrees unless it is something completely immaterial. He fears the *'kra* as a quasi-physical object "would mean the total or 'near total' (whatever that might mean) extinction of the *ɔkra* (soul) upon the death of the person" (Gyekye 1987: 86, 87). He, therefore, sees the ability of the *'kra* to continue to exist independently in the world of the ancestors (*Asamando*) as being more than just a life entity.

Quasi-physicalists accept a transfiguration of the *'kra* because ancestors are only extended beings. I am more inclined to accept this view, even though I do not entirely deny the entitative nature of the *'kra*. The idea of the apotheosized *'kra* is a suprasensible attainment that makes it capable of intervening in the affairs of the living simply because a transfiguration has taken place. At face value, we may deny this as incongruent with Akan thought. But in every practical sense, Akan people believe ancestors are more powerful than the living and can help the living in ways that are beyond their abilities. The honorable status of ancestors in the religious rites is one of the most important in Akan religions. The rationality that living *akra* (human beings) are calling upon departed *akra* (ancestors) for help sustains this argument. It occurs naturally to think that the present state of the *'kra* in the mundane life is not envisioned as possessing such spiritual abilities like the ancestors. A transfiguration must take place to allow it to function in that respect. As to the question of how this transfiguration occurs, I do not intend to enter into that argument here. Danquah had already dealt with this subject in his evolutionary theory of the Akan concept of life in the *Akan Doctrine of God* (1968). For the purpose of this present research, I will focus on Gyekye's view of the *sunsum*, and how his pneumatic conception directly confronts the philosophy of quasi-physicalism.

6.3.3. The Pneumatic Conception of *Sunsum* in Gyekye

The last argument Gyekye draws against the philosophy of quasi-physicalism is the spirituality of *sunsum,* which quasi-physicalists reject. The pneumatic character of *sunsum* is not a recent development. We already encountered the trend taking shape in the works of Captain Rattray and other subsequent scholars. On several occasions, *sunsum* has been confused with *ɔkra* in the same way some use "spirit" and "soul" interchangeably. Gyekye thinks a distinction can be drawn although he sees *sunsum* and *ɔkra* in an *ontic unity* as we will soon discuss.

Gyekye remains one of the few contemporary thinkers and students of the *sunsum* who, like Wiredu, chose a career path in philosophy which, instead of contributing to Akan religions with empirical studies, focused more on the analytical study of existing literature on Akan religions (Müller 2008: 169).[118] Gyekye thinks the term "spiritual" is better rendered in the Akan language as *sunsum*, and since *sunsum* is the principle of animation, Akan ontology is essentially or primarily spiritual. Gyekye believes the *sunsum* is divine, spiritual, and the activating principle in creation. In other words, the spiritual supersedes or transcends the physical. This view makes the spiritual an ethereal part of the physical or as he concludes, "[w]hat is primarily real is spiritual" (Gyekye 1987: 69).

Gyekye continues to maintain a dualistic worldview of a spiritual-physical realm where the physical is dependent upon the spiritual, and the more reason he claims an aspect of the human being, i.e., *ɔkra*, as spiritual. His overall views on the *sunsum* are drawn from his conception of it as a mystical, unempirical, and nonphysical spiritual element. The point of departure between the pneumatic and quasi-physical conceptions is the different point of views of Akan metaphysics. For example, Wiredu's metaphysics is quasi-physical, whereas Gyekye's is spiritual. I will examine in detail the claims of Gyekye on the *sunsum*.

---

[118] Although Gyekye is not an ethnographer, there are considerable amounts of sources that he draws from field work. The most part of his ideas stem from interactions with traditional rulers and persons with traditional knowledge of Akan religions and culture.

6.3.4. The Meaning of *Sunsum* According to Gyekye

Gyekye provides an alternative view of the Akan *sunsum*. He translates *sunsum* as appropriately "spirit." The reason for this stems from the definition he offers that *sunsum* refers "to all unperceivable, mystical beings and forces in Akan ontology, and specifically to refer to the activating principle in the person" (Gyekye 1987: 88). Anthropologically, *sunsum*, the activating principle, is responsible for the formation of an individual's personality, i.e., "a set of characteristics as evidenced in a person's behavior – thoughts, feelings, actions, etc." (Gyekye 1987: 90). Qualities associated with personality include courage, jealousy, gentleness, forcefulness, and dignity. These psychological qualities are not sensible or material (Gyekye 1987: 90). It gives Gyekye reason to characterize the *sunsum* as something immaterial, mystical and nonempirical and the basis for the spiritual universe of the Akan.

To Gyekye, the Akan universe is "endowed or charged with varying degrees of force or power," which means, "all created things, that is, natural objects, have or contain *sunsum*; every deity (*obosom*) is a *sunsum*, but not vice versa" (Gyekye 1987: 72, 73). Thus, Gyekye thinks *sunsum* is something more than a "father's spirit" to his child. He also denies its affiliation with the *ntorɔ*, already given by Busia. He then, however, applies a generic conception that will make it more reasonable for acceptance, that is, *sunsum* derives from God, the omnipotent (Gyekye 1987: 73). The ontological implication here labels the *sunsum* as divine, and consequently immortal, contradicting the perishability of the *sunsum* at death. This also forms the basis of the spiritual unity between *ɔkra* and *sunsum* as advanced by Gyekye. Again, the designation of God as *sunsum* or the ultimate source of *sunsum*, recalls Danquah's theory of *Onyankopɔn*, the *Sunsum* of *Odomankoma*, as the essence of all universal experience.[119] That means *sunsum* is required for experiential activation. This leads Gyekye to characterize Akan worldview using panpsychism; thus, "everything is or contains *sunsum*" (Gyekye 1987: 75).[120]

---

119 *Sunsum* is the subject of experience that makes activity possible. "Experience is the awareness of something" says Gyekye, and since "a purely material thing, such as wood or a dead body, cannot experience anything, it follows that the *sunsum*, *qua* subject of experience, cannot be material" (Gyekye 1987: 91).

120 According to Akan religions, it is not God who is present in creation. The forces identified in natural objects are the pantheon deities. God works through a pantheon

The views of Gyekye are not far from (if not identical with) Minkus' category of *ye sunsum* (exclusively spiritual) and *wɔ sunsum* (the inspirited). Gyekye does not make any direct reference to Minkus, but he states, "the word *sunsum* is used in two different but related senses." As he sees it, the first refers "to any self-conscious subject whose activities are initiated self-consciously." This may include all spiritual beings with intelligence and will. The second, according to Gyekye, refers to the mystical powers in the world that "constitute the inner essence or intrinsic properties of natural objects, and are believed to be contained in those objects" (Gyekye 1987: 73). So, Gyekye uses *sunsum* "in both a specific sense, to refer to the essence of a particular deity or man, and a general sense, to refer to all beings and powers unperceived by man" (Gyekye 1987: 73). The pneumatic character of *sunsum* lies in this rudimentary rationality.

Gyekye gives more details on the notion of *sunsum* and its distinction from *ɔkra*. It has been a matter of difficulty for some to draw a difference or relationship between *ɔkra* and *sunsum*. Rattray first saw the difficulty of distinguishing "between the *'kra* and the next kind of soul, the *sunsum*, and sometimes the words seem synonymous" (Rattray 1927: 154). At different times, Rattray thought of *sunsum* as either the soul or the volatile part of the *ɔkra* (Rattray 1923: 152; 1927: 153, 154). Danquah likewise saw the *sunsum* as the counterpart of the *ɔkra* (Danquah 1968: 112). Perhaps the most constructive among all was Meyerowitz who saw *ɔkra* and *sunsum* as two elements of one soul (Meyerowitz 1951: 27). None of the scholars saw the two as identical. Gyekye expounds on the non-identical nature of the two by referring to specific attributes given exclusively to the *ɔkra* that Akan people do not attribute to the *sunsum*. For example, the Akan will say, "His '*kra* is sad" (*ne 'kra di awerehow*); never, "His *sunsum* is sad." Or "His '*kra* is good," meaning, the person has a fortunate soul. On the contrary, if the Akan say, "His 'kra is not good," it will mean the person is unlucky. To say a person's *sunsum* is not good means that person is an evil person or a witch.

---

of deities who act in His stead. It is the deities who take residence in natural objects, not God. Pantheism is never practiced in the Akan religious experience. Gyekye writes: "Such an impression, however, would be erroneous, for Akan thinkers do not maintain that Onyame (God) is identifiable with the sum of all things. They do not identify the creator with the creature, the author with his work" (1987: 75). God is never identifiable with His creation. It is rather the emanating *sunsum* of God and the other deities who are present in creation.

Again, Akan people will say, "His *sunsum* is heavy" to designate a person who possesses a strong personality. Never will the Akan say, "He has a heavy '*kra*." Gyekye uses these illustrations to demonstrate the nonidentical nature of the *ɔkra* and *sunsum*. However, he is convinced that the two have a constitutive unity or ontological relationality, meaning they form a single spiritual element from God. His emphasis on *ɔkra* as divine and spiritual forms the basis of this assumption. As a result, Gyekye rejects any tripartite view of Akan concept of a person, that is, *ɔkra*, *sunsum*, and *nipadua*, to embrace a dualistic character where *ɔkra* (soul) and *sunsum* (spirit) form one spiritual element, whereas the *nipadua* or *honam* is the material that constitutes a human being. Consequently, an individual is "made up of two principal entities or substances, one spiritual (immaterial: *okra*) and the other material (*honam*: body)" (Gyekye 1987: 99). The "soul" then, according to Gyekye, is *ɔkra* plus *sunsum*. Unlike quasi-physicalists, Gyekye does not see any contradiction between the Akan concept of *ɔkra* and the Western philosophy of mind or soul.

6.4. A Critique of the Pneumatic Conception of *Sunsum*

My response at this point is directly influenced by the evidence provided in this debate and my own conceptual views in this debate. I have already underlined that Gyekye is a comprehensive thinker and one whose analytical approach to Akan religions provides a coherent Akan philosophical framework. However, there are aspects of his views on the Akan *sunsum* that cannot altogether be accepted as entirely indigenous. While Wiredu conceptualizes Akan religions to give them a logical balance that are free from Western conceptualization, Gyekye uses, as Müller commented, "only Western or etic concepts to articulate" Akan spirituality, as though Akan religions are compatible with Western thought (Müller 2008: 175). This is the reason why he accepts "soul" and "spirit" as appropriate terms for translating *ɔkra* and *sunsum*, and more radically embraces an *ontic* unity of *ɔkra* and *sunsum*.

Gyekye's views are not without weaknesses. First, it is unquestionably true that the *ɔkra* is divine, bearer of destiny, and that Akan people believe it is immortal. We find the proof in its character as a life entity. Nobody expects a life principle to die; it is instead a determinant object for life and death. It is also observed that the views of Gyekye on the *sunsum* as cosmic, immaterial, mystical, and nonempirical, conform to the general conception of *sunsum* among Akan people. This definition has been quite recurring in my historiographical investigation, and it resonates well with several scholars studying Akan religions. What is at stake is how Gyekye characterizes the *sunsum* as divine, generic, and having an *ontic unity* with the *ɔkra* in its anthropological conception. These are not entirely indigenous, and it undercuts the Akan religions in several ways, as later analysis will reveal.

Second, besides the overwhelming evidence from our historiographical inquiry about the male's role in transmitting *sunsum*, one example which suggests that *sunsum* is not divine and that it cannot be generic is the notion among Akan people of *sunsum bōne*, often referring to as evil spirit, witch or wizard, and *Onyame Sunsum*, translated here as God's *Sunsum*. Is the *sunsum* in both cases the same generic divine *sunsum*? I doubt it. Even if one takes the two, for argument's sake, as generic, it still cannot be accurate because it will raise a theological question. How can the *sunsum* from *Onyame* in its practical experience be manipulated for an evil course? In reality, Akan people do not associate evil with God, and since evil is found on the side of the *sunsum*, it cannot follow that this *sunsum* is generically divine because, for all practical intents and purposes, the essence of the Supreme Being is morally good.[121] This is exactly so for the *ɔkra*, whose essence shares in the divine attributes of being deathless and without evil. Danquah says the *ɔkra* "is in its nature divine, and no contamination with sin or evil is possible for it... God never made a decree for an evil soul. God never made an evil man" (Danquah 1968: 87). He then designates *sunsum* as the depository of evil in an individual. He thinks evil "exists but only in the *sunsum* side; the world of the *sunsum* not the world of *okara*." There is evil in the world which, through neglect and submission of the *sunsum*, perpetuates evil in the individual. In other words, no one is born evil. Evil is

[121] Gyekye himself identifies the cause of evil from the malevolent lesser deities (witches and other spirits) and the human freewill. The lesser deities "are held either to be good and evil or to have powers of good and evil." Their potency to cause evil stems from their very nature that is partly evil. They have the power to cause sickness, natural disasters, and even to kill individuals without strong *sunsum*. Gyekye notes that "though the deities were created by God, they are believed to operate independently of God and in accordance with their own wills: they can, and do, use their independent wills to pursue evil." The human freewill involves "character, conscience, thoughts and desires." The freewill makes human beings architects of their moral standards. A person always has the capacity to choose to do what is good as well as evil (Gyekye 1996: 12).

an inclination of the *sunsum* due to the evil in the world. It is a contradiction to perceive *sunsum* as immanent to God and at the same time, susceptible to do evil. *Sunsum* can be evil because other means, other than God, transmit it. Onyame *Sunsum* should be distinct from all other *sunsum* we might consider.

Third, it follows that the *ontic unity* theory is also questionable. Gyekye articulated this theory to explain why the *ɔkra* is active and why it can take a message or transmit one. According to this theory, the *sunsum* is a part of *ɔkra* and is the bearer of consciousness responsible for thoughts. The *ontic* in unity theory justifies the capacity of the *ɔkra* to possess thought or to have consciousness. It justifies why Gyekye embraces a dualistic soul-body anthropology, rather than a tripartite (soul-body-spirit) conception. Nevertheless, the theory belittles the Akan belief of the disembodied *ɔkra* and *sunsum* at the death of the individual. When death occurs, it is the *ɔkra*, not the *sunsum*, which is apotheosized to travel to the realm of *Nananom Nsamanfo* (The Eminent Ancestors). The *sunsum* returns to the father's family to wait for the next embodiment. This is what led Busia to see the *sunsum* as a patrilineal biogenetic that runs through the father's family (Busia 1954: 198). This recycling process is not same with the *ɔkra*. Minkus confirms that it is the *sunsum*, rather than the *ɔsaman*, of the deceased or ancestor that influences the character disposition of the one who bears his or her name (Minkus 1981: 186). Rattray and other ethnographers saw a dichotomy between the *ɔkra* and *sunsum*, with the former being divine and the later terrestrial. Danquah was the architect of the divine origin of *sunsum* and its *ontic* in unity with the *ɔkra*. He considered the mind to be the spiritual, the end of the evolution of the *sunsum* and *ɔkra*. Danquah avoids several traditional conceptions in his attempt to demythologize Akan religions and to make them more pro-Western, if not Christian.[122] We can observe the same tendency in Gyekye's logical conclusion in his attempt to make the Akan concept of mind compatible with other metaphysical systems and more straightforwardly against the philosophy of quasi-physicalism.

Fourth, another implication following the ontic unity theory is that it relegates to the background the fact that only males can transmit the *sunsum*. Akan people do not say that just for natal purpose, but it has to do with

---

[122] Danquah is quoted as saying, "Christianity is a fulfillment of the religious conceptions of our own people" (Danquah 1968: xxv).

the position of males in society. A Ghanaian Akan highlife musician, Akosua Agyapong, mentions in one of her songs titled, "*Frema*": "*Mmarima sunsum kata mmaa so*," which I have translated as, "The *sunsum* of men hovers over women."[123] Besides the lyrical evidence of the *sunsum* of a man, she explains why majority of Akan people believe that the agency of the *sunsum* is masculine and more powerful than that of the woman. Another example is from one Yaw Tano, from Wiamoase in the Asante region. Mr. Tano has been an adherent of the Akan traditional religion for more than thirty years and happens to be my uncle. He served as one of the officiants of the god *Jenchu*, whose priest is Kwaku Anokye, also from Wiamoase. When asked about the *sunsum*, Tano said to me that it is the father's "spirit" to his child. Although he now professes, to an extent, the Christian faith, he did not allow his new faith to influence his traditional conception. The views he expressed agree with what Ephirim-Donkor has recently concluded, namely that "only males are bearers of the *Sunsum* making males progenitors of life, their offspring... *Sunsum* (spirit) is transmitted through a father's semen (*huaba/ntoro*) during a sexual act" (2016: 83).[124] Ephirim-Donkor also commented that "the *Sunsum* of a father hovers over all things physical as well as spiritual" (2016: 86). The *sunsum* places men in a position of significant influence and authority over their offspring, and it tends to have significance in Akan social setup. The *ontic* in unity theory of the *ɔkra*, whereby *sunsum*, instead of being transmitted by the father, comes directly from God, takes away this important masculine role in Akan anthropology.

Fifth, Gyekye contradicts all others to further argue that "*sunsum* cannot derive from the child's father" (Gyekye 1987: 91). The reason behind his objection is that trees, plants, and other natural objects also contain *sunsum*. Gyekye's denial is only an attempt to support his general conception of *sunsum* as deriving directly from God, and to formulate a logical system that can better position Akan philosophy in the academic sphere. Others have asked Gyekye whether trees should have human fathers for their *sunsum* to be passed on to their offspring. The logical conclusion would be that the reproductive activities of trees and animals would be adequate to pass on their *sunsum* to their offspring (Coetzee & Roux 1998: 220). The meaning of *sunsum* is so polarizing that a generic definition is difficult.

---

123 "*Frema*" was her first album released on January 1, 1990.

124 Ephirim-Donkor discusses this subject in detail in his book *African Personality and Spirituality: The Role of Abosom and Human Essence* (2016: 83-89).

Sixth, having disputed the divine origin of *sunsum*, it follows that the *ɔkra* cannot have an ontic unity with it. I, therefore, stand with others who see *ɔkra* as distinct and as having a sort of superpersonal wholeness. What then do we do with the ontic unity theory? Should it be out of the question, or there is a place for it in Akan religions? I will answer these questions in favor of the theory, but not in the way Gyekye explained. In life, a logical conclusion can be made to suggest that an *ontic unity* occurs when *ɔkra* and *sunsum* are reunited in the same way the *ntorɔ* of the father and *mogya* of the mother unite to form the human body. Rattray and Meyerowitz give us a reason to accept such a proposal. Rattray, for instance, suggested that perhaps the *sunsum* is the volatile part of the *ɔkra*, and the reason a person may die when the *sunsum* is attacked. Meyerowitz too saw an *ontic unity* when she referred to the *ɔkra* as the unconscious and *sunsum* as the conscious, together they make two elements of one soul (Meyerowitz 1951: 27). The newborn child is a developing personality in whom the unity of the *ɔkra* and *sunsum* play vital roles. Both *ɔkra* and *sunsum* have distinct roles to fulfill, but they are interwoven into a unified whole.

So far, Rattray, Danquah, Meyerowitz, and Gyekye all agree on an *ontic* in unity of the *ɔkra* and *sunsum*, but they disagree when it comes to the origin of *sunsum*.

6.5. Evaluation of Quasi-Physicalism and the Pneumatic Conception

The ongoing debate has brought forward two important views of Akan spirituality. The first has been the philosophy of quasi-physicalism, which argues that Western conceptualizations have influenced the study of Akan religions, and therefore a philosophical decolonization is required to get rid of conceptual blunders and misunderstandings. Part of that effort has been the question of the English translation of *ɔkra* and *sunsum* as "soul" and "spirit." Although Gyekye strongly maintains that these translations are appropriate, Wiredu, the precursor of quasi-physicalism, disagrees and thinks *ɔkra* is not spiritual but quasi-physical. He says the same of the *sunsum*, namely that it is not categorically a spirit or spiritual, but quasi-material. A great deal of his disagreement has been that "soul" and "spirit" have philosophical connotations that are not the same as the Akan notion of *ɔkra* and *sunsum*; as such, they cannot be identical. From this background, Gyekye constructs his philosophical defense against the philosophy of quasi-physicalism.

The strength of Gyekye's argument is in the fact that *sunsum* is an immaterial entity that can be rightly translated as spirit, as well as the bearer of consciousness. Gyekye sees the *sunsum* as the basis for psychological phenomena. That is, the mind is not just thought as the quasi-physicalist imagines it to be. The mind is a spiritual entity, a substance synonymous to *sunsum*, which makes a thinking being in essence partly spiritual (Gyekye 1987: 88, 164). Gyekye uses sleep peregrination of the *sunsum* to illustrate the connection between the mind and body:

> The fact that dreaming occurs only in sleep makes it a unique sort of mental activity and its subject, namely *sunsum*, a different sort of subject. A purely physical object cannot be in two places at the same time: A body lying in bed cannot at the same time be on the top of a mountain. Whatever is on the top of the mountain, then, must be something nonphysical, nonbodily, and yet somehow connected to a physical thing – in this case, the body (Gyekye 1987: 93).

Given this is the rationale behind Gyekye's duality of the concept of a person, Wiredu says it is a hypothesis which does not have a place in Akan thought, on the account that mind is not a substance of the body, and neither is it identical with *sunsum*. Wiredu argues in favor of the nonsubstance conception of mind (Wiredu 1987: 160). The *sunsum*, too far removed from being identical with the mind, would have to be a possessor of mind in order to act in dreams (Wiredu 1987: 163). How can *sunsum*, a spiritual entity *qua* mind, act in dreams without a mind of its own? It is true that dreams do not occur in the material world even though it is a mental activity. However, because every human being possesses a *sunsum*, everyone is capable of participating in the mystical world.

My own conclusion supports Wiredu, for the following reasons: the *sunsum*, which is on the top of the mountain in the dream, is not logically the person's physical body. It has to be something that Wiredu considers as a quasi-physical being. It is represented as the person's double in the dream, possessing a complete physiological identity and in a quasi-physical world. Whatever one comes to experience in dreams is just a replica of some physical realities. This accounts for the identification of familiar persons and places in dreams because they are all perceptions of physical elements presented in quasi-physical images. That world that the *sunsum* dramatizes in dreams is not a spiritual world; neither is it a physical world. It is a quasi-physical world, and the *sunsum* does not belong there.

Regarding the expression "quasi-physical," both Gyekye and Majeed did not consider it as a philosophical subject worth dealing with. A thorough assessment of the expression does not seem to concern them any more than the nature of the *ɔkra*. Gyekye understood "quasi-physical" to mean "seemingly physical" or "almost physical" (Gyekye 1987: 86). Majeed, on the other hand, relied mainly on Safro's definition to engage the theory in detail. Based on their analysis and understanding of the term quasi-physical, both arrive at a conclusion to reject quasi-physicalism for other philosophical interpretations that support the spirituality of the *ɔkra*. Gyekye thinks the *ɔkra* may be subject to total or "near total" extinction upon the death of the person if characterized with quasi-physical properties (Gyekye 1987: 86, 87). This assumption is contrary to the philosophy of quasi-physicalism because the quasi-physicalist believes in the immortality of the *ɔkra*. Wiredu believes the apotheosized *saman* (ghost) in the netherworld is an extended form of the *ɔkra*.

Gyekye and Majeed misunderstood the concept of quasi-physicalism due to their definition of the term as "almost physical." The quasi-physical and paraphysical character of the *ɔkra* makes its activity a paranormal phenomenon. It does not have any straightforward physical properties. Nevertheless, it relates to a physical phenomenon, a kind of "parasitical on material analogies" for which no adequate laws of physics or scientific explanation exists.[125] There is no scientific explanation to ascertain how the *ɔkra* subsumes the body. Neither do the traditional concepts offer any clue. The physical proof is that its presence means life and its departure is death, and that traditional medicine men who possess extrasensory abilities can enter into communication with the *ɔkra*. This is the background that shapes Wiredu's conception of why any theory of souls or spirits is an empirical theory (Wiredu 1987: 170).

Majeed criticizes Wiredu for being rationally misled by the hypothesis of Hans Werner Debrunner, the Swiss-German historian and theologian, that the *ɔkra* "is sometimes said to be a person's double, conceived in his material image complete with a head, hands, legs and all" (Wiredu 1987:

---

125 Borrowed phrase from Wiredu (1987: 175).

161). Majeed thinks it is not sensible to use phrases like my *ɔkra's* leg and my *ɔkra's* head, or even say that her *ɔkra*'s chin is like this or that his *ɔkra*'s hand has done that (Majeed 2013: 27, 28). Simply put, the *ɔkra* has no such parts as claimed by Debrunner. Indeed, there are no statements like that in Akan oral traditions. Majeed rightly suggested that the shape that the medicine man sees may not be the *ɔkra's* own shape or perhaps it assumes "the shape of the person it was known to inhabit just for the purposes of easy identification of its bearer" (Majeed 2013: 28). All these may seem true of how the *ɔkra* looks like, but the most obvious evidence is the image of the deceased that Akan people assume as the *ɔsaman* (ghost or ancestor). Alternatively, it may be the image of the *ɔkra* that the body bears, just like printing a photo from a digital camera. In whichever way, several Akan people will perceive the *ɔkra* in anthropomorphic images. There are expressions like *Wo reku me 'kra,* meaning, "You are killing my *ɔkra*;" *Me kra redi awerehoɔ,* meaning, "My *'kra* is aggrieving." Most Akan people use these statements to express diverse emotional experiences in a person's life. Even if those statements are considered metaphorically, they may lead to the notion of the *ɔkra* as an entity with human sentiments and consciousness, just as a person may feel in the physical world. *Ɔkra*'s chin or leg, or hand, etc. may be quite unknown in the Akan languages. However, certain aspects of the *ɔkra*, as analyzed above, exhibit anthropological properties.

Moreover, the preexistence of the *ɔkra* with God, where it also received its *nkrabea* (destiny), makes it capable to negotiate its destiny, as some accounts indicate. It would have to possess consciousness and the capacity to reason for its destiny. Unless the *ɔkra* is a personality, it cannot reason with God for its destiny. It is, therefore, not an error to conceive of the *ɔkra* as possessing anthropological properties, even if such characteristics are absent in the ordinary Akan languages. Wiredu calls the *ɔkra* a living entity, i.e., it constitutes the body as a substance, not an astral being (Wiredu 1987: 162).[126]

There are several characteristics of the nature of *ɔkra* to contest its pneumatic conception. A spirit has non-spatial constraints, whereas *ɔkra* has a spatial constraint. The restriction of the *ɔkra* to giving life to the body precludes it from acting in spiritual directives like a "spirit" does. Its separation from the body is death. On the contrary, the *ɔkra* attains spirituality

[126] Akan people do not think of the presence of the *ɔkra* as possession or an astral entity. It is just a substance that forms part of the whole body.

after death when it has realized its destiny. There is no return to God after that transfiguration.[127] The *ɔkra* departs with the image of its bearer to become an ancestor (spirit) in a world called *Asamando* (world of spirits), a replica of the physical world. The spirit does not lose consciousness, since it can now identify other predeceased ancestors, interact with other spiritual beings, and respond to the call of the living when summoned in the pouring of libation. In this state, it becomes acceptable that the *ɔkra* has attained spirituality because it can travel across space and time.

The following tables give a summary of the nature of the *ɔkra* and *sunsum* as understood by Kwesi Wiredu and Kwame Gyekye.

Table 3: Summary of the character of the ɔkra according to Wiredu and Gyekye

	Definition	**English**	**Nature**	**Origin**	**Generic**	**Posthumous**
Wiredu	That whose presence in the body means life and whose absence means death and which also receives the individual's destiny from God.		Quasi-physical, Life-giving entity	God		Spirit in Asamando (quasi-physical world)
Gyekye	That which constitutes the innermost self, the essence, of the individual person…the individual's life…the embodiment and transmitter of the individual's destiny (fate: *nkrabea*) …a	Soul	Non-physical, Spiritual	God		Spirit in Asamando (spiritual world)

[127] There have been some authors who have asserted the return of the *ɔkra* to God: see for example (Neville et al. 2009: 51). This may not exactly correspond to most Akan traditional concepts about the death of a person. Such treatment of the *ɔkra* may be found in some Christian teachings, but may be far removed from Akan traditional anthropology. The ancestors do not live with God; neither do they live with the lesser gods. Their world is different from that of the other spirits according to Akan traditions.

	spark of the Supreme Being (Onyame) in man. It is thus described as divine and as having an antemundane existence with the Supreme Being.					

Table 4: Summary of the character of the sunsum according to Wiredu and Gyekye

	Definition	**English**	**Nature**	**Origin**	**Generic**	**Posthumous**
Wiredu	That which is responsible for the total effect communicated by an 'individual's personality.'		Quasi-material	Through the father		Perishes at death
Gyekye	To all unperceivable, mystical beings and forces in Akan ontology, and specifically to refer to the activating principle in the person.	Spirit	Spiritual, has ontic unity with the *ɔkra*	God	Yes	Together with the *ɔkra* becomes the ancestor

6.6. Summary

This chapter has offered an evaluation of the ongoing debate between the philosophy of quasi-physicalism and the pneumatic conception of the *ɔkra* and *sunsum*. How relevant is this debate to the present research? The purpose has been to see the various implications for the construction of contextual Akan Christian pneumatology. The critique of quasi-physicalism questions the fundamental basis for contextual Akan Christian pneumatology, namely the *ɔkra* and *sunsum*. Is there anything at all spiritual in Akan worldview? The merit in quasi-physicalism relies on its attempt to decolonize Akan concepts and to provide an alternative way of interpreting Akan realities. Gyekye, on the other hand, gave alternative conceptions about what ought to be philosophically expedient in the Akan understanding of the spiritual. In his attempt to defend the pneumatic notion of *ɔkra* and *sunsum*, he offered a philosophical framework that appeals to various philosophical systems, even though aspects of it is considered nonindigenous by others. From my analysis of the argument, it is observed that neither quasi-physicalism nor the pneumatic conception adequately conveys the meaning of the Akan doctrine of *ɔkra* and *sunsum*. It is the understanding of their nature and the roles they play in Akan anthropology that give reason to the existence of the argument of quasi-physicalism and the pneumatic conception of Akan spirituality.

The chapter that follows will deal with some Akan terms that are frequently confused with or closely related to *sunsum*. I will articulate my understanding of *sunsum* through a comparative analysis of some of these terms.

7. Contemporary Analysis of Commonly Confused Terms With *Sunsnum*

> *"In Akan thought, for instance, Rattray noted different ideas of the sunsum ('spirit') of a person with some of his informants saying that the sunsum and the ōkra (soul) are the same, and others disagreeing. He noted the 'sometimes contradictory' nature of 'all these quotations" referring to the statements of his informants."*—Kwame Gyekye.[128]

The present attempt to develop a contextual Akan Christian pneumatology has been the reason for the historiographical investigation into the nature of the Akan concept of *sunsum*. So far, I have retraced and analyzed the evolution of the term, from its pneumatological conception to the contemporary argument of quasi-physicalism. The different perspectives scholars draw from the nature of *sunsum* serve to lay the foundation for a broader framework of understanding. However, there are some other Akan terms that often nuance a comprehensive understanding of *sunsum*. Most of the nuances, already discussed in the previous chapter, stem from various conceptions about *sunsum* from both Western and indigenous scholars studying Akan religions. This chapter aims to draw a synthesis from the different discussions in order to examine the relationship between *sunsum* and other commonly confused terms with it. The purpose is to present the most compelling argument for the distinctiveness of *sunsum*, with a particular focus on how it informs my research towards the articulation of a contextual Akan Christian pneumatology.

[128] Gyekye (1987: 47).

7.1. The Relationship Between *Sunsum* and *Ɔkra*

The relationship between *sunsum* and *ɔkra* has been a problem to scholars. The majority of scholars studying Akan religions understand the two to be distinct aspects of the human being. Gyekye thinks the relationship between the two constitutes an inseparable unity of *ɔkra* and *sunsum*, i.e., consisting in a single unity. I have responded to Gyekye in the previous chapter with a critique, arguing this cannot be so. Most scholars envision a distinctiveness of the two, although both form a single essence of the human being. *Sunsum* is a patrilineal essence. The idea of coming from the father suggests that it is not just a concept or idea, but something immaterial which forms the basis for the spiritual bond between the father and his offspring. The *ɔkra*, on the other hand, is a divine essence responsible for life and the bearer of a person's destiny. Akan people know too well that *sunsum* and *ɔkra* are distinct but correlates in constituting each human person. However, the distinction has not always been quite easy for scholars studying Akan religions. The most significant reason for this difficulty has to do with their anthropological conception.

Rattray saw the problem but did not engage it in any sustained manner. He thought it was difficult to distinguish between the two because they sometimes seem synonymous (Rattray 1955: 154). Dietrich Westermann (1875-1956), a German writer, philologist, and student of Akan religions, assumed *sunsum* and *ɔkra* to be one and the same thing.[129] Sam Akesson says, "the distinction between the 'kra and the sunsum is not quite clear nor is it easy to follow" (Akesson 1965: 286).[130] He opined that the difficulty arises from synonymous usage of the two terms. Nevertheless, he believed a distinction is still possible. Akesson called the *ɔkra* the life-soul responsible for life in the body, and the *sunsum* the personality-soul upon which functionality depends. As a functional element, *sunsum* exists only in the

[129] Westermann came to this conclusion after observing a ritual cleansing of the *ɔkra* in a river, which he called the *asumguare*, explained by him as "washing of the sum (=sunsum=okra)" (Tehle 1907: 407). Tehle explained that *asumguare* is a contamination of the Twi phrase *asu mu guare*, which means "washing in the water." Tehle gives the root to why some Akan scholars still believe in the ceremonial washing of the *sunsum*. As it stands now, however, the shreds of evidence do not support that idea. Captain Rattray rectified this error by saying, "an Ashanti would never talk of washing his sunsum" (Rattray 1955: 154). Rattray was aware of the ritual washing of the *ɔkra*, and several scholars favor his position.

[130] The two terms, *kra* and *sunsum*, are capitalized in the original text.

material world. However, he also thought *sunsum* is a conscious counterpart of the *ɔkra* in the body (Akesson 1965: 286). Most philosophers believe consciousness involves thoughts, awareness, and experience. To the Akan, consciousness is a phenomenal experience carried out by the *sunsum*, the inward energy, or the capacity that affects a person's spiritual and emotional disposition.[131] Danquah came to the same conclusion, seeing *sunsum* as "a form of consciousness or embodied one" (Danquah 1944: 116). Akesson further came to grips with the numinous essence of the *ɔkra* as the reality which receives worship and offerings, whereas *sunsum*'s role is to fight the evils that attempt to contaminate the *ɔkra* (Akesson 1965: 286).[132] This observation rightly agrees with Rattray's description of *sunsum* as an advance guard that protects the individual (Rattray 1955: 154).

There are enough reasons to show that Akan people believe the *ɔkra* and *sunsum* are not ontologically identical. Although Gyekye proposes the ontic in unity theory, he does not consider the two to be identical – despite their constitutive spiritual unity. He argues in favor of a nonidentical theory, stating that to characterize the two as "identical would logically mean that whatever can be asserted of one can or must be asserted of the other" (Gyekye 1987: 95). Gyekye is right to see both terms as having their distinctive attributes and predicates that makes them nonidentical.

7.1.1. Characteristics of *Ɔkra*

Gyekye highlights some of the nonidentical attributes or predicates of the two terms with my comments (Gyekye 1987: 95):

131 This does not suggest a dualistic or tripartite conception of the human being where *sunsum* may be seen as an indwelling entity to carry out such animation. Those who think this way often encounter the problem of how *sunsum*, a purely spiritual element, could have any interaction with the *nipadua*, a purely material component.

132 I am not totally convinced about what Akesson had wanted to say here. Akan religions do not associate evil with the *ɔkra*. In fact, Akan people believe no one is born evil, neither can the *ɔkra* become evil. Hence, the *'kra* endowed by Onyame is without evil. This is what Danquah meant when he said evil exists on the *sunsum* side rather than the *'kra* side (Danquah 1968: 87). The *ɔkra* is unconscious to evil. In spite of this, I do agree with Akesson that *sunsum* "tries to conquer the weaknesses to which the Akan is exposed" (Akesson 1965: 286). Instead of the *ɔkra*, it is rather the *nkrabea* (destiny) of the *ɔkra* that *sunsum* tries to protect.

1. "Ne 'kra redi awerɛhoɔ' (His *'kra* is sad). Never his *sunsum* is sad." Many Akan use the statement, *Wo reku me sunsum,* "You're hurting my *sunsum,*" to denote emotional anguish. Since the *ɔkra* is deathless, it is almost a contradiction to say, "*Wo rekum me 'kra*" (You are killing my *ɔkra*) even though the statement is common.
2. "Ne 'kra teetee' (His *'kra* is worried or disturbed)." Alternatively, most Akan will say, *Ne 'kra abotõ,* meaning "My *'kra* is downcast."
3. "Ne 'kra adwane' (His 'kra has run away) to denote someone who is scared to death." The departure of the *ɔkra* signifies death. Hence, the expression is used in the face of danger to one's life.
4. "Ne 'kra ye' (His *'kra* is good), referring to a person who is lucky or fortunate. The negative of this statement is 'His *'kra* is not good.' If you used *sunsum* in place of *'kra*, and made the statement 'His *sunsum* is not good' (*ne sunsum nnye*), the meaning would be quite different; it would mean that his *sunsum* is evil, that is to say, he is an evil spirit, a witch:" A person's *'kra* is the bearer of destiny, i.e., the total expression of a person's wellbeing in life. Prosperity, riches, and everything that progresses an individual's life is attributed to good fate. So, Akan people often say, *Ɔkraa ne Nyame*, literally, "He bid farewell to his God." When used figuratively, it means the person received blessings from God. On the contrary, unfortunate circumstances are attributed to the *'kra*. Akan people will say, *Wo 'kra nyɛ a, wonya asafo nsam amanne"* – "If your soul is not a lucky one, you fall into the hands of a 'company'."[133]
5. "Ne 'kra afi ne ho' (His *'kra* has withdrawn from his body)." This expression means the individual is dead. There is no breathing or functionality of the vital organs.
6. "Ne 'kra dii n'akyi, anka owui' (But for his *'kra* that followed him, he would have died)." Some Akan scholars saw the *'kra* as the double of the individual. My discussion with Meyerowitz has given more details on this subject. Akan people have another expression that goes like this, *Ne ti ye* (His head is good), meaning the person was fortunate.
7. "Ne 'kra aniagye*"* (His *'kra* is happy). In recent times, a statement like *Sunsum sɔre yi Nyame ayɛ* (Arise my *sunsum* to praise God)

[133] Proverb and translation taken from Rattray (1915: 45).

> has become synonymous with *Me kra to dwom,* or "Sing my *'kra.*" The identical conflict is real and wages on.

There are observations to point out in the above analysis. First, the usage of *ɔkra* is more expressive of reflexive sensations or emotions. Note the following expressions, "My *ɔkra* is sad or worried," and "My *ɔkra* is happy." Both involve the awareness of subjective experiences, i.e., conscious feelings. But if the *ɔkra* can feel, why do we reject its entitative nature? Or which one experiences emotions: *ɔkra* or *nipadua* (body)?

There is a relational ontology between the *ɔkra* and body. Gyekye talks of the relationship as "an indissoluble or indivisible unity, and that… a person is a homogeneous entity" (Gyekye 1987: 99). How then is the concept of a person dualistic according to Gyekye? The case for the duality theory is related to the Akan belief of disembodiment of the *ɔkra* and the body at death. Dualists perceive the *ɔkra* as a spiritual entity (substance) of the body with corresponding causal influences, i.e., whatever happens to the body reflects in the conditions of the *ɔkra* and vice versa (Gyekye 1987: 101). A happy *ɔkra* is a healthy body, but a sick body makes the *ɔkra* unhappy. The ritual of soul washing (*Kraguare*) and destiny (*nkrabea*) affirm the reality of the causal relationship.

On the contrary, the quasi-physicalist is anti-dualistic. The human being is hylomorphic, meaning, composed of a non-entitative substance (*ɔkra*) and a material one (*nipadua*). The human body is, therefore, an embodied life. It also accounts for Safro's thought that "as our discovery of physical laws proceeds and our scientific knowledge increases, we may come to accept some or all the quasi-physical objects as bona fide physical objects" (Safro 1992: 193). To the quasi-physicalist, the reflexive emotions of the *ɔkra* are dependent on the thoughts and actions of the body, but not vice versa.

Further, the concept of *ɔkra* is the rationality behind life, livelihood, and death. The *ɔkra* as the determining factor for life is firmly established; that also makes it an underlining factor in the ethical process of life. There are two Akan terms to define life: the first is *nkwa*, often translated in English as "life." *Ɔkra* is life (*nkwa*), literally referring to the biological process of existence, i.e., growth, procreation, etc. Its survival of death grounds the concept of ancestorship and immortality. The second word is *ɔbra*, also translated in English as "life." It is not easy to offer a straightforward definition of *ɔbra*. It appears to me as the whole process of a person's ethical life, and how one lives out one's existence. It thus includes the person's choices and activities in life. The closest concept to *ɔbra* is *nkrabea* (destiny), which signifies the individual's act towards specific goals in life. *Nkrabea* finds its course in *ɔbra* (the ethical life). Both *ɔbra* and *nkrabea* are related to the *ɔkra* in some way. For that reason, Akan people have understood the concept of *sunsum* acting as an advance guard to protect one's *nkrabea* for a commendable ethical life (*abrabɔ*).

7.1.2. Characteristics of *Sunsum*

As for the characteristics of the *sunsum*, Gyekye presents compelling arguments in order to show that it is distinct and never identical with *ɔkra* (Gyekye 1987: 95, 96). I will present his analysis here with my comments.

1. "*Ɔwɔ sunsum* 'He has *sunsum*,' an expression they use when they want to refer to someone as dignified and as having a commanding presence. Here they never say, 'He has *okra*,' soul, for it is believed that it is the nature of the *sunsum* (not the *okra*) that differs from person to person; hence they speak of 'gentle *sunsum*,' 'forceful *sunsum*,' 'weak or strong *sunsum*,' etc." *Sunsum* makes an individual distinct in terms of personality. The Akan phrase, *Wo sunsum* (Your *sunsum*) means it is your distinct intrinsic force or identity. The Akan will also say *Ne sunsum* (His *sunsum*) to talk about the peculiar character of an individual or a thing. Thus, *sunsum* is not foreign to the object in which it is identified. Other expressions may include, "The *sunsum* of the river," "The *sunsum* of the tree," "The *sunsum* of God," etc. Busia concludes that *sunsum* is an individual's ego, personality, distinctive character, and disposition (Busia 1954: 197).
2. "*Ne sunsum yɛ duru* (His *sunsum* is heavy or weighty); this means that the person has a strong personality." The statement shows the dynamic nature of *sunsum*, unlike the *ɔkra*. *Sunsum* can grow from weak to strong or vice versa. It is a constant dynamic force that experiences the intrinsic as well as the external world.
3. "*Ne sunsum hyɛ me so.* 'His *sunsum* overshadows mine.'" Unless the *sunsum* is a force, it cannot overshadow a person. It is a person's *sunsum* that is always seeking for vengeance. The Akan will never

say, *Ne 'kra hyɛ me so* (His *'kra* overshadows mine), because the *'kra* is latent and only a life-force.

4. "*Obi sunsum so kyɛn obi deɛ* 'Someone's *sunsum* is bigger or greater than another's.' 'To say 'someone's *'kra* is greater than another's' would be meaningless.'" There is the reason why a person's *sunsum* can knock down the *sunsum* of another. There is also a reason why some people can resist a witchcraft attack, and others cannot. People with weak *sunsum* are vulnerable to witchcraft attack.
5. "*Ɔwɔ sunsum pa* (He has a good *sunsum*); that is, he is a generous person." So far, the majority of Akan scholars believe the *sunsum* is the operational force for morality. It is responsible for *suban* (character) and personality formation. Human moral and ethical qualities are not dependent on the *ɔkra* but the *sunsum*.

The above expressions of *sunsum* are personality traits of individuals in the material world. Much of the *ɔkra* expresses reflexive emotions relative to life and death. This is not exactly the case with regard to the *sunsum*, which is responsible for the distinctive characteristics of the person in the world of experience. Danquah says a person's *sunsum* is in fact the matter or the physical basis of reality (Danquah 1944: 115). It is the basis of the spiritual sphere from where the individual's distinct features are projected into the world. *Sunsum*, not the *ɔkra*, is what is known in life. Persons are known by their distinct characters. So, Akan people say, *Yɛnim wo a, na yɛnim wo*, "Once we know you, you are known." Social identification is dependent on the individual's *sunsum* or personality, not the *ɔkra*.

The nonidentification of the two terms appears in the definitions of Captain Rattray. He talks of *sunsum* as "that spiritual element in a man or woman upon which depends not life, i.e. breath, for that is the kra – but that force, personal magnetism, character, personality, power, soul, call it what you will, upon which depend health, wealth, worldly power, success in any venture, in fact, everything that makes life worth living" (Rattray 1923: 46).[134] He was again convinced of the paternal transmission of the *sunsum* to the child, and its counterpart with the *ɔkra* in the body. He further talks of the *ɔkra* as the stranger from without (divine). He also says it is the *ɔkra*, rather than the *sunsum*, that causes the body to breathe (Rattray 1927: 154). In sleep, breathing continues because the *ɔkra* does not leave the body as

[134] The *kra* is in capital letters in the original text.

the *sunsum* does in dreams. In its nightly peregrination, Akan people believe the *sunsum* can get knocked about by other *sunsum,* leading the person to fall ill or to die. This is what led Rattray to conclude that "[p]erhaps the *sunsum* is the more volatile part of the whole *'kra*" (Rattray 1927: 154). Captain Rattray explains that oneiromancy, i.e., the reading of omens from dreams, is the natural consequence of the Akan belief in dreams (Rattray 1959: 192).[135] To the Akan, dreams are as real as the physical world.

We can further underline the fact that the *ɔkra*, unlike the *sunsum*, does not attack or seek revenge. It is a general belief among Akan that if a woman is unfaithful to her husband, the *ɔkra* of the man will inform his *ɔbosom* (*ntorɔ*), which will then let his *sunsum* know, and the latter will take revenge on the woman to kill her.[136] The *ɔkra* cannot seize the woman because it "is not volatile in life, as the *sunsum* undoubtedly is" (Rattray 1959: 154). The *sunsum* in my conception is an emanating force from the deities. I will present various arguments in support of this assertion in my discussion below.

7.1.3. *Ɔkra* and Otherworldly Realities

Akesson concluded that *ɔkra* is anthropic, i.e., a characteristic of human beings, never to be identified with animals and trees (Akesson 1965: 287). He relied largely on the ideas of Rattray who had come to a similar conclusion that *ɔkra* "seems to be used only of human beings," since Rattray claimed never to have "heard of the *'kra* of an animal" (Rattray 1959: 153). Asare Opoku shares the same idea (Asare Opoku 1978: 95). Ephirim-Donkor, on the other hand, shares a contrary view: he thinks *ɔkra* is the very

---

[135] Rattray recounts incidences where a dreamer may be liable for committing certain offenses when the person's dream is disclosed. If a person dreams of having sexual relation with a married woman, the dreamer will be fined for committing adultery. It is believed his soul is seeking to desire the soul of that woman. Or as Rattray was also informed, "If you dream that you have had intercourse with a woman with whom you have never had sexual relations, it means that you will never in all your life have sexual intercourse with that woman, because "your soul has already devoured her"" (Rattray 1959: 193).

[136] This is not the case for the man who commits adultery because the *sunsum* of the woman is not strong enough to cease the husband. Akan laws consider adultery a tribal taboo. A man caught in the crime of adultery will be asked to pay adultery damages. But this, of course, will depend on the gravity of the crime. Rattray wrote extensively on the crime of adultery among the Asantes (Rattray 1929: 313-323).

essence of God, and which is present in human beings and all living things (Ephirim-Donkor 1998: 62). He sees *ɔkra* as a life principle for all living things because it takes life to create life, and only God is the giver of life (Ephirim-Donkor 2016: 105).

I fully share the views of Ephirim-Donkor on the *ɔkra* of animals, even if it is inferior to that of the human being. There are statements from Akan folklore to support the view. For example, Ghanaian Highlife music legend, Nana Kwame Ampadu, ascribes *ɔkra* to animals.[137] In the lyrics of his song "*Anibre Nyɛ*" (Covetousness is evil), he says, "*Ɛsono ɔdabo ne 'kra na ɛsono eyuo deɛ. Ɛsono akokɔ ne 'kra na ɛsono brekuo deɛ*" "The 'kra of the bay duiker differs from that of the black duiker. The 'kra of the chicken differs from that of the coucal bird."[138] Similarly, Amakye Dede, another Ghanaian Highlife legend, in the lyrics of the song, "*Sufrɛ Wo Nyame"* (Call upon your God), says: "*Akokɔnini 'kra nso, ɛne obrekuo deɛ nsɛ,*" meaning "The *'kra* of the rooster is unlike the *'kra* of the coucal bird." The rationale behind these statements is their direct reference to destiny, which varies from one person to another. In a much deeper sense, they present facts concerning what informs the Akan mind about life. As proposed by Ephirim-Donkor, life is dependent upon *ɔkra*, and since animals have breath like human beings, they should possess *ɔkra*. How can human beings share *'kra* with inferior creatures like animals? The answer is straightforward: *Ɔkra* is not a homogenous life principle for all living things. Since the *nkrabea* (destiny) of animals differs widely from human beings, it follows that their *'kra* is not the same.

---

[137] Nana Kwame Ampadu was one of the pioneer Akan musicians of the traditional Ghana highlife music. His musical career began in the mid 60's. He remains the most prolific songwriter of all time in Ghana and the diaspora with more than seven hundred songs on albums. In 1973, he was crowned as *Nwontofohene* "King of Musicians" by the Arts Council of Ghana. Highlife is a musical genre which originated from Ghana and later on spread to the Western Anglophone African countries such as Liberia, Sierra Leon, Nigeria and Gambia. The lyrics of Highlife music are based on the traditional values and philosophy of the culture.

[138] *Brekuo* is a kind of brownish bird, with a grey chest, red eyes, and black tail. I have chosen to call it the coucal although others mistakenly call it wood pidgeon. The name of the bird comes from two Akan words, *brɛ* means "tired of too much effort" and *guo* "fruitless." Together, *brekuo* (*brɛguo*) means fruitless effort. There is a legend about the bird that makes Akan people follow its cry as *Me brɛ gu yɛ ya* "My fruitless efforts are painful." The bird reminds Akan people that determination and hard work do not always yield the desired results.

Some people have identified the *ɔkra* with the blood of the mother. Gyekye has disputed the latter as suppressing the Akan concept of disembodiment of the body and life after death (Gyekye 1987: 99). Gyekye perhaps feared such a theory would materialize the *ɔkra*, which Akan people firmly hold as spiritual. Danquah had earlier seen life and blood as co-extensive, though he was not very clear whether he ever associated the *'kra* with blood. He asserted that the usage of "blood is a metaphor for offspring, because upon it hangs the racial life" (Danquah 1944: 179). Akan people do not postulate any other life outside the *ɔkra*, the spark of God. It follows that non-living objects do not have *ɔkra*, since there is no biological experience of life processes. But we know from the start that natural objects are inspirited with *sunsum*.

It is worth noting, in my opinion, that if non-living things, e.g., rocks/stones, for instance, cannot experience any biological process of life, although they are inspirited with *sunsum*, then we can conclude that *sunsum* is not the spirit of life, neither is it synonymous with the *ɔkra*.

7.1.4. The Meaning of *Sãsã*, the Revengeful Spirit

Akesson thought animals have *sãsã* (the revengeful or agitated spirit) instead of *ɔkra* (Akesson 1965: 287). The assumption is not altogether clear. My analysis in the previous section answered the question of animals having *ɔkra* as their principle of life. What then is *sãsã* among the Akan?

The basic idea of *sãsã* is the spirit of the deceased that has become an agitated spirit in the limbo (Ephirim-Donkor 2008: 76). The Akan word *sa* is polysemic and can mean the following: "to dance," "to gather," "to be picky," etc. It is also used to describe a situation in which a person or thing is following or stalking or pursuing. For example, *Adɛn na wo sã me saa*? "Why are you pursuing me?" Or, *Ɔsã no* "He is being followed."[139] In these two instances of the usage of *sã*, the repetitive form *sãsã* will give the idea of persistent pursuit. With that in mind, we understand Rattray's definition of *sãsã* as "the invisible spiritual power of a person or animal, which disturbs the mind of the living, or works a spell or mischief upon them, so that they suffer in various ways... [It] is essentially the bad, revengeful, and hurtful element in a spirit" (Rattray 1959: 153). People who die in battle, are executed or murdered, are said to hunt their perpetrators by their *sãsã*.

---

139 The root word *sa*, is given extensive explanation in Christaller (1881: 398-402).

According to Rattray, persons who are always taking life, such as executioners, hunters, butchers, and, as a later development, sawyers who cut down great forest trees, are vulnerable to *sãsã* influence and attacks (Rattray 1959: 153).

Akesson further says *sãsã* is that part of the deceased spirit which is conscious of the cause or nature of the person's death (Akesson 1965: 288). This observation is true. The *sãsã*, having known the cause of its death, pursues the murderer to cause a state of mental agitation or remorseful feeling until the person confesses, commits suicide, or is killed by the *sãsã*. Hence, Akan people will say, "*Ne sãsã annya no*," literally (as translated by Akesson), "His revengeful spirit has got him or his *Sãsã* has rendered him weak." It seems to me that there is no apparent difference between *sãsã* and *saman* (ghost), except that the former is revengeful and the latter travels to *Asamando*.[140] If that is the case, then it follows that *sãsã* is the same as the departing *ɔkra* that has become agitated.[141] The only part of a living thing that can survive death to act in this respect is the *ɔkra*. Therefore, my conclusion is that *sãsã* is related to the *ɔkra*, but not to the *sunsum*. If this is correct, it is as I see it a compelling sign that animals indeed have their own proper life principle (*ɔkra*).

We can further be sure that *sãsã* is neither exclusive to animals nor human beings. Akan people do not consider all animals as having *sãsã*. There are certain animals known as *sãsã mmoa* "*sãsã* animals." Rattray enlists the

---

140 The etymology of the word *saman* is disputed. There are some who take the prefix *sa*, as explained earlier, to mean "finish" or "end." The suffix *man* (or *mang*) means "nation" or "community." *Saman* then is someone without the nation or out of the living community. Hence, others say *w'asa wɔ 'man mu* "He is done or finished with the living." Akesson (1965: 289, 290) explained the word in this sense: "The Akan word OSAMANG is descriptive of the privileged powers which death grants the ghost-soul of the deceased Akan. The root word SA means "to run after"; the suffix MANG means "the body of inhabitants of a country united under the same government, a nation, tribe, people or state." The name OSAMANG could be understood as the person from the body of inhabitants who run after the violator of the customs. The prefix "O" is the third person singular in the Akan grammar. The ghost-souls or the spirits of the dead watch the affairs of the state with keen eyes, and it is well known that they do not let a member of a community who may break a taboo go unpunished. Literally speaking, Osamang runs after those who violate the customs laid down by the ancestor."

141 Several Akan drama and movies showcase this aspect of the Akan culture of *sãsã* and *saman*. In some instances, the *sãsã* of the murdered has been called *saman*. The movie industry has become an avenue to showcase most Akan traditions.

following: "the bongo (*otromo*); the elephant (*esono*); the roan (*oko*); the waterbuck (*fusuo*); the duyker (*otwe*); a very small antelope called *adowa*; the black duyker (*ewiyo*); the yellow-backed duyker (*kwaduo*). Of all these *sãsã* animals, the bongo is the most dangerous and most feared" (Rattray 1959: 183). *Sãsã* can be repelled by following certain spiritual practices such as putting on amulets or bathing *sãsã duro* (*sãsã* antidote).

7.2. The Relationship between *Sunsum* and *Ntorɔ*

The social anthropologist has little difficulty in studying the *ntorɔ* - thanks to the vast extent of materials existing on the subject today. Rattray had to extact this knowledge from the memory of the Asantes. He, in particular, thought *ntorɔ* was synonymous with *nton*, *sunsum*, or *ɔbosom* (god) (Rattray 1959: 318). Later studies, however, suggest that *ntorɔ* is not synonymous with *nton*, or with *sunsum* (Danquah 1968; Busia 1954; Denteh 1967; Gyekye 1987; and others). As for Rattray's later assumption of the *ɔbosom*, there is no doubt as to its affinity with *ntorɔ*. Most Akan scholars accept *ntorɔ* as a tutelary spiritual attribute. My analysis in previous chapters agrees with the others. The relationship between *ntorɔ* and *sunsum* is the focus of this section.

7.2.1. The Meaning of *Ntorɔ*

In this study, I have defined *ntorɔ* as a social biogenetic responsible for paternal group membership, proto-psychological temperaments, and character resemblance (not physical) of the father or his patrilineage. *Ntorɔ* determines the "physiological mysteries of conception" (Rattray 1923: 46). During sexual intercourse, a man transmits his *ntorɔ* through the semen to mingle with the *mogya* of the woman. This biological process may equal what is scientifically known as fertilization in human reproduction. But among native Akan, conception is beyond biological formation. A child is composed of several spiritual elements, namely the *ntorɔ* of the father, the *sunsum* of the father, the *sunsum* of the person after whom a child is named, the *sunsum* of an ancestor from the mother's lineage, and *sunsum* of tutelary deities related to the child (Denteh 1967: 92).

Every Akan belongs to *ntorɔ* group, in the same way each of them belongs to *abusua*.[142] The father's lineage determines the *ntorɔ* group membership, whereas the mother's bloodline determines the *abusua* group membership. Despite these two significant social groupings, Akan people place more importance on the *abusua* group membership than the *ntorɔ*. One reason is the fact that Akan citizenship is by the *abusua*, not *ntorɔ*. Rattray understood the *abusua* differently from the *ntorɔ*, in the sense that it determines the whole succession of property (Rattray 1923: 37). The idea is conveyed in the proverb, *Ɔba sɛ ɔse nanso ɔdan ne na abusua,* meaning "A child may look like the father, nevertheless he is dependent upon the mother's *abusua*." The male *ntorɔ* is only protective and psychological. The *ntorɔ* of the male child is inherited or transferable at death to the man's next of kin, mostly the nephew. In contrast, *ɔkra* and *sunsum* are not transferable.[143] The *ntorɔ* of the female returns to its source (i.e., the river deity) at death. How does the tutelary concept of the *ntorɔ* affect gender roles among the Akan?

---

142 Akan marital taboos are construed after the *ntorɔ* ideology. People of the same *ntorɔ* group are not permitted to marry in the same way persons of the same *mogya* or *abusua* cannot marry themselves. This taboo is one of the surviving taboos in some modern Akan societies. The twelve charismatic traits of the *ntorɔ* of the Akan with their twelve tutelary deities are: *Bosompra* (Tough/Strong/Firm), *Bosomtwe* (Humane /Empathetic), *Bosompo*/*Bosomnkóteaa* (Proud/Audacious), *Bosomafram* (Liberal/Kind/Empathetic), *Bosommuru* (Respectable/ Distinguished), *Bosomkonsi* (The Virtuous), *Bosomdwerébe* (Eccentric/Jittery), *Bosomayensu* (Truculent), *Bosomsika* (Fastidious), *Bosomkrete* (Chivalrous), *Bosomakim* (Fanatic), *Bosomafi* (Chaste). The *Bosommuruntorɔ* is the name of the golden sword held by the Asante king to swear allegiance to the kingdom. It is believed to be the most important of all the *ntorɔ* divisions. In 2002, the late and former United Nations Secretary, Kofi Annan, was conferred with the title of *Bosommuru* by Otumfuo Osei Tutu II, Supreme King of the Asante kingdom in Ghana, for his distinguished humanitarian service.

143 *Sunsum* is not transferable as underlined in the study. It ceases its operation upon the death of the individual. However, *sunsum* cannot be destroyed. In cases where a child is named after an ancestor, the *sunsum* of that ancestor may come upon the child whereupon the child will exhibit similar character or charismatic traits of that ancestor. This happens because the naming ceremony takes place on the eighth day after the birth of the child when he is still under the protection of the father's *sunsum*. It is believed that a child masters his own *sunsum* when he has come of age. Here, we have every reason to understand why the operation of *sunsum* is spiritual. Besides this, *sunsum* is not inherited in the same manner as the *ntorɔ* is inherited.

Akan people consider the essence of the deities to be masculine. This masculine character is the reason why only males are capable of transmitting *ntorɔ*. Ephirim-Donkor sees the masculine essence of the deities to be essentially the attributes retained in terms of the activity of the child in life (Ephirim-Donkor 2016: 83). He thinks the father is a representative of the *abosom* whose *sunsum* he draws upon to protect his offspring (Ephirim-Donkor 2016: 82-83). Rattray called the *ntorɔ* the male totemic spirit from a father to his offspring. He also added: "Like all supernatural elements it is powerful" (Rattray 1956: 8). The *ntorɔ* is powerful because it is part of the essential qualities of the deities whose essence are *sunsum*.

7.2.2. The Difference between *Ntorɔ* and *Sunsum*

Too often, many people tend to confuse *ntorɔ* with *sunsum*, as if the two were synonymous terms. Rattray wrote that *ntorɔ* "appears to be used at times synonymously with *sunsum*" (Rattray 1923: 46). The reason for this assumption, in my opinion, might have been the idea that both *ntorɔ* and *sunsum* are derived indirectly from the father. Such confusion is bound to occur, especially when one observes the characteristics of the *ntorɔ* and *sunsum* as personality traits. However, the two are not synonymous, even if they are relative in some respect. In my previous discussion with Busia, some of the similarities were analyzed.

The distinction drawn by Busia follows that "*ntorɔ* is the generic term of which *sunsum* is a specific instance" (Busia 1954: 197). What does Busia mean by the term "generic?" Does it mean the general kind of common class of species from which emerge other specific characters? Or could it be related to the concept of the *abusua* where several kinsmen are connected in a natural affinity? More plausibility supports the latter since Busia concluded: "A man's *sunsum* is a child of his *Ntorɔ*; and all who belong to the same *Ntorɔ* are believed to have similar *sunsum*. Hence, it can be rightly said that a man transmits his *ntorɔ* to his children" (Busia 1954: 198). The analogy used here is directly pointing to the traditional concept of a father-child relationship. In conclusion, *sunsum* is the result of the *ntorɔ* (*ɔbosom*).

Now, we have a puzzle to solve. There is an identification of the *ntorɔ* with the *sunsum*, which shares a measure of ontological relationality with it. To accept that relationship is to admit also that *sunsum* is the spiritual essence of the *ntorɔ* (*ɔbosom*), incarnated in its spiritual dispositions as ego, personality, and distinctive character of an individual in life. The experience of the individual in the world is a direct reflection of the mysteries of the spiritual bond that exists between the father's family and the pantheon deities. Busia accepted this view: he talked of *sunsum* as the personal power or cast of countenance from the father (Busia 1954: 197). Akan rituality, indeed, recognizes and affirms these mysteries in diverse religious ceremonies, which in effect become the source of profound practices that the skeptic or the foreigner may see as mere superstition. An example is the ritual of *ntorɔ* washing, which is a ceremonial bathing in the *ntorɔ* river or in a basin with water fetched from the river in case the ceremony takes place indoors.[144]

Given the above explanation of the relationship between *ntorɔ* and *sunsum*, we have little doubt to question how the father imparts his *sunsum* to his offspring. We have one more question left to answer: how does one differentiate the nature of the *ntorɔ* from that of the *sunsum*?

Scholars of Akan religions have accepted *ntorɔ* as the semen which a man transmits to a woman during sexual intercourse. In *Ashanti*, Captain Rattray writes, "the semen is actually sometimes called *ntoro*" (Rattray 1923: 37). He repeated this statement, writing that "the male-transmitted *ntoro* (spirit) seems sometimes used in the sense of semen" (Rattray 1923: 78). Parrinder calls the *ntorɔ* a seminal soul (Parrinder 1951: 20, 58). Some Akan informants in Wasa-Amanfi in the Western region of Ghana told Meyerowitz that *ntorɔ* is related to *wo ho nsu*, 'the water of yourself,' i.e.,

---

[144] Some of the rituals include the *washing* days, i.e., special days reserved for the *ntorɔ* group. These days are set aside for the pacification of the individual. In most cases, if a person wants to know the *ntorɔ* to which you belong, the person may ask you, "*Wo guare ntorɔ bɛn*," literally, "Which *ntorɔ* group do you *wash* or *bath* (belong))." The idea of washing infers to the ceremony of washing during these ceremonial days of the *ntorɔ*. Rattray observed one of these ceremonies in the following words, "Every Tuesday the King of Ashanti 'washed' in his own palace while all the chiefs and populace went to the Suben River. Here the people of lesser importance entered the water and bathed, while for those of more importance water was drawn in brass pans and taken up on the banks. Some water was also drawn from the special spot called *kwasu* and put in a gold *kuduo* (called *akra yawa*, souls' basin), and this was brought back to the palace and placed in a room known as *Bosommurudan* (*Bosommuru* room), sometimes called *Akrafieso* (Souls' House) …The ordinary person does not wash every week when his *ntoro* day comes round, but when his *obosom* (god) tells him that he should, and when, as my informant said, 'it is thought necessary'" (Rattray 1923: 52, 53).

semen (1951: 28). Gyekye came to a similar conclusion, seeing *ntorɔ* as "sperm-transmitted characteristic" by relating it to genetic factors responsible for inherited characteristics (Gyekye 1987: 94). Other scholars agree (Wiredu 1990: 244; Ephirim-Donkor 2016: 82).

The idea of *ntorɔ* as a tutelary spirit stem from its watery nature. Rattray states: "the *ntoro* element in man seems to be often connected with water or liquid, such as saliva, in some form, and from it to have derived its origin" (Rattray 1923: 53, 54).[145] He further added that "water has a divine origin – it comes from Onyame, the greatest of Gods – the Sky God" (Rattray 1923: 54). As Akan people associate water with the pantheon deities, so it follows that *ntorɔ* (*ɔbosom*) is nothing but the semen. Meyerowitz surmised everything in the following words: "Just as a male river fertilizes the female land, so the husband causes his wife to conceive, and therefore river water and semen became equated. The husband has to mould his character after the river sacred to his *ntorɔ*, and he has to adopt the characteristics which the river (or lake) is believed to possess" (Meyerowitz 1951: 29I).

The conclusion we reach from the above analysis is that the semen is the material form of the *ntorɔ* (*ɔbosom*), from which emanates the *sunsum*, the immaterial form. This conclusion answers the question of the spiritual origins of the *sunsum*, and it explains why the father's *ntorɔ* is so powerful. The traditional Akan, through their religious expressions, have known the secrets of biological mysteries of life of which today's advanced science appear to confirm.

To sum up, we have seen that Akan people will not say a man transmits his *sunsum*, but rather that he transmits his *ntorɔ* to his offspring. In this sense, we understand *sunsum* to have its mysterious mode of passage from the father to the child, which from my analysis is associated with the *ntorɔ*, the *ɔbosom* (spirit) incarnate, or literally the semen. Minkus was convinced that "the father's transmission of his *sunsum* [is] by means of the semen"

---

145 The Akan Twi word *ntorɔ* can mean "to lie to someone." The root *toro* means slippery or slimy. For example, Akan people use the word to describe the slimy nature of *okro*/*okra* vegetable. The word is also used to describe a slippery surface. In some instances, the *toro* is used to refer to a sharp object that can no longer cut sharply. For example, *wo be toro sekan no ano*, means "You'll destroy the cutting edge of the cutlass." Or, when a charm loses its powerful effect, Akan people will say *aduro no ano atoro*, meaning, "the spell has lost its effectiveness." It is not a coincidence that semen is associated with *ntorɔ* because of its slimy or slippery nature.

(Minkus 1980: 186). *Sunsum*, therefore, is the force, energy, or the emanating spiritual power that accompanies the *ntorɔ*. Here, it becomes logical to infer once again that if *ntorɔ* does not follow the deceased to *Asamando*, as already established, then the *sunsum* does not either, since the former is the source of the latter. For any theologization of *sunsum* to be meaningful, the essential power of *sunsum* cannot be detached from its source, herein seen as the pantheon deities. This is the reason why my conclusions favor the claim made by Busia that all who belong to the same *ntorɔ* are believed to have a similar *sunsum*.

7.3. The Relationship between *Sunsum* and *Suman* (charm)

Suman is an Akan term often translated in English as a "charm." Most English dictionaries define charm as any inspirited object kept or worn to ward off evil and bring good luck. Synonymous words include amulets, talismans, and mascots. Rattray translated *suman* as fetish, an English term erstwhile missionaries regularly used in describing Akan traditional religions (Rattray 1923: 90, 91; 1959: 9-24). Recent research has concluded that the term "fetish" is not appropriate to describe Akan traditional religions (Idowu 1973; Asare Opoku 1978; Ephirim-Donkor 2016). However, Rattray's characterization of suman as "fetish" is correct because it is a part of the objects of thc Akan traditional religions.

According to Rattray, *suman* "is an object which is the potential-dwelling place of spirit or spirits of an inferior status...closely associated with the control of the powers of evil or black magic, for personal ends, but not necessarily to assist the owner to work evil since it is used as much for defensive as for offensive purposes" (Rattray 1959: 23). Both Dickson and Danquah came to a similar conclusion, viewing *suman* as a repository object of power worn on the body for protection and as a mascot for luck (Danquah 1944: x, 7).

When compared to what Rattray, Minkus, and Gyekye wrote on this aspect of Akan superstition, Danquah and others had little to say about it. Minkus was right to follow her academic predecessors in viewing *suman* as something you hold, giving the idea of "a material object such as a pot, leather pouch, beads, broom, headband, etc. which may be worn on the person or put in the user's house or, in the case of a bad *suman* in the victim's house" (1981: 188). *Asuman* (pl) are inspirited objects believed to contain some form of power. Inspirited objects are not in themselves distinct spiritual but votary objects of spiritual beings. In other words, we can adequately characterize *suman* as a channel of spiritual force emanating from a spiritual agent. There is a legend that says human beings learned the preparation of *suman* from dwarfs who are said to possess magical powers (Rattray 1923: 23; Minkus 1981: 188).

There is one important question which we must now consider, and which concerns the use of idols to represent the *ɔbosom* in shrines. Should one consider the idols as *suman*? As pointed above, early colonial writers mistakenly classified the *ɔbosom* as fetish, and their priests "fetish priests." The implication demonized the Akan religions as without any divine revelation. Although Rattray dealt with that erroneous interpretation, its consequences remain in the memory of some Akan who perceive the *ɔbosom* as *suman* and often confuse *ɔbosom* with the idols. However, the *ɔbosom* is a spirit that the Akan experience through objects. The carved objects are never called *asuman* by the Akan. Rattray treats this subject with great caution and precision. In general, Rattray makes the following distinctions between *ɔbosom* and *suman* (1959: 22-23):

1. An *ɔbosom* (shrine of a god) is carried and has its own *ɔkomfoɔ* (priest) who gives oracular utterances. *Suman* have not their *ɔkomfoɔ,* though an *ɔkomfoɔ* may have *suman* of his own.
2. *Suman* may form a part of an *ɔbosom*, but the two are themselves distinct.
3. The main power of the *ɔbosom* comes directly or indirectly from Nyame, the Supreme God, whereas the power in *suman* may come from *sunsum* of plants or trees, and sometimes – directly or indirectly – from fairies, forest monsters, witches, etc.
4. An *ɔbosom* is the god of the many, the family, the clan, or the nation. *Suman* is personal and helps its owner personally.

The differentiation given by Rattray implies that *ɔbosom* and *suman* are not synonymous. Even though Rattray asserts that *suman* may form a part of the *ɔbosom*, the two are not identical. The distinction between them, in my view, is more about their nature rather than in the actual exercise of their power. Gyekye sees the distinction in reverse, that is, they are not distinct by nature as they are in the actual exercise of their powers (Gyekye 1987: 74). I will reaffirm further that *ɔbosom* is a spiritual agent, but *suman* is not.

Dickson underlined that *asuman* derive their power from the *ɔbosom* (Danquah 1944: x). The superiority of the *ɔbosom* permits the extension of their powers to other elements for mystical activities such as protection and luck for people. *Suman*, on the other hand, is man-made, not a shrine, and derives its source of power from the combined forces (*sunsum*) of nature and spirits of its materials. This is the reason why a traditional priest once told Rattray that Ta Kora, the great *ɔbosom*, needs no help from ordinary *suman* (Rattray 1923: 182).

It is not a taboo to put on *suman* among Akan people. So, the one who wears a *suman* cannot be prejudiced as seeking to harm others, unless in the cases of people with a bad *suman* (*adubɔne*) which they normally cast on the path, house, farm or the immediate environs of their victims. However, this latter use of *suman* seems to be a misuse of its original intent. As Rattray pointed out, *suman* is for defensive purposes rather than for attacks.

Akan kingship has an office, called *Nsumankwaa* division, comprising individuals who are in charge of spiritual medicines used for protecting the king. The *Nsumankwaahene* (the chief of the *Nsumankwaa*) is in charge of the royal physicians, and he is the chief spiritualist who sits on the left side of the king, forming part of the left wing of the throne.[146] His position on the left side of the king is strategic. The position makes him a point of contact before anyone shakes hands with the king, as Akan people shake hands from right to left. The *Nsumankwaahene* will avert any spiritual attack intended to harm the king. He ensures the protection of the king in all public functions and takes care of his traditional medicines; he is also the custodian of the *asuman* in the *Nsumanfieso* (room for keeping the *asuman*). We can observe how much of *sunsum* surround the kingship. The idea of *suman* shows how traditional medicinal experts can manipulate the *sunsum* of natural objects to their advantage.

There is one significant aspect that needs to be mentioned as it is crucial to understanding the relationship between *suman* and *sunsum*, that is, the

---

[146] The political administration of Akan kingship functions like a military regiment because it was originally created for warfare. The divisions include *Gyasehene* (leader of interior affairs), *Adontenhene* (Chief commander of the whole army), *Twafohene* (leader of the advance guard), *Benkumhene* (leader of the left division), *Nifahene* (leader of the right division), *Kyidomhene* (leader of the rear-party division), and *Ankobeahene* (leader of the body-guard of the Chief) (Rattray 1929: 90). These regimental divisions form the order of seating in all public functions.

Golden Stool, the shrine of the *sunsum* of the Asantes. As explained in previous chapters, the Golden Stool descended from the sky under the auspice of the great traditional priest Ɔkomfo Anɔkye. It is believed to represent the unity and authority of the Asante nation. Anɔkye assured the Asantes of the potency of the Stool to bestow prosperity and to ward off adversity. The fact that the Golden Stool contains the *sunsum* of Asantes does not make it a *suman*. The degree of its intrinsic *sunsum* makes it supernatural, enabling it to exercise a wide scope of protection over all the Asantes.

The Stool forms the basis of the political unification of the Asante kingdom. Some aspects of the Stool are anthropological; for example, it bears a name following the pattern of Akan "day names." The Asantes call it *Sika Dwa Kofi*, "The Golden Stool born on Friday" (Kyerematen 1969). To maintain its potency, it receives sacrifices and food offerings after the manner of rituals performed for the *ɔkra* of an individual. Kyerematen notes that there are several *asuman* added to the Golden Stool by the Asante kings. Therefore, we can deduce that *suman* is a wearable object and cannot be identified with the *Sika Dwa Kofi,* which is the shrine of the whole nation.

We may thus conclude that the power of *suman* is derived from the *sunsum* of spiritual entities, which by their essential qualities as spirit-beings extend their potency in material objects to protect beneficiaries in the physical world. *Suman* is another expression of Akan beliefs in the supernatural.

In contrast to *akɔm*, where a spiritual deity selects his own agent, *suman* is a general commodity: people benefit from its economy. Whoever wears *suman* believes it can fetch greater luck and protection. This raises the question of how much or what degree of *sunsum* does a person need for protection? Whether a person has a strong or weak *sunsum*, the rationale behind *suman* is a power greater than oneself. The owner of *suman* may be aware or oblivious of its source of power, especially those bought from the marketplace. The spiritual ingredients of *suman* will exert its power as long as its taboos are observed. Minkus found out that not all *suman* might require periodic rituals to keep them. Only few of them may require ritual ceremonies (Minkus 1981: 188).

As long as a *suman* is properly handled, there is no limit in the execution of its power. On the contrary, a violation of its taboos, or contact with what is inimical, may render a *suman* ineffective, making its activating *sunsum* impotent and exposing the person to attacks (Minkus 1981: 188). Akan people usually say *Aduro n'ano atoro* – "the charm has lost its potency." A *suman* losing the potency of its *sunsum* is equivalent to an individual who loses his or her life when the *sunsum* is knocked about. It follows that every inspirited object is bound to lose its *sunsum* or its power when desecrated by inimical practices unless the necessary ritual is performed, and in this case the *suman* is no exception. *Sunsum*, defined in this present study as an emanating spiritual force, is indestructible. Although certain taboos may render it weak, or a more powerful *sunsum* may overcome it, only a disconnect with its primary possessor (the human being or an object) will occur. *Sunsum* will always return to its source. This concept is an underlining principle in Akan cosmology.

8. General Conclusion

Throughout this study, I have reached some specific conclusions on the nature of *sunsum* and shown the various possibilities of analyzing it. Generally, Akan people believe in an inspirited universe in which everything is animated and interpenetrated by an immaterial force or power called *sunsum*. The overall implication has been that everything in its natural state is inspirited to exercise power. Hence, the relationship between nature and the Akan is the most sacred thing. It is the source of the Akan's energy and their link to the supernatural. Scholars of Akan religions grapple with the nature of *sunsum* – whether it is supposed to be a "spirit" or spiritual force.

Through a historiographical investigation, I identified the different schools of thought within the historical-scholarly discussions regarding the nature of *sunsum*. Christaller, the chief architect of Twi scholarship, translated *sunsum* as soul, i.e., the spirit of the human being, and in most part of his publications, especially the Twi translation of the Bible, he used *honhom* to translate the divine spirit in the entire Bible. Captain Rattray, by far the most distinguished European anthropologist of Akan religions, translates *sunsum* as both soul and spirit, giving way to a pneumatic view of *sunsum*. Danquah, the first indigenous scholar to launch a thorough investigation into Akan religions, rejects the pneumatic view of *sunsum* by erstwhile foreign writers. He designates *sunsum* as only a prototype called *esu* (nature) from God and the basis of personality, not spirit. Meyerowitz regards *sunsum* as the personal soul, the ego or conscious part of the individual. She likens *sunsum* to a shadow and concludes that it is the *sunsum* that becomes an ancestor after death. Busia thought of *sunsum* as a spiritual gift responsible for personality, personal power, and a spiritual bond between a father and child. The overall understanding of Busia makes *sunsum* only a personality or charisma. Minkus climaxes the pneumatic construction of *sunsum* by her two categories of the nature of *sunsum*: the exclusively spiritual (*ye sunsum*), and the inspirited, i.e., those that have *sunsum* (*wɔ sunsum*). Ephirim-Donkor defines *sunsum* in relation to the *Abosom* (pantheon deities) whose essence are thought to be *sunsum*, and the transmission of their *sunsum* results in creating human beings. Hence, the human being is the *Ɔbosom* incarnate.

In contemporary Akan philosophy, the approach to the study of *sunsum* shifts from objectivity to subjective interpretation. Wiredu challenges the pneumatic character of *sunsum* as not outrightly spirit, but quasi-material. He does not translate *sunsum* into English in order to prevent compromising Akan philosophical ideas. His philosophy of quasi-physicalism argues that there is nothing spiritual in Akan religious ideas except what is quasi-physical or quasi-material. Safro accepts Wiredu's quasi-physicalism. Gyekye and Majeed, on the other hand, oppose the philosophy of quasi-physicalism and argue that it is philosophically indefensible. Their argument favors the pneumatic nature of *sunsum* as correctly a "spirit."

Besides the different perspectives each scholar draws from the discussion, I have shown in the study that they do not disagree much on the reality of *sunsum* as a spiritual essence or substance of natural objects, i.e., all things are inspirited with the potential quality for good or evil. Therefore, the Akan is aware of the spiritual world and how spirits and spiritual forces impinge on the physical. As a result of this background, my research raises some fundamental questions about whether *sunsum* may serve as the basis of a contextual Akan Christian pneumatology, or whether there are other ways to speak of contextual Akan Christian pneumatology. How do we speak of the Holy Spirit among the Akan people of West Africa?

Throughout the study, I used the term Akan pneumatology to articulate the concept of spirits and the spiritual in Akan cosmology. My research has carried out a critical investigation into the spiritual worldview of the Akan people, particularly on *sunsum*, to understand the notion of the "spirit" and how that understanding affects a contextual application of the doctrine of the Holy Spirit. These have been the main theses that have occupied the entire study, and my answer has been that *sunsum* as an Akan spiritual reality, emanating force responsible for personality development, and an essential quality of objects and "beings," is correct. With reference to the question whether there is another possibility of speaking about Akan pneumatology, my research has answered this question with a categorical and firm yes, and that opens up new possibilities for articulating contextual Akan Christian pneumatology.

I will now move to propose some approaches towards the study of contextual Akan Christian pneumatology for the future. This shows that my research is not an end in itself but a means to an end. The entire study has shown that there is a growing interest in African pneumatology. This growing interest is not detached from the way the majority of African people want to live their lives. In the end, contextual Christian pneumatology is a spiritual revival that has a profound impact on questions of identity, i.e., the "being" of the human and its various paradigms of human progress. It seeks to elevate ethical and moral standards for people to live by the spiritual values of the Spirit. This kind of a pneumatological framework requires serious research by and among theologians, and the adoption of right approaches. Methodologies help researchers to review specific procedures, from both present and historical information available and relevant to the research subject. The approaches in the next paragraphs are proposed to recognize the different pathways to the study of contextual pneumatology.

The first is a historiographical approach to contextual pneumatology. A historiographical approach traces the historical development of the construction of Akan spirituality throughout the various phases of Akan scholarship. It investigates ideas that have impacted and shaped the thinking of scholars with the purpose of drawing the best possible perspective from the theories, interpretations, and approaches employed by different Akan scholars. With this approach, two things need to be considered, that is, 'emic' and 'etic' perspectives. The emic approach takes an objective view from the cultural context, whereas the etic approach is a descriptive view of the researcher's own understanding. A historiographical approach should deal with both approaches to clearly spell out an indigenous conception from ideas of the researcher. This in no way means a reduction of any evolution of cultural ideas; instead, it ensures that adaptations and dynamisms are properly construed. In keeping with this, a historiographical approach attempts to assess the various ideological developments in Akan pneumatology and the contradictions existing between the historiographical framework and theoretical ideas. When it comes to the meaning and nature of spirits among the Akan, there are various theories existing, including ideological discrepancies, disguised Christian ideas, and subjective ideas. Therefore, a historiographical approach will help future researchers to investigate the ideological dynamisms of the historical thinking of scholars, and how that investigation impacts on academic discussions.

The second is the anthropological approach to contextual Christian pneumatology. Anthropological studies on Akan pneumatology were basically the works of Christaller, Rattray, Meyerowitz, Busia, Minkus, and Ephirim-Donkor. Their approach was anthropological due to its focus on sociocultural elements of Akan religions: folklore, rituals, beliefs, taboos, and symbols. Several other scholars have significantly contributed to this area of research. Early anthropologists used an ethnographic approach to conclude that *sunsum* is the basis of Akan spirituality. A majority of them regarded *sunsum* as a patrilineal spirit responsible for personality formation and the basis for a person's spirituality. Further investigation shows that *sunsum* is indirectly a divine spiritual element manifesting itself through the pantheon deities and finally through the father to his child. That conclusion is not limited to the human being, but to the natural objects. The anthropological approach should acknowledge the current evolution of Akan spiritual realities and their appropriate definition of the human being and society. Students of Akan contextual Christian pneumatology should be able to explore and establish that there is apparently no distinction between the spirit of the human being and the divine spirit. As a consequence, they should be able to reconstruct Akan pneumatology from a single object of God's omnipresence.

The third is a philosophical approach to contextual pneumatology. A philosophical approach deals with questions and logical constructs of conceptualizations. Its purpose is to analyze results of events in a logical and scientific method. Akan philosophers of *sunsum* use epistemological and critical analyses of available information to explain the spirituality of the human being. Notable scholars in this field include Danquah, Kwasi Wiredu, Kwame Gyekye, Kwame Safro, and Majeed. These philosophers approach Akan studies from an analytical subjectivism. Different opinions exist among the philosophers concerning the nature of the *sunsum*. For instance, Danquah thinks it is only an experience or personality and not necessarily a spirit. When Danquah said Onyankopɔn is the *Sunsum* of Odomankoma, he did not mean to say Nyankopɔn is a spirit or is spiritual but is instead an experience or personality of Odomankoma in the world (Danquah 1968: 113). Wiredu and Safro think *sunsum* is quasi-material and not pneumatic as it perishes with the deceased. Wiredu is not convinced that a spirit can perish since it is supposed to be immortal. Gyekye and Majeed emphatically regard *sunsum* as a spirit contrary to the philosophy of quasi-physicalism. Gyekye's understanding of *sunsum* and *ɔkra* turns out to be constitutive of a single entity. The philosophical arguments in the larger context of Akan studies reveal the value the scholars place in search of a better understanding of Akan pneumatology. Future contextual Akan Christian pneumatology should consider all the philosophical assumptions to align (not disregard) them to the research methodology. With the philosophy of quasi-physicalism, a contextual Akan Christian pneumatology based on a philosophical assumption is almost here with us. In other words, theologians should prepare to embrace an open discussion from various interpretations of Akan concepts of the spirit and to engage with them responsibly.

The fourth is a theological approach to contextual pneumatology. There are different theological methods existing simply because different perspectives of faith and religion exist. In general, a theological approach is a scientific study of religion that seeks to understand the ways in which the internal tenets of a particular religion or religions are understood or expressed in a rational way for its adherents. This approach is content based, i.e., internal analyses of information deriving from within the particular religious context. Within the Akan religions, a theological approach has been an ongoing work and this, to a greater extent, underlies the study of Akan pneumatology. For example, Danquah, Busia, and Minkus related *sunsum* indirectly to God. Gyekye defines *sunsum* as mystical, unempirical, and nonphysical. He categorically refers to it as deriving from Onyame with a strong emphasis that *sunsum* is "a universal spirit, manifesting itself differently in the various beings and objects in the natural world" (Gyekye 1987: 69-73). The conception designates *sunsum*, from the onset, as the essence of God manifesting in a panentheistic manner. All these definitions are theological motives of some sort about Akan religions. The theological approach heightens upon the introduction of Agyarko's *sunsum* pneumatology. Agyarko's use of an ecumenical approach in dialogue with Akan religions is a significant step towards the outcomes of theological methodologies in the studies of Akan pneumatology. Theological branches such as practical theology, biblical studies, systematic and ethics, and history of Christianity, and their subdivisions are all capable of theologizing a contextual Akan Christian pneumatology.

The fifth is a scientific approach to contextual pneumatology. Should we envision an empirical approach to the study of Akan pneumatology? My answer to this question is affirmative. With this, I am not referring to the post-modern idea of spiritual but not religious; rather, I am interested in a more progressive view that will allow scientists to discover that the Akan notion of *sunsum* is compatible with physical science. Kwame Safro is keen about this when he writes, "the modern quasi-physicalist does not deny that as our discovery of physical laws proceeds and our scientific knowledge increases, we may come to accept some or all the quasi-physical objects as bona fide physical objects" (Safro 1992: 193). Quasi-physicalism is a philosophical term that describes a category of objects that lie between the world of natural objects and the realm of the spiritual or immaterial. Quasi-physical objects somehow respond to limited laws of physicalism (Safro 1992: 193). The future proposal of a scientific discovery of quasi-physical objects makes the theory a hypothesis for further investigation. Our current understanding of *sunsum* as a spiritual force may one day become material; this would be the beginning of the relationship between traditional pneumatology and science. On the contrary, advancement in science should cause Akan scholars to worry about the future of religious spirituality as the world appears to some as moving away from an immaterial cosmology to a totally material one.

Overall, my research has shown that the description of *sunsum* as the intrinsic power of a being or an object or an emanating spiritual force is compatible with the general understanding of the Akan concept of *sunsum*. This conclusion does not in any way diminish the various roles *sunsum* play in Akan culture and religions. Nonetheless, is *sunsum* the be-all and end-all for the formulation of an Akan pneumatology? What is the next step in the various ways of speaking of Akan pneumatology and the development of contextual Akan Christian pneumatology? In response to these questions, my inquiry attempts to provide a theological framework for a contextual Akan Christian pneumatology that takes into account another term for the spirit, namely *honhom*. This is the subject of my second book, which is also published by LIT Verlag.

FIGURES

Figure 1. Map showing the Akan ethnic group in the tropical areas of Ghana and the southeast of la Cote d'Ivoire.

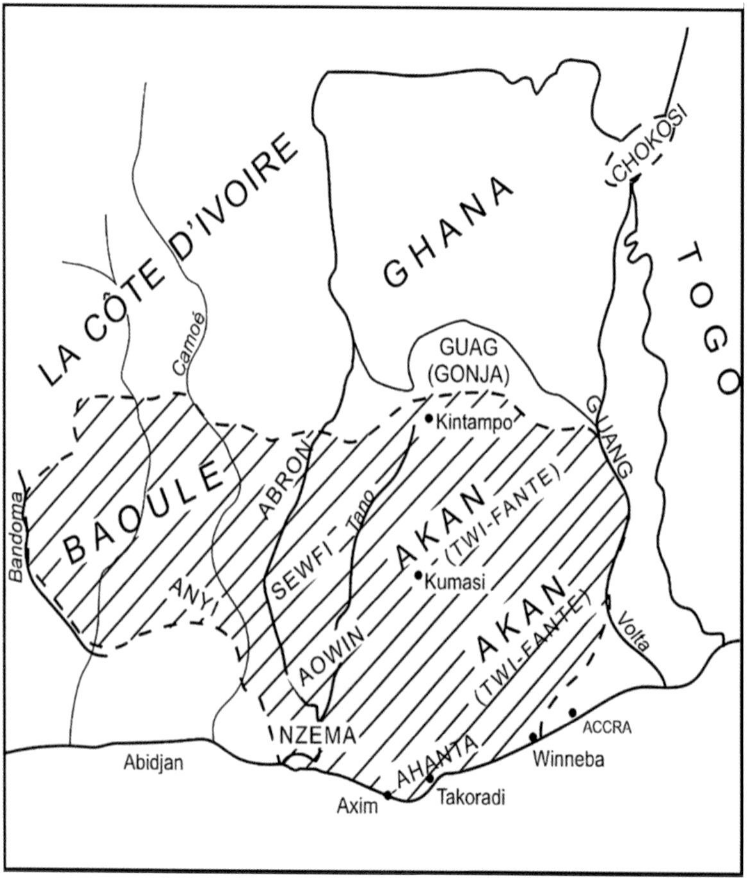

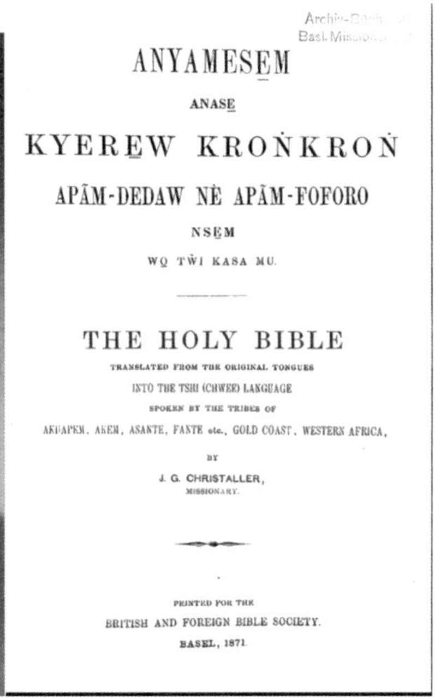

ANYAMESEM

ANASE

KYEREW KROṄKROṄ

APÃM-DEDAW NÈ APÃM-FOFORO

NSEM

WO TWI KASA MU.

THE HOLY BIBLE

TRANSLATED FROM THE ORIGINAL TONGUES

INTO THE TSHI (CHWEE) LANGUAGE

SPOKEN BY THE TRIBES OF

AKUAPEM, AKEM, ASANTE, FANTE etc., GOLD COAST, WESTERN AFRICA,

BY

J. G. CHRISTALLER,

MISSIONARY.

PRINTED FOR THE

BRITISH AND FOREIGN BIBLE SOCIETY.

BASEL, 1871.

Figure 2 Left. Rev. Johann Gottlieb Christaller (19 November 1827–16 December 1895), the architect of Ghanaian Twi literary scholarship.

Figure 3 Right. The inside cover of the first Twi Bible translation by Christaller and published by the British and Foreign Bible Society in 1871.

Figure 4: Image of the Golden Stool alongside *asuman* (amulets).

Glossary of Akan Terms

Abosom (pl)	Pantheon gods
Abrewa	Old lady (Nana)
Abusua	Clan
Adinkra	Symbols
Adwene	Mind
Akɔm	Prophesy
Asamando	Hades
Bayie (pl. Abayifoɔ)	Witch
Benkum	Left side
Esu	Nature
Esum	Darkness
Ɛboɔ	Stone
Fante	Fante tribe
Honhom	Breath/wind/spirit
Honhom Kronkron	Holy Spirit
Huaba	Semen
Hyɛbea/hyɛbrɛ	Appointed time
Mmoatia (pl)	Dwarfs
Mogya	Blood
Mpanyinfoɔ (pl)	Elders/Ancestors
Nana	Eminent one
Nananom (pl)	Elders/Ancestors
Nifa	Right side
Nkrabea	Destiny
Nsamanfo (pl)	Ghosts/Ancestors
Nsɛm	Words
Nsumankwaa	Medicinal Division
Nsumankwaahene	Chief of Medicines
Nton	Totem
Ntorɔ	Semen/ Paternal spirit
Odomankoma	God (Creator)
Onipa ('Nipa)	Human being
Onyame ('Nyame)	God (generic)

Onyame sunsum	God's power/Spirit
Onyankopɔn	God
Ɔbosom	Pantheon deity
Okomfoɔ (Akomfoɔ)	Traditional priest
Ɔkra	Life principle/ Soul
Ɔkrateasefo	Living soul
Saman	Ghost
Samanadzie	Ancestral world
Sankofa	Go back to take
Sasabonsam	Forest monster
Sãsã	Revengeful spirit
Sika Dwa Kofi	The Golden Stool
Suban	Character
Suman	Charm
Sunsum	Personality, Spirit
Sunsum bɔne	Evil spirit
Sunsum Kronkron	Holy Spirit
Sunsum mu	Spiritual/Mystical
Sunsuma	Shadow (spirit in Ga language)
Ta Kora	The deity Tano
Tumi	Power/Authority
Tweduampɔn	Dependable God
Twi	An Akan language
Wiase	World (under the sun)

Bibliography

Akessen, Sam K. "The Akan Concept of the Soul." *African Affairs*, vol. 64, No. 257 (Oct. 1965), pp. 280-291.

Allou, René K. *Les populations Akan de Côte d'Ivoire: Brong, Baoulé Assabou, Agni.*Paris: L'Harmattan, 2012.

Awuah-Nyamekye, Samuel. *Managing the Environmental Crisis in Ghana: The Role of African Traditional Religion and Culture with Special Reference to the Berekum Traditional Area.* Newcastle upon Tyne, UK: Cambridge Scholars Publishing, 2014.

Basden, G. T. "Book Review: The Akan Doctrine of God." *Theology*, Vol. 47, no. 294, Dec. 1, 1944, pp. 282-283.

Bavaj, Riccardo. *Intellectual History*. St. Andrews: The University of St. Andrews, 2010.

Bediako, Kwame. *Theology and Identity: The Impact of Culture Upon Christian Thought in the Second Century and in Modern Africa.* Oxford: Regnum Books, 1999.

Bill, George. *Until All Have Heard: The Centennial History of Church of God World Missions*. Cleveland, Tenn: Church of God World Missions, 2010.

Bishop, Paul. *Synchronicity and Intellectual Intuition in Kant, Swedenborg, and Jung*. USA: The Edwin Mellen Press 2000.

Boaduo, Nana A.-P, and Kofi P. Quan-Baffour. *Sankofaism: Reinventing Africa from Its Indigenous Philosophies.* Saarbrücken, Germany: Lambert Academic Publishing, 2011.

Burke, Peter. *What is Cultural History*? Cambridge, UK: Polity, 2008.

Brown, E K, and Sarah Ogilvie. *Concise Encyclopedia of Languages of the World*. Oxford: Elsevier, 2009.

Busia, Abrefa K. "The Ashanti of the Gold Coast," In: *African Worlds: Studies in the Cosmological Ideas and Social Values of African Peoples*. London: Oxford University Press, 1954.

——— "The African World View." *Présence Africaine*, Nouvelle série, No. 4 (Octobre-Novembre 1955), pp. 16-23. Address given on 3rd May at the Conference on the Christian Faith and African Culture of the Christian Council of the Gold Coast.

Cardew, Michael. *Pioneer Pottery*. London: A. & C. Black, 2002.

Christaller, Johann G. "A collection of 3,600 Tshi Proverbs in Use Among the Africans of the Gold Coast as Speaking the Asante and Fante Language, Collected, together with their Variations, and Alphabetically Arranged," Basel, 1879.

——— "A Dictionary of the Asante and Fante Language Called Tschi (Chwee, Twi) With a Grammatical Introduction and appendices on the Geography of the Gold Coast and Other Subjects," Basel, 2nd rev. ed., edited by J. Schweizer in 1893, published as "A Dictionary of the Asante and Fante Languages Called Tshi (Twi)," Basel, 1881.

——— "A Grammar of the Asante and Fante Language Called Tschi (Chwee, Twi) Based on the Akuapem Dialect, With Reference to Other (Akan and Fante) Dialects" – "Twi *mmebusem mpensa-ahansia mmoaano*", Basel, 1875.

——— *Anyames̱em anas̱e̱ Kyere̱w Kroṅkroṅ apãm-dedaw nè apãm-foforo ns̱em wo̱ tw̆i kasa mu. The Holy Bible translated from the original tongues into the Tshi-Chwee-language, spoken by the tribes of Akuapem, Akem, Asante, Fante, etc., Gold Coast*. Basel: B. & F.B.S., 1871.

——— *Christian Messenger for Basel German Mission Church on the Gold Coast, W. Africa*. (a bimonthly paper) 2, no. 12 (December 1888).

——— *Dictionary of the Asante and Fante Language Called Tshi (Twi)*. Basel: Basel Evangelical Missionary Society, 1933.

Christaller, Johann G. Asante, David, Opoku, Theophilus. "*Anyamesem anase Kyerew Kronkron Apam-dedaw ne Apam-foforo nsem wo Twi kasa mu*" (The Holy Bible translated from the original tongues into the Twi language), Basel, 1871.

Christaller, J. G., Locher, C. W., Zimmermann, J. *A Dictionary, English, Tshi (Asante), Akra; Tshi (Chwee) Comprising as Dialects: Akan and Fante; Accra connected with Adangme; Gold Coast, West Africa*. Basel, 1874.

Coetzee, P H, and A P. J. Roux. *The African Philosophy Reader*. London: Routledge, 1998.

Collingwood, Robin G. "Human Nature and Human History," In *The Idea of History*. Oxford: Oxford University Press, 1946, pp. 204-231.

Conservation International. *Handbook of Totems in Ghana: Traditional Mechanisms for Biodiversity Conservation.* Accra: Innolink, 2003.

Danquah, J B. *The Akan Doctrine of God: A Fragment of Gold Coast Ethics and Religion*. London: Cass, 1968.

——— *Ancestors, Heroes and God: The Principles of Akan-Ashanti Ancestor-Worship and European Hero-Worship*. Kibi, Gold Coast: George Boakyie Pub. Co, 1930.

——— *Gold Coast: Akan Laws and Customs and the Akim Abuakwa Constitution*. London: G. Routledge & Sons, 1928. Internet resource.

Danquah, J. B. *The Gold Coast Akan*. London: Lutterworth Press, 1945.

Dawson, Christopher. *Religion and Culture*. Washington: The Catholic University of America Press, 2013.

Debrunner, W. Hans. *A History of Christianity in Ghana*. Accra: Waterville Publishing, 1967.

——— *Witchcraft in Ghana: A Study on the Belief in Destructive Witches and Its Effect on the Akan Tribes*. Accra: Presbyterian Book Depot, 1961.

Denteh, A. C. "Ntorō and Nton." I.A.S. *Research Review*, vol. 3, No. 3, 1967, 91–96.

E. W. S. "112. Robert Sutherland Rattray: 1881-14th May, 1938." Man 38 (1938): 107-08. www.jstor.org/stable/2792895.

Emerson, Ralph W. *Essays: First Series*. Waiheke Island: Floating Press, 2009. Online archives: http://www.emersoncentral.com/selfreliance.htm. Last visited April 25. 04, 2019.

Ephirim-Donkor, Anthony. "Akom: The Ultimate Mediumship Experience Among the Akan." *Journal of the American Academy of Religion*, vol. 76, no. 1, March 2008, pp. 54–81.

——— *African Personality and Spirituality: The Role of Abosom and Human Essence*. Lanham, MD: The Rowman & Littlefield Publishing, 2016.

——— *African Religion Defined: A Systematic Study of Ancestor Worship Among the Akan*. Lanham, MD: University Press of America, 2010.

——— *African Spirituality: On Becoming Ancestors*. Trenton, NJ: Africa World Press, 1997.

Field, Margaret Joyce. *Search for Security: An Ethno-Psychiatric Study of Rural Ghana*. (London: Faber & Faber, 1960).

Gordon, E. Peter. "What is Intellectual History? A Frankly Partisan Introduction to a Frequently Misunderstood Field." Unpublished article, 2012. https://ces.fas.harvard.edu/uploads/files/Reports-Articles/What-is-Intellectual-History-Essay-by-Peter-Gordon.pdf. Last visited May 3, 2020.

Green, Ronald M. "Religion and Morality in the African Traditional Setting." *Journal of Religion in Africa*, vol. 14, no. 1, 1983, pp. 1–23. JSTOR, www.jstor.org/stable/1594931.

Gyekye, Kwame, "African Ethics," *The Stanford Encyclopedia of Philosophy (Fall 2011 Edition)*, Edward N. Zalta (ed.), https://plato.stanford.edu/archives/fall2011/entries/african-ethics/. Last visited May 3, 2020.

Gyekye, Kwame, and Wiredu, Kwasi. *Person and Community: Ghanaian Philosophical Studies, vol. I.* Washington, D.C: Council for Research in Values and Philosophy, 1992.

Gyekye, Kwame. *African Cultural Values: An Introduction*. Philadelphia, PA: Sankofa Pub. Co, 1996.

——— *An Essay on African Philosophical Thought: The Akan Conceptual Scheme*. Cambridge: Cambridge University Press, 1987.

Hallett, Edward Carr. *What is History?* 2nd edition. London, England: Penguin Books, 1990.

Hauser-Renner, Heinz. ""Obstinate" Pastor and Pioneer Historian: The Impact of Basel Mission Ideology on the Thought of Carl Christian Reindorf." *International Bulletin of Missionary Research*, Vol. 33, No. 2, April 2009, pp. 65-70.

——— "Examining Text Sediments–Commending a Pioneer Historian as an 'African Herodotus': On the Making of the New Annotated Edition of C.C. Reindorf's History of the Gold Coast and Asante." *History in Africa*, vol. 35, 2008, pp. 231–299.

Herskovits, M. J. "Robert Sutherland Rattray." *American Anthropologist*, Vol. 41, 1939, pp. 130–131.

Idowu, E. Bolaji. *African Traditional Religion: A Definition.* Maryknoll, N.Y: Orbis Books, 1973.

Jawanza, E. Clark. *Indigenous Black Theology: Towards an African-Centered Theology of the African American Religious Experience*. New York: Palgrave Macmillan, 2012.

Kyerematen, A. "The Royal Stools of Ashanti." *Africa: Journal of the International African Institute*, vol. 39, no. 1, 1969, pp. 1–10.

Lovejoy, Arthur O. *The Great Chain of Being: A Study of the History of an Idea*. New Brunswick, N.J: Transaction Publishers, 2009.

Majeed, Mohammed. "A Critique of the Concept of Quasi-Physicalism in Akan Philosophy." *African Studies Quarterly*, vol.14, Issues 1 & 2. Nov. 2013, pp. 23–33.

Martey, Emmanuel. *African Theology: Inculturation and Liberation.* Maryknoll, NY: Orbis Books, 1993.

Mbiti, John. *Introduction to African Religion (2nd ed.)*. Long Grove, Illinois: Waveland Press, Inc, 2015.

——— *Introduction to African Religion (2nd ed.)*. Oxford: Heinemann Educational Publishers, 1991.

McCaskie, T. C. *State and Society in Pre-Colonial Asante*. Cambridge and New York: Cambridge University Press, 1995.

Meyerowitz, Eva L. R., "Concepts of the Soul among the Akan of the Gold Coast." *Journal of the International African Institute*, Vol. 21, No. 1 (Jan., 1951), pp. 24 –31.

Minkus, Heleine K. "Causal Theory in Akwapim Akan Philosophy," In: Wright, Richard A. *African Philosophy: An Introduction*. Lanham: University Press of America, 1984.

——— "The Concept of Spirit in Akwapim Akan Philosophy." *Africa: Journal of the International African Institute*, Vol. 50, No. 2 (1980), pp. 182–192.

Molefi, K. Asante, and Abu S. Abarry. *African Intellectual Heritage: A Book of Sources*. Philadelphia: Temple University Press, 1996.

Müller, Louise, "Ghanaian Films and Chiefs as Indicators of Religious Change among the Akan in Kumasi and Its Migrants in Southeast Amsterdam", in Robert W. Hefner, John Hutchinson, Sara Mels, Christiane Timmerman (eds), *Religions in Movement: The Local and the Global in Contemporary Faith Traditions*. New York: Routledge, 2013.

——— "The Reality of Spirits: A Historiography of the Akan Concept of Mind." *Quest: An African Journal of Philosophy*, XXII (1–2), 2008, pp. 163–185.

——— *Religion and Chieftaincy in Ghana: An Explanation of the Persistence of a Traditional Political Institution in West Africa.* Zürich: Lit Verlag, 2013.

Neville, A. Helen, Brendesha M. Tynes, and Shawn O. Utsey (Eds). *Handbook of African American Psychology*. Thousand Oaks, Calif: SAGE, 2009.

Nkrumah, Kwame. *Neo-colonialism: The Last Stage of Imperialism*. London: Panaf, 1970.

Opoku, Asare K. "Review: African Spirituality: On Becoming Ancestors by Anthony Ephirim-Donkor," *Journal of the American Academy of Religion*, vol. 66, no. 4, 1998, pp. 947–949.

Opoku, Asare K. *Traditional Religion: Interviews with Priests, Priestesses, and Other Shrine Officials*. Accra, Ghana: Institute of African Studies, University of Ghana, 1978.

Owusu Agyarko, Robert. "'Sunsum' the Spirit of Life: Pneumatology in the [Akan] West African Context." Paper presented at the International Conference on Pneumatology and Contextual Theology, Geneva, March 2014.

——— "God of Life: Rethinking the Akan Christian Concept of God in the Light of the Ecological Crisis." *The Ecumenical Review,* Vol. 65, March 2013, pp. 51–66.

——— "The Sunsum of Onyame: Akan Perspectives on an Ecological Pneumatology." Journal of Reformed Theology, Vol. 6: 3, (2012), pp. 251-261.

——— *God's Unique Priest (Nyamesofopreko): Christology in the Akan Context (Doctoral dissertation)*. University of the Western Cape, South Africa, 2009.

P'Bitek, Okot. *African Religions in Western Scholarship*. Kampala: East African Literature Bureau, 1970.

Parrinder, Edward G. *West African Psychology: A Comparative Study of Psychological. and Religious Thought*. London: Lutterworth Pr, 1951.

Pescheux, Gérard. *Le royaume Asante (Ghana): parenté, pouvoir, histoire, XVIIe–XXe siècles*. Paris: Karthala, 2003.

Pobee John S. *Toward an African Theology*. Nashville: Abingdon, 1979.

Rattray, R S. *Ashanti Law and Constitution*. Oxford: Clarendon, 1929.

——— *Ashanti proverbs: (the primitive ethics of a savage people)*. Oxford: The Clarendon Press, 1916.

——— *Ashanti*. Oxford: Clarendon Press, 1923.

——— *Religion and Art in Ashanti*. Oxford: Clarendon Press, 1927.

Renier, Gustaaf Johannes. *History Its Purpose And Method*. London: George Allen & Unwin Ltd., 1950.

Roberts, Pamela. *Black Oxford: The Untold Stories of Oxford University's Black Scholars*. Oxford: Signal Books, 2013.

Safro, Kwame. "Why I Am Not a Physicalist." *The Personalist Forum*, Vol. 8, No. 1, Supplement: Studies in Personalist Philosophy. Proceedings of the Conference on Persons (Spring 1992), pp. 191–196.

Sanneh, Lamin. *Encountering the West: Christianity and the Global Cultural Process, the African Dimension*. Maryknoll, New York: Orbis Books, 1993.

Shoup, John A. *Ethnic Groups of Africa and the Middle East: An Encyclopedia*. Santa Barbara, Calif: ABC-CLIO, 2011.

Skinner, Quentin. "Meaning and Understanding in the History of Ideas." *History and Theory*, 8(1). Wesleyan University, Wiley, 1969, pp. 3–53.

Smith, W. Edwin. "The Akan Doctrine of God, a Fragment of Gold Coast Ethics and Religion," *African Affairs*, vol. 43, Issue 173, 1 October 1944, pp.186–187.

Van der Geest, Sjaak. "From Wisdom to Witchcraft: Ambivalence towards Old Age in Rural Ghana." *Africa: Journal of the International African Institute*, vol. 72, no. 3, 2002, pp. 437–463.

Welbourn, F B. "J. B. Danquah, The Akan Doctrine of God" (Book Review). *Journal of Asian and African Studies*.vol. 4, Iss. 4, Oct 1, Leiden,1969, pp. 315-320.

Wilks, Ivor. "Asante Nationhood and Colonial Administrators 1896-1935." In: Lentz, Carola, and Paul Nugent (eds). *Ethnicity in Ghana: The Limits of Invention*. Basingstoke: Macmillan, 2000.

Wiredu, Kwasi, et al. *A Companion to African Philosophy*. Malden Mass.: Blackwell, 2004.

Wiredu, Kwasi. "African Religions," In: *The Routledge Companion to Philosophy of Religion*. Chad V. Meister, Paul Copan (eds). London: Routledge, 2007.

——— *Cultural Universals and Particulars: An African Perspective*. Bloomington: Indiana University Press, 1996.

——— *Philosophy and an African Culture. Cambridge, New York: Cambridge University Press, 1980.*

——— "The Concept of Mind with Particular Reference to the Language and Thought of the Akans," in: Fløistad Guttorm (Ed.), *Contemporary Philosophy: A New Survey*. Dordrecht: Martinus Nijhoff Publishers, 1987, pp. 153–179.

——— "Toward Decolonizing African Philosophy and Religion." *African Studies Quarterly*, vol.1, Issue 4, 1998, pp. 17–46.

Worae, Yaw. "Some Translation and Exegetical Problems in the New Testament of the Asante-Twi Bible (2012)." A Thesis Submitted to the School of Graduate Studies, Kwame Nkrumah University of Science and Technology, Kumasi, in Partial Fulfillment of the requirement for the award of Master of Philosophy (MPhil.) degree in religious studies, November 2016.

Yankah, Kwesi. *Speaking for the Chief: Ȯkyeame and the Politics of Akan Royal Oratory*. Bloomington: Indiana University Press, 1995.

Filmography

Owuo Sunsum (The Spirit of Death) I, II, III&IV. Dir. Theophilus Amoabeng. United Pictures, 2013. Film.

Sunsum mu awarea (Spiritual Marriage) I&II. Dir. Asare Bediako. Power Based Studio/Trinity Computers, 2012. Film.

Sunsum Mu Ndwuma (Spiritual works). Dir. Theophilus Amoabeng. United Pictures, 2011. Film.

Sunsum Mu Nsɛm (Spiritual matters). Dir. Frank Gyimah. Globalense Ventures & Above All Films, 2012. Film.

Sunsum Mu Oyɛfoɔ (Spiritual enemy) I, II, III& IV. Dir. Isaiah Kofi Appiah. Country Man Movie Production, 2013. Film.

Websites

"Busia, Kofi Abrefa." *The Columbia Encyclopedia, 6th ed.* Encyclopedia.com. (June 19, 2018). http://www.encyclopedia.com/reference/encyclopedias-almanacs-transcripts-and-maps/busia-kofi-abrefa. Last visited June 22, 2022.

Gyekye, Kwame. "African Ethics," *The Stanford Encyclopedia of Philosophy*, (Fall 2011 Edition), Edward N. Zalta (ed.), https://plato.stanford.edu/archives/fall2011/entries/african-ethics/. Last visited March 22, 2020.

Lorenz, Hendrik. "Ancient Theories of Soul", *The Stanford Encyclopedia of Philosophy* (Summer 2009 Edition), Edward N. Zalta (ed.), http://plato.stanford.edu/archives/sum2009/entries/ancient-soul/. Last visited March 22, 2020.

The Merriam-Webster.com Dictionary, Merriam-Webster Inc., https://www.merriam-webster.com/dictionary/historiography. Last visited Mar. 22, 2020.

Afrikanische Theologie / African Theology / Théologie Africaine

Clifford Owusu-Gyamfi
The Spirit With Us
Towards A Contextual African Pneumatology and Theological Anthropology
vol. 11, 2022, 208 pp., 29,90 €, pb., ISBN-CH 978-3-643-80335-1

Emmanuel Njoku
Youth Development in Nigeria
A Means to Poverty Alleviation and the Promotion of Peace, Justice, and Security. A Study in the Light of the Principles of the Catholic Social Teaching
vol. 9, 2020, 606 pp., 69,90 €, pb., ISBN-CH 978-3-643-91341-8

Henry Chukwudi Okeke
Igbo-Religion und Christentum – ein unversöhnlicher Gegensatz?
Die Spiritualtität des Igbo-Volkes als Beispiel von Religion in einer globalen Welt. Mit einem Geleitwort von Prof. Dr. Detlev Dormeyer
Bd. 8, 2019, 184 S., 24,90 €, br., ISBN 978-3-643-14528-4

Anthony Kofi Sackey
The Beginnings of Mission on the Gold Coast (present-day Ghana)
With special Emphasis on Basel and Catholic Missions
vol. 7, 2018, 352 pp., 34,90 €, pb., ISBN-CH 978-3-643-91048-6

Angelo Chidi Unegbu
The Institution of the Seminary and the Training of Catholic Priests in South-Eastern Nigeria (1885 – 1970)
A historical evaluation
vol. 6, 2018, 400 pp., 59,90 €, hc., ISBN-CH 978-3-643-91043-1

Claude Adouma Bonsou
Fruchtbarkeit in der Ehe
Überlegungen zur Bevölkerungsentwicklung und Empfängnisregelung in Schwarzafrika aus theologisch-ethischer Sicht
Bd. 4, 2016, 282 S., 34,90 €, br., ISBN 978-3-643-13331-1

John Chidubem Nwaogaidu
Jesus Christ – Truly God and Truly Man
Towards a Systematic Dialogue between Christology in Africa and Pope Benedict XVI's Christological Conception
vol. 3, 2016, 268 pp., 34,90 €, pb., ISBN-CH 978-3-643-90732-5

Benjamin Nzenekwesi Eze
Challenges of Health Care Workers Vis-a-vis Evangelical Mission of Jesus Christ in Igboland, Nigeria
vol. 2, 2014, 440 pp., 44,90 €, pb., ISBN-CH 978-3-643-90399-0

LIT Verlag Berlin – Münster – Wien – Zürich – London
Auslieferung Deutschland / Österreich / Schweiz: siehe Impressumsseite